Hierarchies in Distributed Decision Making

Springer
Berlin
Heidelberg
New York
Barcelona
Hong Kong
London
Milan
Paris
Singapore
Tokyo

Christoph Schneeweiss

Hierarchies in Distributed Decision Making

**With 68 Figures
and 5 Tables**

 Springer

Prof. Dr. Christoph Schneeweiss
University of Mannheim
Lehrstuhl für Operations Research
D-68131 Mannheim
Germany

ISBN 3-540-65585-9 Springer-Verlag Berlin Heidelberg New York

Library of Congress Cataloging-in-Publication Data
Die Deutsche Bibliothek – CIP-Einheitsaufnahme
Hierarchies in distributed decision making: with 5 tables / Christoph Schneeweiss – Berlin;
Heidelberg; New York; Barcelona; Hong Kong; London; Milan; Singapore; Paris; Tokyo:
Springer, 1999
   ISBN 3-540-65585-9

© Springer-Verlag Berlin · Heidelberg 1999
Printed in Germany

Hardcover-Design: Erich Kirchner, Heidelberg

SPIN 10656015   42/2202-5 4 3 2 1 0 – Printed on acid-free paper

Two funnels disguised as hierarchies

Die Trichter*

w
u.s.
Waldweg
auf ihren
still und heiter
fließt weißes Mondlicht
Durch ihres Rumpfs verengten Schacht
Zwei Trichter wandeln durch die Nacht.

The funnels**

h
ug
thro
and cheerful
flue in flowing pale
employs their bodies' narrow
a sylvan moon's canescent light
Two funnels travel through the night

*Christian Morgenstern and the translation of **Max Knight

Preface

Distributed decision making can be regarded as a means of reducing organizational or computational complexity. Thus, large organizations are split up into various divisions, and complex decision problems are separated into more tractable components. With the increased capability for handling and communicating huge amounts of data, these decomposed units need no longer be treated as being almost isolated but may be coordinated more closely. Multi-agent systems, networking or principal agent theory point towards these modern developments.

Frequently distributed decision systems do not just build a network of equally ranked subsystems but exhibit distinct hierarchical phenomena ranging from one-person hierarchical planning - as in traditional hierarchical production planning - to multi-person antagonistic agency problems. Taking into account the ongoing paradigmatic shift from monolithic one-person decision problems to multi-person asymmetric settings, it now seems timely to develop a conceptual framework within which all these diverse phenomena may be treated in a unified way. Such a unified approach is not only desirable for theoretical reasons but it also allows for a simultaneous treatment of one- and multi-person decisions as they occur, for instance, in modern supply chain management.

The idea of trying to establish a theory on hierarchies in distributed decision making was born at the European Summer Institute on Hierarchical Planning in Mannheim in August 1993.

The diversity of contributions presented called for a common language and a sound conceptual basis. Since that time, together with my doctoral students and colleagues at our department in Mannheim and with the continuous support of many friends in the international OR community, I have been working to develop such a theory. Recently a EURO Working Group on Hierarchical Organizational Planning was set up which tries to focus the interest of European Operational Research to this fascinating field.

The treatise is fairly innovative. Many new concepts and notions had to be introduced and besides embedding a considerable amount of existing theory a significant amount of new original work had to be integrated. Thus the MIT theory of hierarchical production planning or the Dantzig/Wolfe coordination scheme, as well as principal agent theory, had to be described within the wider theoretical frame of hierarchies in distributed decision making. New fields, such as implementation and design problems, or modern cost accounting and hierarchical negotiations were based on the developed theory, demonstrating its ability to provide a sound theoretical framework to new areas in management science.

Developing a general theoretical framewok and proving its usefulness for various fields of management science would not have been possible without the continuous scientific efforts of my doctoral students and colleagues at my department in Mannheim. Not only have we developed new approaches to hierarchial production planning, investment-oriented costs, the design of flexibility, hierarchical negotiations, and the concept of implementation uncertainty, we also worked hard in preparing the material from a didactical point of view. For many years I have given lectures to my Mannheim students, and in summer 1996 to graduate students at the University of Mining and Metallurgy in Cracow on selected subjects of the theory. Their comments, and the many problems and problem solutions we prepared, greatly helped to improve the presentation.

My sincere thanks are due to Dr. Bill Dowsland and Dr. Don Leech, University of Wales, Swansea, UK who not only checked the English of parts of an earlier version of the manuscript, but gave also valuable comments on the presentation of some of the material. Thanks are also due for helpful comments of many other colleagues, particularly of Prof. Dr. Gülay Barbarosoglu, Istanbul and Prof. Dr. Rudolf Vetschera, Wien. Moreover, I gratefully acknowledge the permanent support of my colleagues and doctoral students Dipl.-Wi.-Ing. Thorsten Bender, Dipl.-Wirtsch.-Inf. Rüdiger Eichin, Dipl.-Wirtsch.-Inf. Erich Kleindienst, Dipl. math. oec. Kirstin Zimmer as well as Dr. Michael Hauth and Dr. Hans-Joachim Vaterrodt who carefully looked at large parts of various versions of the manuscript and who contributed a considerable number of substantial improvements. Most of all I am indebted to Dr. Carsten Homburg with whom I could discuss the entire manuscript. Many improvements are due to his comments, and what is more, Chapters 11 and 12 are based on his doctoral thesis. Finally, I would like to express my whole-hearted thanks to Mrs. Gabriele Eberhard and Mrs. Ruth Einig who did the irksome work of preparing the many versions of the manuscript and who often helped me with the English.

Mannheim, October 1998   Christoph Schneeweiss

Contents

Chapter 1

Introduction

Modern society, with its overwhelming diversity of interests and developments and its ever growing complexity, can no longer be understood and governed by the paradigm of centralized decision making. In fact, rather than following a monolithic approach, distributed decision making has become the predominant methodology of handling complex systems. Democratic structures tend to transfer decision rights to those parts of the society that are actually affected, companies are separating into profit centers or are even outsourcing parts of their activities, and complex decision problems are solved in splitting them up into their components. Indeed, former well-defined relationships, particularly those of a strict hierarchical nature, are becoming obsolete and are being replaced with free display of activities.

In view of this development, considering *hierarchies in dis-*

tributed decision making may seem to be contradictory or at least anachronistic. At second glance, however, the contrary is the case. In fact, hierarchical structures and distributed decision making are intimately related. This is mainly due to the fact that distributed decisions have to be coordinated and this adjustment is often not achieved through a self-coordination. In most cases, there is a hierarchically superior power that has the right to coordinate or at least to set the rules for coordination.

Thus, *hierarchies in distributed decision making* addresses an important and rapidly developing field in general decision theory. It comprises areas as diverse as hierarchical optimization, hierarchical production planning, multi-agent systems, principal agent theory, behavioral cost accounting, hierarchical negotiations, group decision making, and many other domains. In most cases these areas are part of different disciplines like Operations Research, Computer Science, Economics, Game Theory, Management Accounting, Organizational Theory, Psychology, Sociology, and others.

In view of this diversity, what is the unifying element in all these activities? Why might it be rewarding to design a framework that allows us to approach these seemingly diverse areas in a unified way?

A first answer points to a more practical reason. There is a lot of overlap between the different fields and some areas may even be considered as specifications of others. This overlap should be identified to take advantage of possible synergies.

A second reason for identifying and developing a uniform concept is more guided by the inherent systemizing claim of science to discover and understand general principles and to describe various fields of activity in a unified way.

General systems theory, cybernetics, and particularly decision theoretic concepts for cognitive action-oriented sciences provide general frameworks. These frameworks, however, are often too general to be of particular practical impact. What is needed, is to enrich the existing conceptual frameworks with those elements that are specific to a substantial class of problems. Thus, for the important area of hierarchies in distributed decision making, the general framework of cognitive decision theory has to be enriched with those structural elements that allow a unified approach to hierarchical phenomena. Clearly, these concepts should be general enough to comprise diverse areas but, on the other hand, sufficiently meaningful to provide significant insight into the general structure of a specific problem.

From a decision theoretic point of view the above mentioned areas of hierarchies in distributed decision making span from one-person settings, as in hierarchical optimizations, to antagonistic multi-person situations, as in non-cooperative negotiations. Thus, considering applications, this requires us to cover an area from structural mathematical problems to real-life hierarchical interference. For the one-person situation, distributed decision making can be useful in order to better understand and/or manipulate a complex decision situation. This will particularly be necessary for dynamic systems when decisions have to be made 'distributed' over time and when new information is acquired. For the multi-person situation, distributed decision making is even more obvious. Apart from the diverse information the decision makers might possess, one particularly has to consider the distinct decision rights and decision competence as well as the communication flows between the decision making units.

Distributed decision making has to do with different decisions being made in different parts of a (general) system, and subsequently with the task of coordinating these decisions. No hierarchical elements other than those being present in the coordination procedure seem to be involved. Taking a closer look, however, it is not only the coordination task that gives rise to a consideration of hierarchies. In fact, characterizing hierarchies as systems exhibiting an asymmetric structure, distributed decisions that do not possess some hierarchical features are rather the exception. Decisions made in different points in time and under different states of information, for instance, are prominent examples of (hierarchical) asymmetries.

	One-Person Situation	Multi-Person Situation
Strong Hierarchical Character	High Information Asymmetry, Traditional Hier. Prod. Pl.	**High Preferential and Informational Asymmetry in Hier. Planning, Leadership**
Weak Hierarchical Character	Near Optimal Hierarchical Optimizations	Game Theory, Negotiations of Almost Equally Ranked Parties, Multi-Agent Systems

Fig. 1.1: Hierarchical Features in Distributed Decision Making

Of course not all settings of distributed decision making can be viewed as hierarchies. Fig. 1.1 may be useful to gain some general impression. For a one-person situation, hierarchical (or multi-level) optimization often plays an important role [Anandaligam/Friesz]. The closer a solution is to optimum (i.e., the more it equals a 'simultaneous' solution), however, the less distinct is its hierarchical character. On the other hand, high information asymmetry and low integration of the hierarchical levels as in the case of traditional hierarchical production planning [Hax/Candea] intensify the hierarchical nature. For the multi-person situation, specific decision rights and high preferential and informational asymmetries usually result in significant hierarchies. These hierarchies can be found in general hierarchical planning and leadership situations, particularly in principal agent relationships [Milgrom/Roberts] and in behavioral management accounting [Demski]. Game theory (e.g., see [Fudenberg/Tirole]), on the other hand, and multi-agent systems (MAS) of distributed artificial intelligence, particularly so-called blackboard systems (e.g., see [v. Martial]), and, moreover, group decision making [Jelassi et al.] often show only a limited asymmetry and hence possess only weak or even no hierarchical features. The same is true for negotiations between equally ranked antagonists. However, for negotiations particularly within organizations, one might have typical hierarchical interrelations.

Hierarchies in distributed decision making will be concerned with most of the fields mentioned in Fig. 1.1. Particular emphasis, however, will be put on hierarchical planning, i.e., on the area indicated in the upper right field of Fig. 1.1. But, of course, the general theory we are going to develop will cover all the above mentioned domains, though some areas can only be treated as limiting cases in which the theory will be of less significance than for the central parts.

As mentioned earlier, distributed decision making has not only the problem of separating a system into partial subsystems but it is mainly concerned with the coordination task. In fact, one may distinguish at least four different degrees of coordination (see Fig. 1.2):

(1) **Data integration** describes the lowest level. This is the typical kind of integration one primarily finds in computer science. It is mainly concerned with data and structural consistency guaranteeing a smooth exchange between different systems.

(2) **Integrating systems through negotiations** describes a

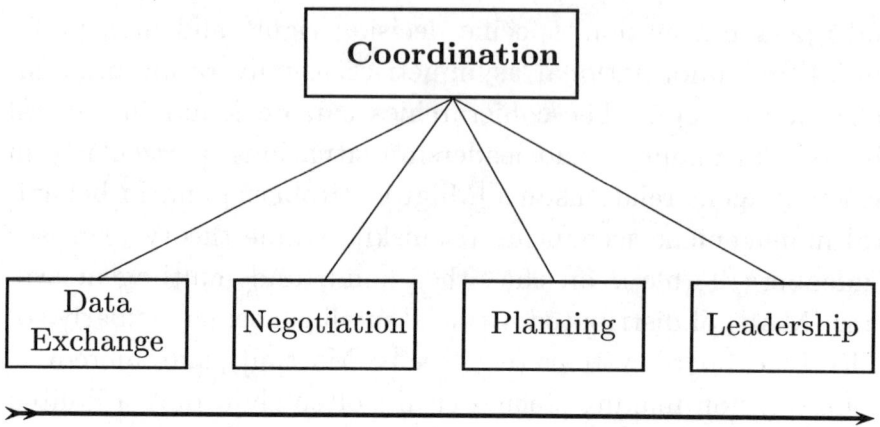

Increasing Sophistication of Communication and Integration

Fig. 1.2: Degrees of Coordination

market-like self-organizing situation. Multi-agent systems
are often of this character. In many situations, however,
there is a coordinating agent who has the (hierarchically)
superior right to set negotiation rules and to promote the
communication process.

(3) **Integration through planning activities** tries to coordinate the decision processes of the separate systems. This
is usually achieved in influencing either the preference structure or the decision field of the concerned systems. The
influence, however, is limited to *transactional* changes, i.e.,
no modification of the general preference attitude is attempted. A change is only temporarily achieved and confined to
the particular coordination task at hand.
For an integration through planning activities the *concept of
anticipating* the behavior of the system that is to be influenced plays an important role which clearly is in contrast to
the more myopic on-line concept of negotiations.

(4) **Integration through leadership activities** particularly
tries to influence the involved parties' general decision be-

havior. Thus not only transactional changes of the preference structure are attempted but one rather endeavors to achieve long lasting *transformational* shifts. Therefore the communication process between the involved parties plays a predominant role, and hence problems of how to convince the other party are becoming a main concern.

As mentioned above, the theory to be developed on *hierarchies in distributed decision making* will mainly focus on the planning aspect and will particularly elaborate hierarchical relationships in such systems. Besides planning activities negotiations will be considered as well. However, they will not be assumed to evolve between parties of equal ranking but will exhibit hierarchical features which are typical within stable organizations. In addition, negotiations will be treated as part of a more comprehensive planning task. Questions having to do with the nature of the communication process, as in modern management accounting (e.g., see [Demski] or [Horngren et al.]) will only be of marginal interest. It should be clear, however, that the general framework to be developed will be comprehensive enough to capture particular features of the communication process as well.

According to the main focus of the investigation the following part of this introductory chapter will provide a rough general characterization of hierarchical situations which will finally result in a broad outline of the proposed *theory of hierarchies in distributed decision making*.

1.1 Some Typical Examples for Hierarchical Situations

Thinking of hierarchies, one immediately has in mind strategic and operational planning activities or typical hierarchical leadership relations in an organization. In fact, there are numerous structures that turn out to be of a hierarchical nature. Fig. 1.3 gives nine examples showing the diversity of hierarchical settings.

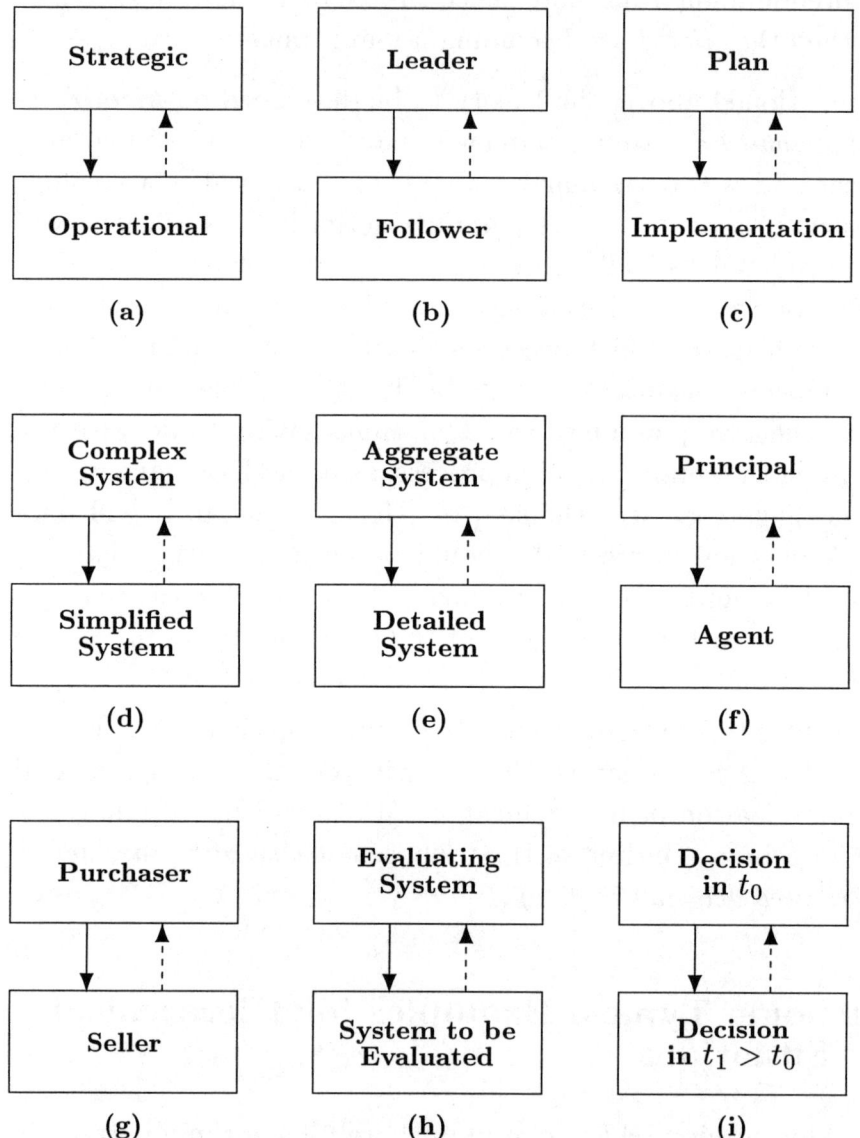

Fig. 1.3: Examples of Hierarchical Situations

Some hierarchies in Fig. 1.3, like *strategic-operational* (a), *leader-follower* (b), or *decision in t_0 – decision in $t_1 > t_0$* (i), show 'strong hierarchical features'. For other situations, for instance, the *principal agent setting* (f) or the *purchaser-seller relationship* (g), the hierarchical character might not be that obvious, i.e., it is not definitely clear, 'who is the master and who the servant'. In what follows, however, we interpret the phrase 'hierarchical' in broad terms, *characterizing a situation of at least two objects (levels) which exhibit some asymmetric relationship as to their decision rights or their information status*, or simply by the fact that one level is making its decision earlier than the other.

As a first characterization one may distinguish between the important classes of
– *constructional* and
– *organizational hierarchies.*

(1) Constructional hierarchies

Constructional hierarchies may primarily be characterized by the *symmetry of their information status*, that is, there exists only one decision maker for all levels of a hierarchy who has to make decisions at a specific point in time using the information available at that very moment. Thus, the hierarchy is mainly defined by the different objectives and decision rights at the different levels.

Constructional hierarchies result from imposing a hierarchical structure on a non-structured system. Hierarchy (e) of Fig. 1.3 with its imposed aggregate description of a detailed system may serve as an example.

(2) Organizational hierarchies

Organizational hierarchies may primarily be characterized by the *asymmetry* of their information status. In the case where there is just *one* decision maker one has the typical situation of a *decision time hierarchy* (case (i) in Fig. 1.3). If, on the other hand, each level has its own decision maker possessing his (or her) own information, one has the case of a *leadership hierarchy* (see (b) in Fig. 1.3).

The **decision time hierarchy** consists of levels which make decisions at different points in time and which therefore are usually based on different information. If, for instance, the upper level's decision is made at time $t = t_0$ and that of the lower level at time $t = t_1$ with $t_1 > t_0$, then, at most, the upper level only possesses the information available at t_0. As prominent examples think of strategic, tactical, and operational planning levels (case (a) in Fig. 1.3). In particular, the tactical-operational hierarchy characterizes the interrelationship between the tactical provision of resources at the upper level and their operational usage on the lower level. Thus design and the operational use of a design or a plan and its implementation ((c) in Fig. 1.3) form typical examples of a decision time hierarchy.

The **leadership hierarchy** describes the relationship between leader and follower. Here information asymmetry is not caused by the different points in time at which a decision has to be made but by the existence of different decision makers who might possess different information and, in addition, might follow different objectives. As a typical example think of a coordination hierarchy where a control unit coordinates several subunits. Fig. 1.4 summarizes the different categories.

Remark: As a further example one might think of leadership hierarchies which describe the relation between two *antagonistically* behaving parties. These important hierarchies will not be discussed under the category of *organizational hierarchies* but will be treated under the separate heading of principal agent problems ((f) in Fig. 1.3). Organizational hierarchies will be confined to *non-antagonistic* situations, i.e., to situations in which the levels do not exploit their (private) knowledge in an opportunistic way as in principal agent settings.

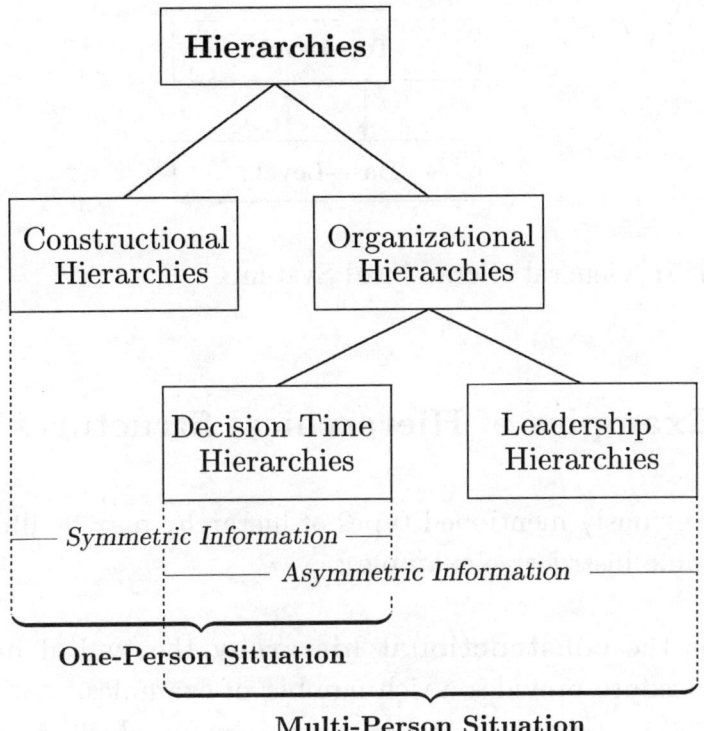

Fig. 1.4: Characterizing Constructional and Organizational
Hierarchies

In general, most of our analysis will be confined to hierarchies
having just two levels. Let us call the more powerful level the
top-level and the more dependent one the **base-level**. Fig. 1.5
depicts this general relationship with a solid and a broken arrow.

To illustrate these general introductory remarks on hierarchical
systems, let us give, in Section 1.2, several typical examples.
Section 1.3 will then introduce some important notions to characterize the general relationship between the levels of a hierarchical system, which, in Section 1.4, will finally enable us to
present a broad outline of the proposed theory on *hierarchies in
distributed decision making.*

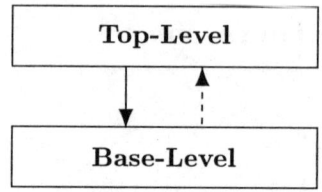

Fig. 1.5: General Hierarchical System

1.2 Examples of Hierarchical Structures

The previously mentioned types of hierarchy may be illustrated with some instructive examples:

(1) For the **constructional hierarchy** the typical modeling procedure provides a rich number of examples.

- Of particular interest is a hierarchy for which the comprehensive real-life situation is taken to be the top-level and the segment in which one is especially interested is defining the base-level. In view of Fig. 1.3 (d) the 'complex system' is specified to be a comprehensive description of the *entire* system whereas the segment in which one is interested represents the 'simplified system'.

- As another type of constructional hierarchy take the approximation of a non-linear model by a linear one. The non-linear model represents the top-level and the linear one the base-level. In view of Fig. 1.3 (d) the 'complex system' has to be identified with the total system. In fact, both levels describe the same system, with the top-level giving a realistic but rather involved (non-linear) description and the base-level providing a relaxed, less difficult to treat version.

(2) An **organizational hierarchy** can be illustrated with many real-life situations.

- Fig. 1.6 shows the hierarchy of planning activities for the functional areas of production, manpower, and financial planning. For all three areas one has the strategic level at which general business strategies are defined. The subsequent tactical level operationalizes the strategic decisions and provides the subsequent operational levels with the necessary production, manpower, and financial resources, respectively. Finally, at the operational levels

Planning Level	Production	Manpower Capacity	Financing
strategic planning	investment strategies	manpower procurement	external and internal financing strategies
tactical planning	investments	hiring and firing	long and short term loans
medium term planning	medium term production planning	distribution of yearly working time	short term financing
execution planning	short term production planning (MRP)	overtime	short term financing, liquidity planning
scheduling	production scheduling	personnel scheduling	liquidity planning, cash management

Fig. 1.6: Hierarchies of Functional Areas of a Company

these resources are actually employed. It is interesting to see that the functional areas are not only structured by themselves but that there exists a hierarchical relationship between the different functional areas as well. Fig. 1.7 shows a typical example of a supply chain where we assume 'sales' to be the most important functional area.

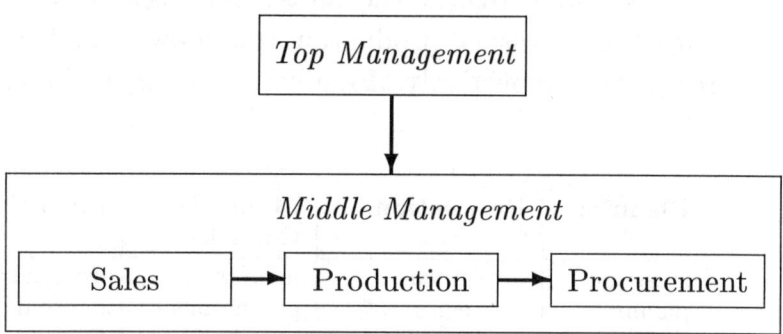

Fig. 1.7: Hierarchy between Functional Areas of a Company

- One of the best known organizational hierarchies is the production planning and control (PPC) system. An example of such a system is depicted in Fig. 1.8. At least four levels of a decreasing degree of aggregation can be distinguished. As Fig. 1.9 shows, at these levels, time, capacities, and production units are appropriately aggregated. Fig. 1.8 indicates on the right hand side the respective information situation and, on the left hand side, the criteria of the different management levels. The hierarchy shows two kinds of top-down influence: the instructions for the next level, and the final influence on the object system, i.e., on the physical production process. To give an example: medium term planning passes a medium term production plan down to the material requirements

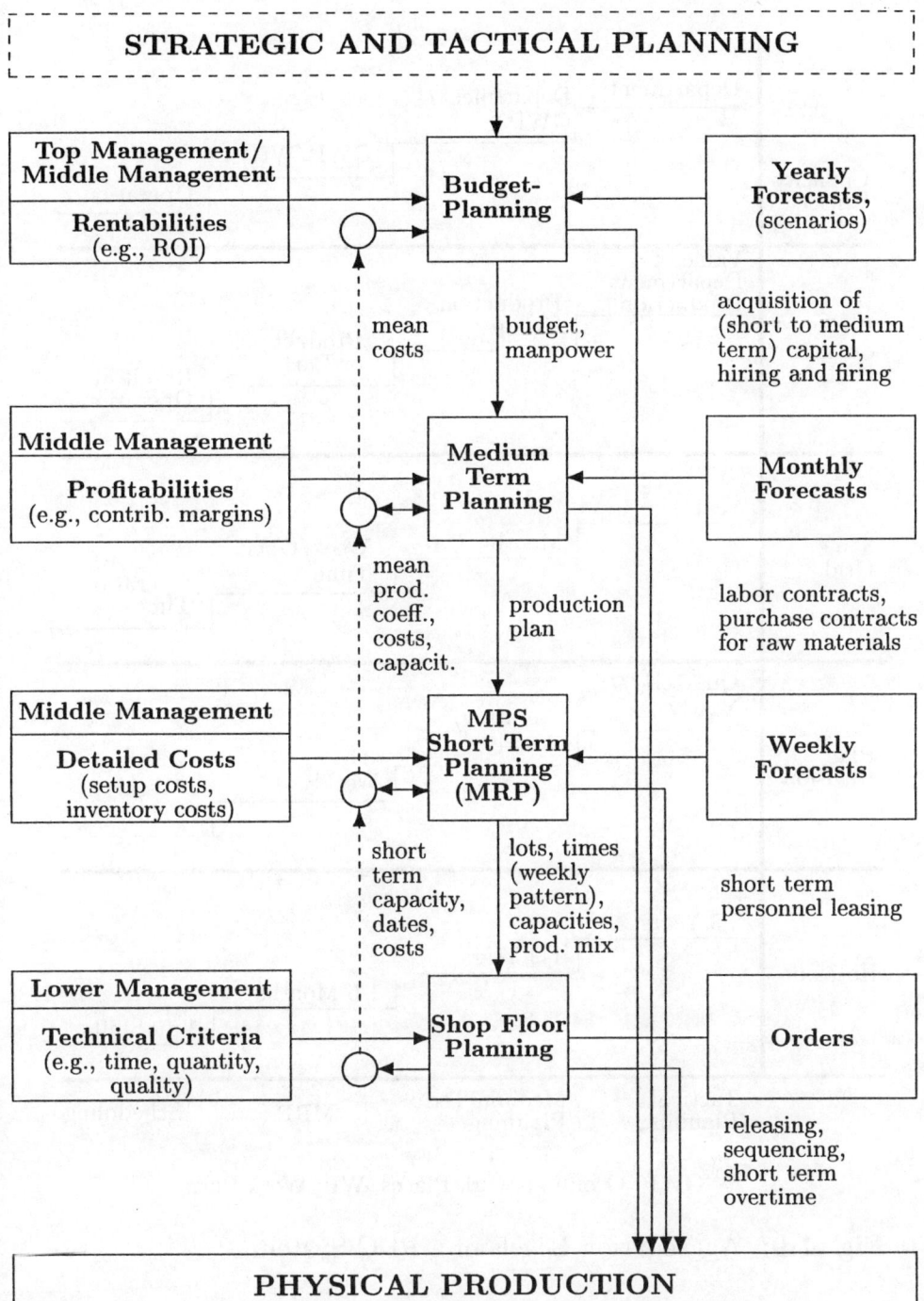

Fig. 1.8: Production Planning and Control System

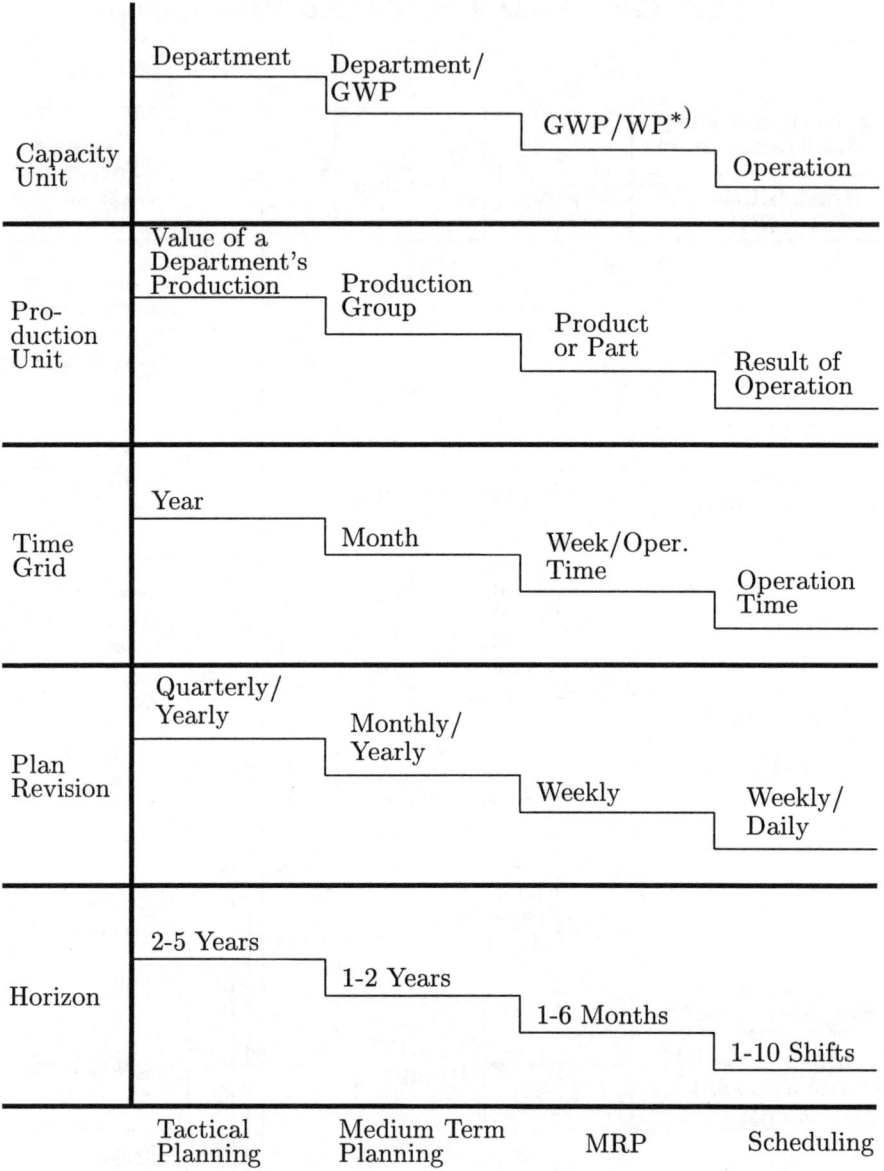

*) GWP: Group of Work Places, WP: Work Place

Fig. 1.9: Aggregation Levels of a PPC-System

planning (MRP)-module which is executed only through the subsequent stages. On the other hand, contracts for raw material, for instance, are executed immediately, that is, these contracts are directly influencing the physical production process.

PPC systems represent typical organizational hierarchies with the budgeting level as the tactical level and with three operational levels. For traditional PPC systems only the two short term operational levels are of interest. More recent systems, however, fully take into account the medium term and tactical levels as well.

Finally, let us consider two examples of hierarchical situations that do not belong to the classes of constructional or organizational hierarchies.

(3) For a **principal agent relationship** let us consider the following example.

- The selling of a house by an estate agent constitutes an asymmetric situation which is typical of hierarchical structures and, in particular, of an *antagonistic* leadership situation. The seller can be represented by the top-level (or the principal) whereas the agent stands for the base-level. Both parties follow different goals, possess different information, and are assumed to behave antagonistically. The seller would like to sell his house at a high price, whereas the agent wants to achieve his task with as little effort as possible. Typical of such a situation is the incentive being offered to the agent depending on the selling price the agent achieves and hence depending on the profit the principal gains.

(4) **Coordinating** subordinates constitutes a typical leadership activity. In contrast to the examples described so far, coordination is often achieved through a *negotiation*.

- Negotiating on a company's budget may serve as an example. Usually, the top-management suggests a budget to the company's different departments which, in most cases, are allowed to present alternative proposals. After some 'negotiation cycles', one reaches a final decision resulting in a definite budget. This negotiation process is hierarchical since the participating parties are not of equal ranking and, in particular, it is the top-management that can finally bring the negotiation to an end.

1.3 Some Important Properties of Hierarchical Systems

Usually the dependencies within a hierarchically structured system are not as simple as depicted in Fig. 1.5. Indeed, a more detailed description is shown in Fig. 1.10. Three different stages of interdependence may be distinguished.

(1) **Anticipation**

In a first step, in finding a feasible decision, the top-level takes into account the base-level's relevant characteristics. These characteristics will be called 'anticipated base-level'. Often an anticipated base-level is just an aggregated base-level or some particularly important aspect that has to be considered. Choosing an anticipated base-level and taking into account its impact on the top-decision will be called an **anticipation**. Generally, an anticipation can be regarded as the base-level's bottom-up influence on the top-level. The anticipation is one of the main concepts to describe hierarchical phenomena.

(2) **Instruction**

Having anticipated the base-level, the top-level makes a decision which influences the base-level. Let us call this decision an **instruction**. As an example, take the base-level's provision with certain resources. Generally, the instruction can be regarded as the top-level's top-down influence on the base-level.

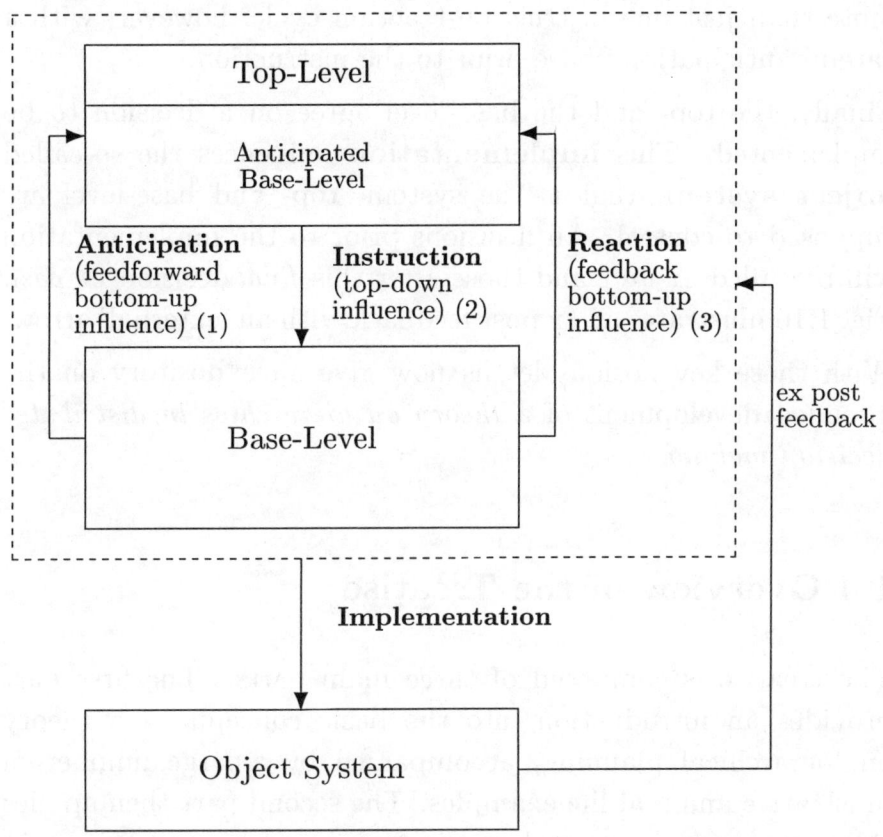

Fig. 1.10: Interrelations between Hierarchical Levels

(3) Reaction

If the base-level is in a position to react to the top-level's instruction, we call this bottom-up influence a **reaction**. A reaction is representing a *feedback* influence whereas the anticipation can be considered as a *feedforward* influence (see Fig. 1.10). A feedback influence is a bottom-up influence *after* the instruction has been exerted, whereas an anticipation describes a bottom-up influence *before* the instruction is determined.

Whenever a reaction is possible, one has a **communication** or even a **negotiation process**. In many cases, there will be no more than just one instruction-reaction cycle, however, with a careful anticipation phase prior to the instruction.

Finally, the top- and the base-level agree on a decision to be implemented. This **implementation** influences the so-called **object system**, that is the system, top- and base-level are supposed to control. All decisions prior to the implementation will be called *ex ante* and those after this *final* decision *ex post*. Fig. 1.10 illustrates an ex post feedback with an 'external' arrow.

With these key notions let us now give an expository on the intended development of a *theory on hierarchies in distributed decision making*.

1.4 Overview of the Treatise

The treatise is composed of three main parts. The first part provides an introduction into the basic concepts of a theory on hierarchical planning, accompanied by a large number of illustrative and real-life examples. The second part then applies these concepts to general application areas aiming to obtain deeper theoretical insights. Finally, Part III is devoted to leadership problems, particularly extending hierarchical planning to negotiation processes.

The treatise follows a simple decision theoretic classification. As Fig. 1.11 shows, it starts with one-party (or one-person) hierarchies making just one decision and ends up with the situation of more than one party being involved in a hierarchical negotiation process. For an early exposition of the theory to be developed here, see [Schneeweiss (1995)].

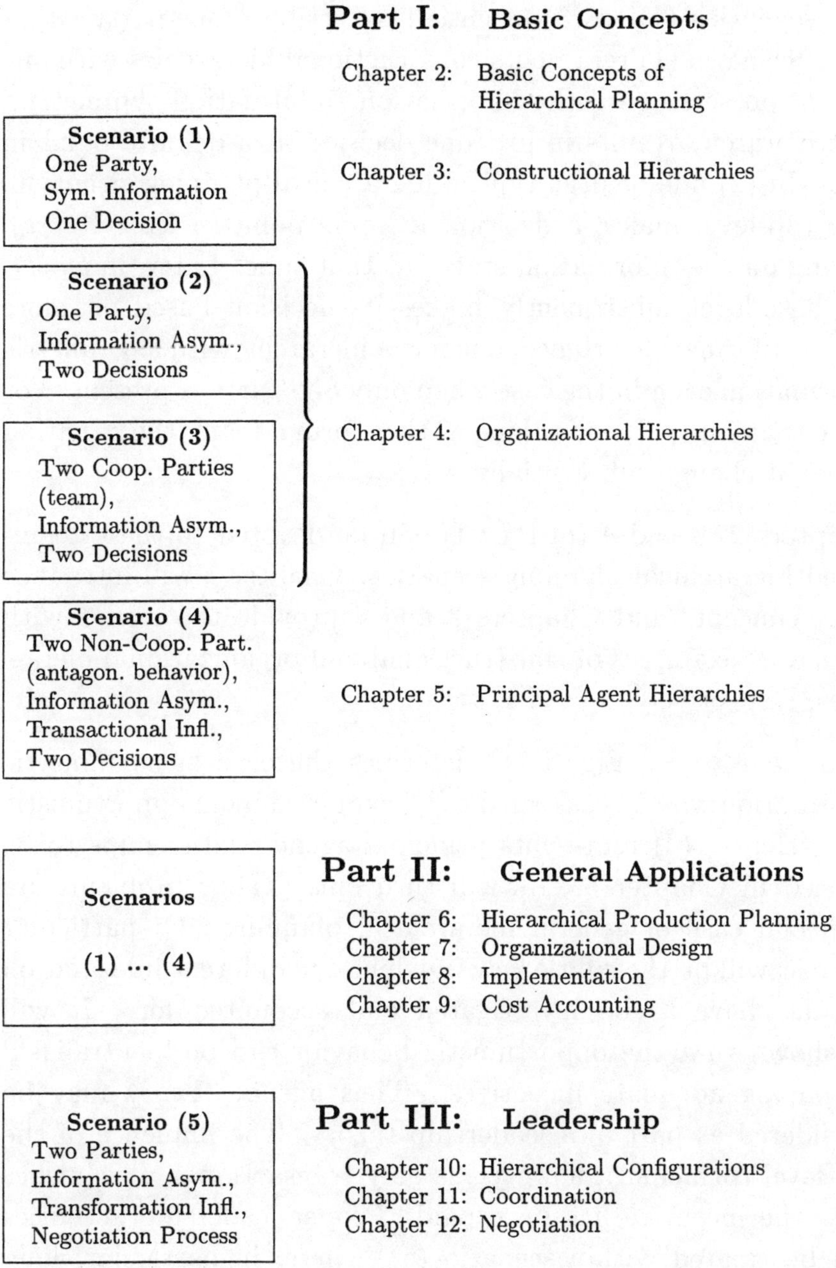

Part I: Basic Concepts

Chapter 2:   Basic Concepts of
                   Hierarchical Planning

| **Scenario (1)** |
| One Party, |
| Sym. Information |
| One Decision |

Chapter 3:   Constructional Hierarchies

| **Scenario (2)** |
| One Party, |
| Information Asym., |
| Two Decisions |

| **Scenario (3)** |
| Two Coop. Parties |
| (team), |
| Information Asym., |
| Two Decisions |

Chapter 4:   Organizational Hierarchies

| **Scenario (4)** |
| Two Non-Coop. Part. |
| (antagon. behavior), |
| Information Asym., |
| Transactional Infl., |
| Two Decisions |

Chapter 5:   Principal Agent Hierarchies

| **Scenarios** |
| |
| **(1) ... (4)** |

Part II: General Applications

Chapter 6:   Hierarchical Production Planning
Chapter 7:   Organizational Design
Chapter 8:   Implementation
Chapter 9:   Cost Accounting

| **Scenario (5)** |
| Two Parties, |
| Information Asym., |
| Transformation Infl., |
| Negotiation Process |

Part III: Leadership

Chapter 10: Hierarchical Configurations
Chapter 11: Coordination
Chapter 12: Negotiation

Fig. 1.11: Overview of the Content of the Treatise

The scenarios (1) to (3) essentially describe a one-party situation. Scenario (1) represents constructional hierarchies with one person possessing all the information (information symmetry). The hierarchy results in just one decision at a definite point in time. In (2) one has the typical hierarchical planning situation. The top-level makes a decision in some point in time $t = t_0$, relying on the information status at that time. Later, in $t = t_1$, the base-level subsequently makes its decision based on more recent information. Hence, one has a hierarchy with asymmetric information even in the case when only one party is present. For more than one person, as long as they form a team, the situation does not change substantially.

Chapters 2, 3 and 4 (of Part I) will be devoted to these team-based hierarchical planning scenarios. Chapter 2 will introduce basic concepts and Chapters 3 and 4 provide the reader with numerous examples of constructional and organizational hierarchies, respectively.

Scenario (4) (see Fig. 1.11) describes the case of asymmetric information which is assumed to be exploited in an opportunistic way. Hence, (4) represents principal agent relationships to be treated in Chapter 5. As will turn out, agency problems are a special case of general hierarchical planning. Of particular interest will be the subtle way in which the different information settings have to be investigated and accounted for. It will be shown that the opportunistic behavior can be 'neutralized' by paying adequate incentives. Thus agency theory may be considered as part of a leadership theory. The influence of the top-level (principal), however, is only transactional. It vanishes after the incentive has been paid. Proper leadership activities will be treated within scenario (5), where, in particular, long lasting transformational influences will be discussed.

Remark: In the literature, the term 'asymmetric information' is usually restricted to the case of antagonistic parties. In our rather broad context, however, it turns out to be particularly convenient to characterize also a team situation or a one-party situation as being in a state of asymmetric information (see scenarios (2) and (3)). This is necessary to differentiate this situation from the symmetric scenario (1) describing constructional hierarchies. Hence, 'asymmetric information' does only characterize the principal agent case if the levels do not behave as a team.

With the basic concepts introduced in Part I, we will then, in Part II, be in a position to discuss the application of hierarchical planning to general management and organizational problem areas. Thus Chapter 6 is devoted to a new approach to hierarchical production planning, and Chapter 7 describes the hierarchical nature of organizational design problems. Chapter 8 then analyzes the fundamental concept of integrating planning and implementation efforts, and, finally, Chapter 9 provides some insight into a possible theoretical foundation of cost accounting.

Leadership questions will be discussed according to scenario (5) in Part III. Before doing so, the whole theory thus far developed has to be raised to a more general level of reflection. Hierarchical phenomena will be understood as the hierarchical superposition of individual decision processes. Hence, in Chapter 10, these processes will be analyzed and the various hierarchical relationships within and between such processes will be investigated. As an outcome of this discussion, Chapter 11 describes coordination processes and Chapter 12 will be concerned with hierarchical negotiations.

The final chapter summarizes the main ideas and gives an outlook on a possible treatment of the management process as a hierarchical intervention of planning and leadership activities. It thus trics to derive a general basis for a comprehensive theory of business administration as an action-oriented normative representation of the management process.

PART I

Basic Concepts

Part I lays the foundations for a comprehensive theory of hierarchical decision structures, starting in Chapter 2 with an introduction into the basic concepts of such a theory. Its focus, however, is rather on planning than on leadership. The discussion of general leadership concepts and hence a full extension to distributed decision structures will be postponed until Part III. Because of its general character, Chapter 2 is a prerequisite for all what follows. It presents the fundamental principles of hierarchical planning culminating and being condensed in the coupling equations to be derived in Section 2.2. The remaining three chapters are then devoted to particular specifications of these equations using as a guideline the scenarios (1) through (4) defined in the overview of Fig. 1.11.

Chapter 3 considers the case of symmetric information which is typical for constructional hierarchies being particularly met in the modeling phase of a problem solution. In this context hierarchical algorithms are playing an important role especially in solving the coupling equations. The subsequent Chapter 4 is then concerned with organizational hierarchies in which the levels are no longer assumed to possess the same information status. Chapter 4 provides numerous examples for various types of hierarchies which are not only of theoretical interest but can be encountered in practice as well.

Agency problems are of particular importance, though somewhat out of the scope of traditional hierarchical planning. The last chapter of this introductory first part is therefore devoted to a brief introduction to the principal agent theory which, in fact, turns out to be a special case of the general coupling equations. The treatment of agency problems does not only achieve a consequent development from scenario (4) to the antagonistic case of scenario (5) (s. Fig. 1.11), simultaneously it extends the theory of hierarchical planning to comprise communication aspects as well. Thus agency problems may already be considered as leadership problems and one therefore might understand Chapter 5 as part of a foundation for the questions to be considered in Part III.

Chapter 2

Basic Concepts of
Hierarchical Planning

This chapter provides the foundations for a theory of hierarchical planning in distributed decision making. It describes in particular the interior structure of a hierarchy in mathematical terms. This description culminates in the derivation of the so-called coupling equations (2.5) which will be the origin for all further developments. Consequently, the equations are purely conceptual, i.e., they solely describe structural relationships. To handle particular situations, a further specification is needed. Some of the more basic concepts, like the team or non-team character of the levels (Sec. 2.3), or the type of anticipation (Sec. 2.4), are presented here. All other specifications, particularly those describing concrete practical situations requiring specific empirical data, are left for subsequent chapters.

Finally, in Section 2.5, three illustrative examples are presented in detail. They are not only helpful to thoroughly understand some of the fundamental concepts, but they also provide the reader with simple 'cognitive anchors' and particularly show how the general coupling equations are to be applied. In addition, these simple examples will be the starting-point for more comprehensive theoretical developments and practical applications. The reader may even want to read at least part of the examples *before* getting involved in abstract conceptual considerations.

2.1 General Characterization of Hierarchical Planning Structures

Hierarchies in distributed decision making are not only limited to hierarchical planning situations but comprise hierarchical negotiations and leadership relations as well. In order to embed hierarchical planning in this broader context, let us start with the general description given in Fig. 1.10 which, more explicitly, can be reformulated as depicted in Fig. 2.1.

Fig. 2.1 shows a hierarchical system with different kinds of subsystems having particular interrelations and outputs. The innermost system is the top-level (or, analogously, the base-level). In order to derive an optimal instruction, the top-level anticipates the base-level and hypothetically applies different instructions IN as 'stimuli' to the anticipated base-level. These instructions give rise to possible (hypothetical) reactions and finally result in an optimal instruction IN^* which is definitely communicated to the base-level. The base-level then takes this instruction into account, derives an optimal reaction RE^* and passes it on to the top-level. After some negotiation cycles, the hierarchical system eventually results in a (contract) decision IN^{**} which is then the basis to influence the (environmental) object system (see Fig. 1.10). The process just described shows several interesting and important features:

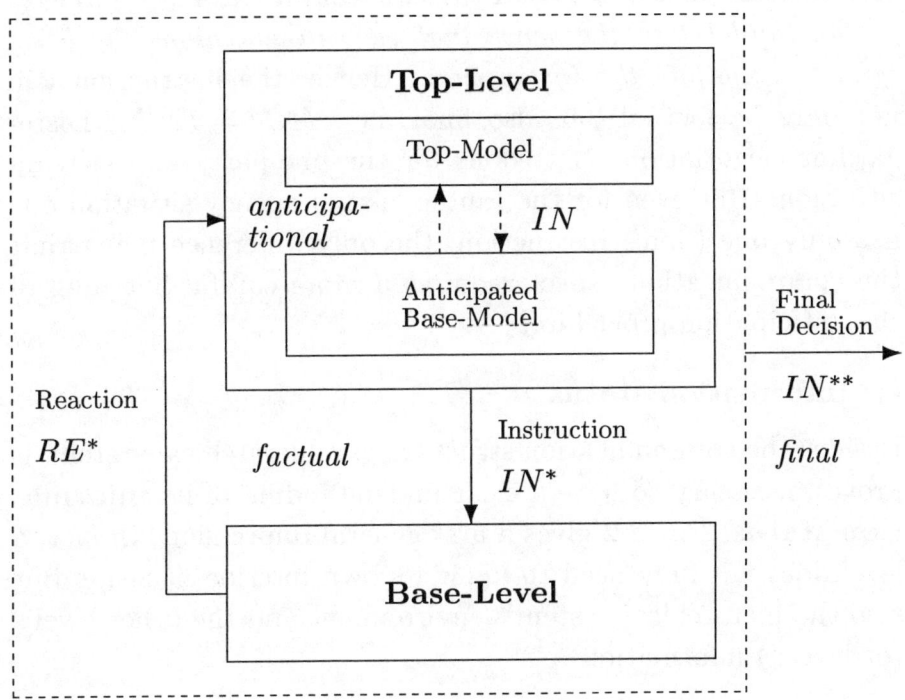

Fig. 2.1: Interdependence of Hierarchical Levels

1. The **anticipational** activities are solely restricted to the top-level. It is only the optimal instruction IN^* that actually leaves the top-level.

2. The communicated instruction IN^* gives rise to a communication process within the wider system, i.e., the proper hierarchical system consisting of top- and base-level. All the signals within this system are called **factual**. They are not final, since they can still be changed.

5. The only **final** decision is IN^{**} which leaves the hierarchical system and is made public. All activities after this final decision will be called **ex post** and all activities prior to IN^{**} **ex ante** (see also Fig. 1.10).

Hierarchical planning (in its strict meaning) will be restricted to the top-level in the sense that we will not allow the base-level to negotiate the instruction. Hence, the instruction will not only be factual but also final, i.e., $IN^* = IN^{**}$. Disregarding negotiations is obvious for the one-party or the team situation. But even for the (antagonistic) agency situation one has only one (final) instruction, the only difference being that the communication aspect requires a more careful handling of the anticipation procedure.

(1) Information status

Besides the communication structure of a hierarchical system, it proves necessary to have a clear understanding of its **information status**. Fig. 2.2 gives a first general impression. In fact, a level does not only need to know its own interior situation but also the hierarchical system's environment and the other level's (or levels') information.

Things are becoming even more complicated if, in addition, one explicitly considers the point in time at which a level possesses particular information. If the top-decision is made at $t = t_0$ and the base-decision at $t = t_1$, one has to distinguish between top- and base-information states at times t_0 and t_1.

Particularly for antagonistic levels, it will be of crucial importance whether the top-level has the same information status as the base-level at the time when the base-decision is made. If the top-level (principal) is not able to observe the base-level's (agent's) action (in $t = t_1$ and later), we have a 'hidden action' case which will require the principal to offer incentives (see Chapter 5).

As already introduced in Section 1.1, let us distinguish between
– *information symmetry* and
– *information asymmetry.*

In case of **information symmetry** both levels possess the same (deterministic or, stochastic) knowledge. This is the typical situation of a constructional hierarchy (see Section 1.1).

The notion **asymmetric information** will be used to describe a situation in which the levels have not the same knowledge. This might be the case even for one decision maker being in different information states in t_0 and t_1 (as for a decision time hierarchy). For different decision makers an asymmetric information situation might occur because both levels possess private information. If, in addition, the levels behave opportunistically they might falsely communicate this knowledge to each other. Often only this last case is called 'asymmetric information situation'. Let us adapt here the wider definition in calling even the simple stochastic decision time hierarchy 'asymmetric'. This allows us to stress the difference between a (one-level) stochastic (symmetric) decision problem and a (two-level) problem in which two decisions are made at different states of information (see also 'remark' in Section 1.4).

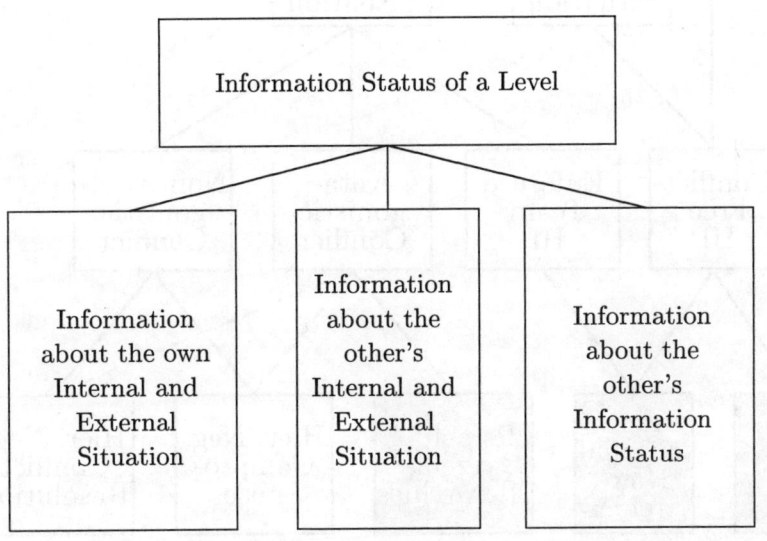

Fig. 2.2: Information Status within a Hierarchical System

(2) **Classification of hierarchical configurations**

As has already been mentioned in the introduction (see Fig. 1.11), hierarchies can be divided into those involving only one decision making unit (DMU) and those which have to do with more than one DMU (see Fig. 2.3). The one-DMU situation leads to conflict-free planning hierarchies. For the multi-DMU case, on the other hand, one has to distinguish between team and non-team based decision situations. Apart from communication aspects, **team based hierarchies** are the same as one-person

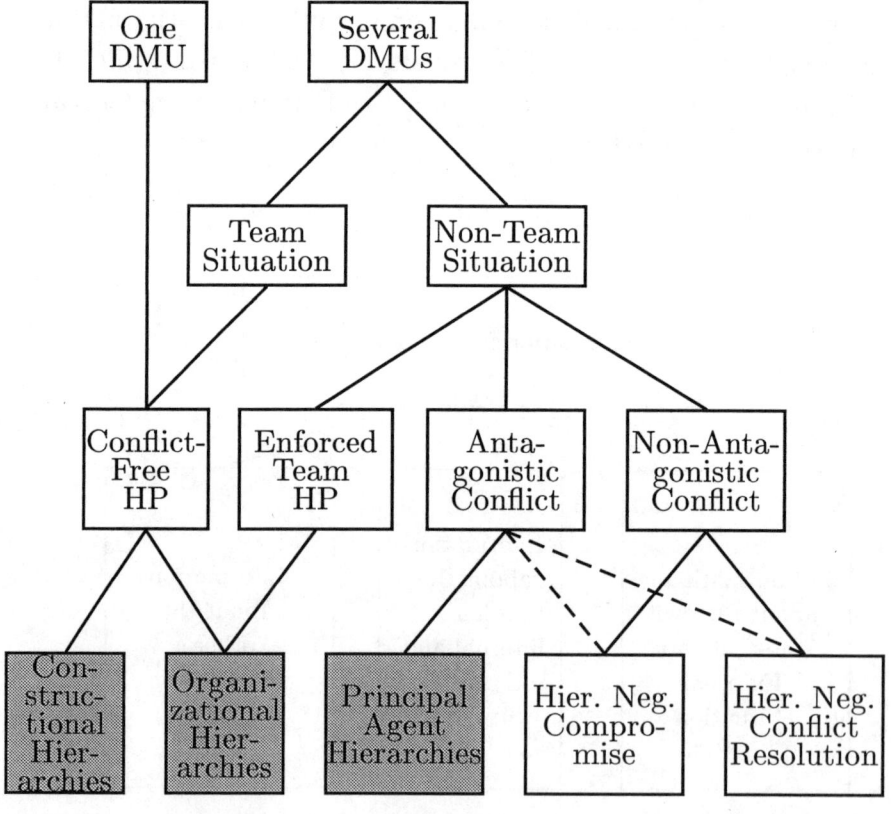

Fig. 2.3: Hierarchies in Distributed Decision Making

hierarchies which are altogether treated as **conflict-free hier-archical planning** problems. Clearly, if the conflict-free levels are following different goals, their improvement is favorable for all parties, i.e., even for competitive goals the parties support each other. (For a further discussion of this point see Section 2.3.)

For the **non-team based case**, the levels follow competitive goals in an egocentric way. In the non-antagonistic case, this results in **'fair' negotiations** without any opportunistic beha-vior, seeking a balance between the levels. This balance can be a compromise or a (proper) conflict resolution. In case of a **compromise**, the levels consider the result as the best solution being achievable without changing their preference structure. For a **resolution**, the situation is different. Here at least one of the levels is adapting its objectives. Clearly, in hierarchical situations in which we are primarily interested, negotiations will be considered within a hierarchical context. Moreover, we will not consider negotiations between antagonistic contracting parties.

Finally, for antagonistic levels, one has a situation which typi-cally is treated in **principal agent theory**. The levels of this so-called **principal agent hierarchy** possess private informa-tion and are behaving opportunistically so that cheating and bluffing has to be taken into account and the compromise is reached at the price of offering incentives. Hence, both DMUs do not consider the compromise as the best that could possibly be achieved through cooperation.

As a limiting case one might consider the **enforced team situa-tion**. In this case there exists a conflict between the levels. The top-level, however, has the power such that (without offering incentives) its instruction represents a compelling obligation for the base-level. This instruction is often called a 'forcing contract', and the hierarchy will be called **'enforced team**

hierarchy'. (For a clear definition of this case see Section 2.3, esp. Fig. 2.5(b).)

According to Fig. 2.3, let us call the (shaded) hierarchies in the bottom line **general planning hierarchies**. Note that constructional and organizational hierarchies were defined in Section 1.1 (Fig. 1.4) as to their information status. Thus, in principle, organizational hierarchies can occur in teams or in non-team settings. Together with the negotiation configurations, general planning hierarchies comprise the entire set of **hierarchical configurations** or **hierarchies in distributed decision making**.

Hierarchical configurations may further be characterized by the interrelationship between the criteria of the levels. Let us therefore postpone this additional clarification after having introduced some further notation.

Chapter 3 will be exclusively devoted to **constructional hierarchies**, while Chapter 4 is reserved for a deeper discussion of **organizational hierarchies**. Antagonistic hierarchies will be treated in Chapter 5 in the framework of **principal agent hierarchies** and, finally, **hierarchical negotiations** are the subject of Chapters 11 and 12.

2.2 Coupling Equations and Anticipation Function

Disregarding hierarchical negotiations, Fig. 2.1 reduces to the case of only one instruction as depicted in Fig. 2.4. In this figure, we adopted a more formal description than in Fig. 2.1. Each level is described by a decision model M depending on a preference structure (criterion) C and a decision field (or action space) A. Hence, one has

$M^T = M^T(C^T, A^T)$ for the top-level and

$M^B = M^B(C^B, A^B)$ for the base-level.

The anticipated base-level is described by the decision model $\hat{M}^B = \hat{M}(\hat{C}^B, \hat{A}^B)$, where the hat ' ^ ' will always be used to denote estimates or variables of an estimated model. The variable $a^T \in A^T$ denotes the decision of the top-level with a^{T^*} being an optimal value. The decision a^T implies an instruction $IN = IN(a^T)$ which is often identical with a^T.

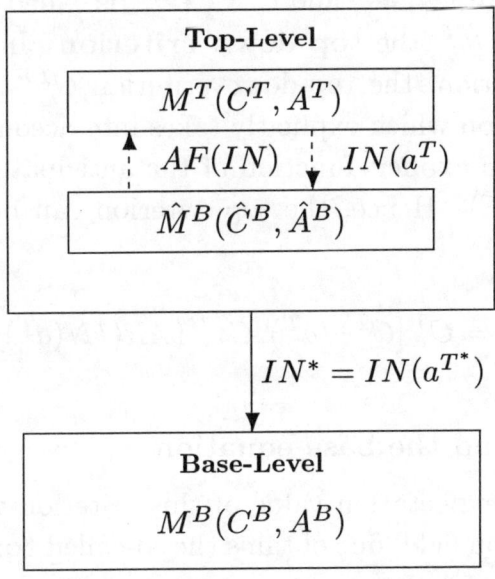

Fig. 2.4: Hierarchical Planning

The most interesting quantity in Fig. 2.4 is certainly the so-called **anticipation function** $AF(IN)$. It describes the base-level's possible reaction with respect to an instruction IN. It is only through $AF(IN)$ that the base-level is taken into account by the top-level. Generally, the anticipation function may be considered as a possible response to the stimulus IN. A formal derivation of $AF(IN)$ will be presented shortly. Let us first look more closely at the top- and base-decision models.

As just introduced, a decision model can be completely defined by a decision field and a performance criterion. For our purposes, however, it will be convenient, in addition, to mark explicitly the information status I and the time at which a decision has to be made. Hence, top- and base-level may be described by

$M^T := \{C^T, A^T, I_{t_0}^T\}$ and
$M^B := \{C^B, A^B, I_{t_1}^B\}$, respectively.

The top-criterion C^T is not a monolithic criterion without any structure. It turns out to be sufficient, however, to decompose it into only two criteria, C^{TT} and C^{TB}. C^{TT} is called the **private criterion**, and C^{TB} the **top-down criterion**. In contrast to the private criterion, the top-down criterion C^{TB} is that part of the top-criterion which explicitly takes into account the base-level, i.e., it is an explicit function of the anticipation function: $C^{TB} = C^{TB}(AF)$. Hence, the top-criterion can be written in greater detail:

$$C^T(a^T) = C^T\big[C^{TT}(a^T), C^{TB}\big(AF(IN(a^T))\big)\big].$$

(1) The top- and the base-equation

Optimizing the expectation value of this criterion with respect to the top-decision field, one obtains the so-called **top-equation** (2.1)

$$a^{T^*} = \arg \operatorname*{opt}_{a^T \in A^T} E\Big\{C^T\big[C^{TT}(a^T), C^{TB}\big(AF(IN(a^T))\big)\big]\big|I_{t_0}^T\Big\}$$

with $\arg f(x) \equiv x$ and $E\{...|I_{t_0}^T\}$ being the mathematical expectation with respect to the information status $I_{t_0}^T$. The optimal value a^{T^*} results in an instruction $IN^* = IN(a^{T^*})$ which, in principle, affects criterion, decision field, and information status of the base-level. Hence, in analogy to Eq. (2.1), the optimal base-decision can be derived from (2.2)

$$a^{B^*} = \arg \operatorname*{opt}_{a^B \in A_{IN^*}^B} E\Big\{C_{IN^*}^B\big(C_{IN^*}^{BB}(a^B), C_{IN^*}^{BT}(a^B)\big)\big|I_{IN^*,t_1}^B\Big\}$$

with C^{BB} being the base-private criterion and C^{BT} a bottom-up criterion. (Notice that, without any loss of deeper insight, we are assuming a^{T^*} and a^{B^*} to be unique).

At least for ordinary hierarchical planning problems (constructional and organizational hierarchies of Chapters 3 and 4) a detailed description of the base-criterion by C^{BB} and C^{BT} proves not to be necessary. Instead of the extensive **base-equation** (2.2) let us therefore simply write

$$a^{B^*} = \arg \operatorname*{opt}_{a^B \in A^B_{IN^*}} E\left\{ C^B_{IN^*}(a^B) | I^B_{IN^*, t_1} \right\}. \qquad (2.3)$$

(2) The anticipation function $AF(IN)$

Eqs. (2.1) and (2.3) describe the general hierarchical planning system. The top-down influence is exerted through the instruction IN^* and the bottom-up anticipative influence enters the top-decision via the anticipation function $AF(IN)$ (possibly based on a cognition inquiry procedure (e.g., see [Bisdorff])). This reaction function can, in principle, be empirically measured or one can try to extract it from past experience. The only aspect which is of importance is its dependence on the possible instruction IN.

For numerous hierarchical planning situations, however, it indeed turns out that $AF(IN)$ can be derived from an estimated base-equation. In this case, $AF(IN)$ proves to be the optimal base-decision $\hat{a}^{B^o}(IN)$ of the anticipated base-level:

$$AF(IN) \equiv \hat{a}^{B^o}(IN) = \arg \operatorname*{opt}_{\hat{a}^B \in \hat{A}^B_{IN}} E\left\{ \hat{C}^B_{IN}(\hat{a}^B) | \hat{I}^B_{IN} \right\}. \qquad (2.4)$$

$\hat{I}^B_{IN}$ denotes the information which the top-level assumes in $t = t_0$ the base-level will possess in $t = t_1$. Note that if $\hat{I}^B_{IN}$ is only known stochastically, $I^T_{t_0}$ contains the corresponding (possibly subjective) probabilities. As a consequence, $AF(IN)$

may often be a random variable. The suffix 'o' always denotes an intermediate optimization. It serves, for instance, to differentiate $\hat{a}^{B^0}(IN)$ from the final decision $\hat{a}^{B^*} := \hat{a}^{B^0}(IN^*)$. Eq. (2.4) will be called the **anticipation relation**.

(3) Re-evaluations

The top-down criterion $C^{TB} = C^{TB}(\hat{a}^{B^0}(IN))$ proves to be one of the key properties of the theory of hierarchical planning. It re-evaluates the assumed optimal behavior of the base-level. This re-evaluation is due to the levels' diverging preferences and information states. For levels building a team, however, a re-evaluation is not needed, implying the criteria C^{TB} and $\hat{C}^B$ to be complementary. If, on the other hand, the levels, and hence the criteria C^{TB} and $\hat{C}^B$ are conflicting, re-evaluating is crucial. In fact, since in hierarchical planning situations the base-level is not allowed to react, a re-evaluation results in an instruction which, as mentioned above, can be considered as a forcing contract. For a more comprehensive discussion see the next section.

(4) The complete set of coupling equations

The Eqs. (2.1), (2.3), and (2.4) will be called **coupling equations** and, for reasons of reference, will henceforth be written in the indicated sequential order as given below.

The coupling equations describe the interdependencies for the case of general planning hierarchies (see Fig. 2.3). They therefore describe as a special case also non-decision time hierarchies, i.e., the case $t_0 = t_1$. Moreover, as a further specification, for constructional hierarchies, the case of information symmetry is included in the Eqs. (2.5). In addition, the anticipation may not only affect the top-criterion but the top-decision space as well: $A^T = A^T_{AF(IN)}$ (e.g., Secs. 2.5.1, 2.5.2, or 6.3.2) indicating, for instance, the result of some learning process of the top-level. Particularly, an implicit anticipation (see Sec. 2.4 below) will influence the top-level via its decision field A^T. Finally, even the optimization operator of the base-level may depend on the instruction: opt $=$ opt$_{IN}$ (see Sec. 8.3), or, to put it more generally, the top-level is assumed to interfere in the base-level's decision process.

Coupling Equations

$$a^{T^*} = \arg \operatorname*{opt}_{a^T \in A^T} E\left\{ C^T \left[C^{TT}(a^T), C^{TB}(AF(IN)) \right] | I_{t_0}^T \right\}$$

$$(2.5a)$$

$$IN = IN(a^T)$$

$$AF(IN) = \arg \operatorname*{opt}_{\hat{a}^B \in \hat{A}_{IN}^B} E\left\{ \hat{C}_{IN}^B(\hat{a}^B) | \hat{I}_{IN}^B \right\} \qquad (2.5b)$$

$$a^{B^*} = \arg \operatorname*{opt}_{a^B \in A_{IN^*}^B} E\left\{ C_{IN^*}^B(a^B) | I_{IN^*, t_1}^B \right\} \qquad (2.5c)$$

The Eqs. (2.5a) and (2.5b) will usually be solved in an iterative way, thus giving rise to a **hierarchical algorithm**. For this algorithm Eq. (2.5b) may be considered as a general updating equation whereas Eq. (2.5a) represents the final step. For intermediate top-equations one would replace a^{T^*} with 'intermediate' optimal decisions a^{T^0}. Section 2.6 will discuss some general properties of the solution of Eqs. (2.5).

2.3 Distinguishing Hierarchical Configurations by their Team Character

Returning to the general exposition given in Section 2.1, we are now in a position to characterize the team nature of the hierarchical configurations listed in Fig. 2.3 in utilizing the criteria just introduced. To this end consider Fig. 2.5 which depicts in its part (a) a team relationship while the remaining figures (b) through (d) represent typical non-team situations.

In case the two levels form a **team**, the criteria C^{TB} and $\hat{C}^B$ are complementary. That is, what is favorable for one party is favorable for the other party as well. Hence, as depicted in Fig. 2.5a, $C^{TB} = C^{TB}(\hat{C}^B)$ is a strict monotonously increasing function of $\hat{C}^B$. Often one will even have $C^{TB} \equiv \hat{C}^B$. In that case there is no re-evaluation taken into consideration, i.e., the top-level truely adopts the base-criterion and the curve in Fig. 2.5a is the diagonal. If, for a team relationship, one still has $C^{TB} \not\equiv \hat{C}^B$, a re-evaluation is performed by the top-level. This re-evaluation, however, is only of a 'technical' nature, transforming, for example, value units of the base-level into those of the top-level. The following chapters will provide numerous examples.

The **non-team based relationship** is depicted in Fig. 2.5b which shows with its strict monotonously decreasing dependence between C^{TB} and $\hat{C}^B$ a conflicting situation. Here a non-trivial re-evaluation is necessary, and the top-level has to make sure, for instance, under penalty of severe consequences, that the instruction communicated to the base-level is actually followed.

In case of a **conflicting but non-antagonistic relationship**, the two levels seek a compromise as indicated in Fig. 2.5c. Since in negotiations one has real actors, the anticipated $\hat{C}^B$ is replaced by C^B. A compromise does not resolve a conflict.

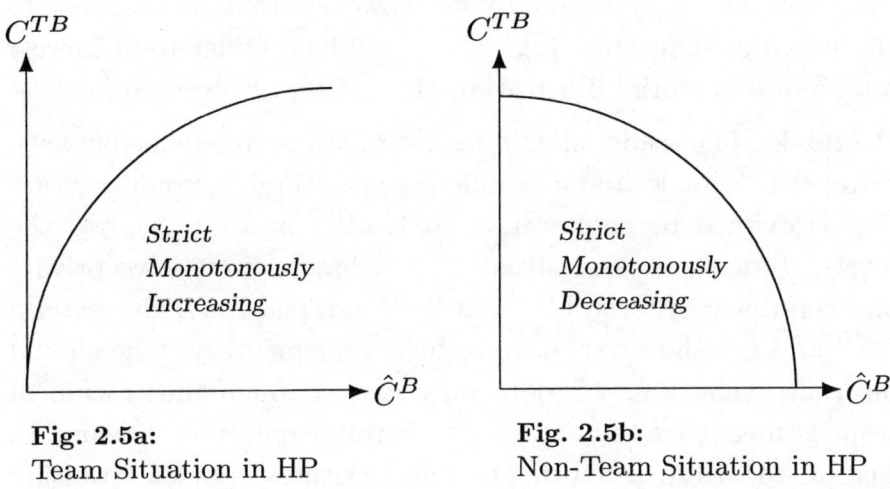

Fig. 2.5a:
Team Situation in HP

Fig. 2.5b:
Non-Team Situation in HP

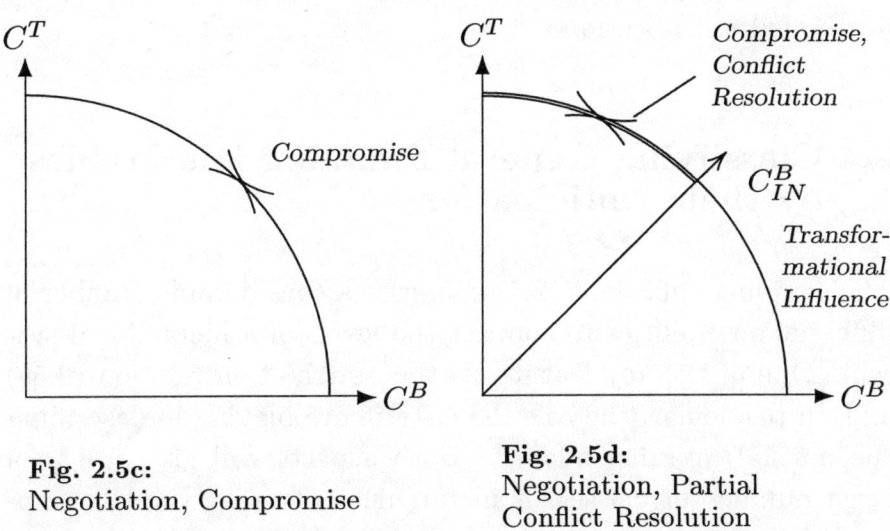

Fig. 2.5c:
Negotiation, Compromise

Fig. 2.5d:
Negotiation, Partial
Conflict Resolution

Fig. 2.5: Characterization of Hierarchical Configurations

Such a **resolution** requires an intrinsic or transformational change of the preference attitudes. Fig. 2.5d shows such a change of the base-level from C^B to C_{IN}^B caused by the influence IN of the top-level. This change reduces the area in which a compromise still has to be found. Note, however, that, in contrast to the previous diagrams, Fig. 2.5d should be understood merely as a simple pictorial illustration of a rather involved context.

Remark: The reader should be aware of the difference between 'competitive goals' and a 'conflicting situation'. A conflict situation is defined by competitive goals C^{TB} and $\hat{C}^B$ 'across' the levels. Indeed, a team situation can have competitive private and top-down criteria, C^{TT} and C^{TB}, respectively; the criteria C^{TB} and $\hat{C}^B$, however, have to be complementary. One should be aware that Fig. 2.5 does only give a rough illustration of what is meant by the not easy to capture notion of a team. In case of stochastic or multi-component criteria, e.g., the situation turns out to be far more involved. An opportunistic behavior, e.g., cannot be depicted in such a simplistic way as in Fig. 2.5. For this case, further considerations are necessary which are postponed until Section 5.4.

2.4 Classifying General Planning Hierarchies by their Anticipation

The coupling equations (2.5) comprise a considerable number of different possibilities to connect the levels of a hierarchical system. One of the key features is the anticipation relation (2.5b) and, in particular, the role the criteria are playing in describing the mutual interdependence. Both aspects will give rise to a large number of classes of hierarchical planning models comprising such prominent model classes as the simple top-down hierarchy, or the tactical-operational planning model.

(1) Grade of anticipation

One may distinguish between two main types of anticipation, the reactive and the non-reactive anticipation (see Fig. 2.6). The

reactive anticipation considers a possible reaction of the base-level with respect to the top-level's instructions. For the **non-reactive anticipation**, on the other hand, no specific reaction is taken into account.

Several types of reactive anticipation may be distinguished, characterizing, in particular, prominent types of hierarchies.

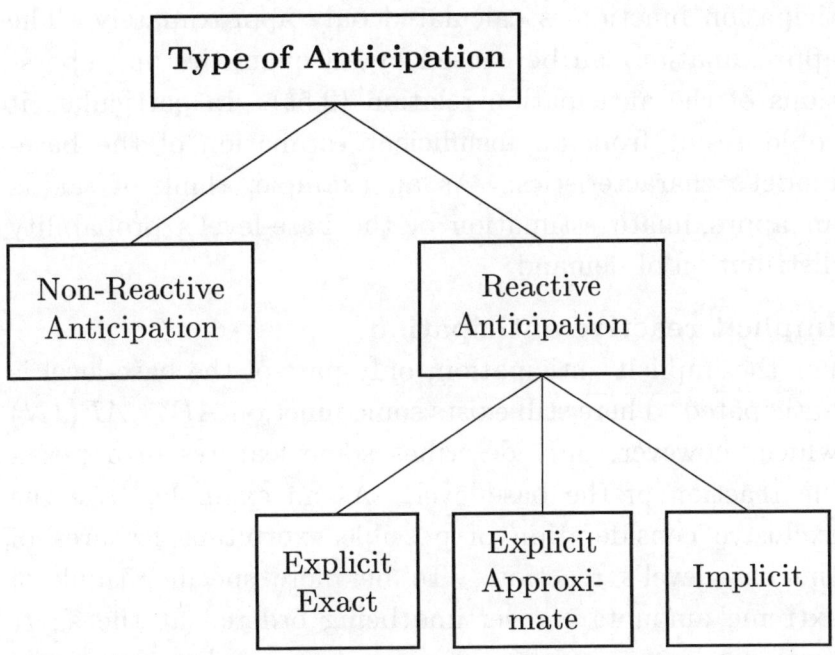

Fig. 2.6: Types of Anticipation

(i) **Exact explicit reactive anticipation**
     For the exact explicit reactive anticipation, the top-level anticipates the base-level exactly apart from uncertainty which is being revealed at the base-level. The anticipation function is exactly calculated via Eq. (2.5*b*) without relying on any approximations, i.e., *it exactly matches the optimization procedure the top-level assumes the base-level*

will follow. In other words: The anticipation is *explicit* since it anticipates the *actual* behavior of the base-level, it is *exact* because the information known to the top-level is processed exactly. For convenience we will occasionally refer to this important idealized case simply as **perfect anticipation**.

(ii) **Approximate explicit reactive anticipation**

For the approximate explicit reactive anticipation, the anticipation function is calculated only approximately. The approximation can be caused by all quantities and operations of the anticipation relation (2.5*b*). In particular, it could result from an insufficient estimation of the base-model's characteristics. As an example, think of taking an approximate estimation of the base-level's probability distribution of demand.

(iii) **Implicit reactive anticipation**

For the implicit anticipation, only part of the base-level is anticipated. There still exists some function $AF = AF(IN)$ which, however, only describes some features of a possible reaction of the base-level. As an example, take the exclusive consideration of possible exorbitant features of the base-level's reaction. To be more specific, think of extreme amounts of overtime being ordered at the short term production level in response to a too low amount of ordinary workforce being provided by the medium term aggregate production level. In anticipating only these extreme values, the top-level can at least ensure the feasibility of its decisions. Implicit reactive anticipations will usually enter the top-equation (2.5*a*) through the top-decision field $A^T = A^T_{AF(IN)}$.

(iv) **Non-reactive anticipation**

For the non-reactive anticipation, an anticipation function no longer exists. The base-level is not taken into account through the anticipation relation (2.5*b*). Instead, some general features of the base-level are accommodated in the components of the top-equation (2.5a). These features, however, do not depend on any particular instruction IN. Of course, the criterion C^{TB} is obsolete.

Obviously, the four cases (i) through (iv), merely represent important prototypes. One will encounter numerous intermediate types of anticipation and, in addition, each prototype generally consists of a variety of particular subtypes.

(2) Types of criteria

Besides the four general kinds of anticipation let us distinguish four prominent hierarchical situations according to the structure of their criteria.

(a) $\bar{C}^T = \{\bar{C}^{TT}, \bar{C}^{TB}\}$: This multi-criterion situation generally describes the influence of the base-level on the top-level (with the bar denoting expected values). All kinds of general design decisions, e.g., such as the design of a flexibility potential, are captured by this criterion (see Chapter 7).

(b) $C^T = C^{TT} + C^{TB}$: This additive form of the general criterion will often be used in conjunction with the exact explicit reactive anticipation (i). Typically, as we shall see in the sequel, for a team situation it describes the large class of **tactical-operational hierarchies**.

(c) $C^T = C^{TB}$: In this case, the top-model relies completely on the base-model. As an example take the case when the top-model is just an aggregate base-model.

(d) $C^T = C^{TT}$: For the non-reactive anticipation case (iv) this describes the typical **top-down hierarchy**. Often only this strict top-down case is known to be 'hierarchical planning' in its strict sense. It should be clear by now that the way how hierarchical planning is treated here describes a far richer concept.

Note, however, that $C^{TB} \equiv 0$ is not completely characterizing a top-down hierarchy. In fact, particularly in case of an implicit reactive anticipation, one still might have a bottom-up influence via the top-decision field $A^T = A^T_{AF(IN)}$.

The characterizations (i) to (iv) and (a) to (d) comprise a large number of different general planning hierarchies which will be further explored in subsequent chapters. First, however, let us give three illustrative examples and add some remarks concerning the general solution properties of the coupling equations.

2.5 Three Illustrative Examples

To illustrate the concepts that have been developed so far, let us consider three simple examples. The first and the second example compare, for a tactical-operational hierarchy, a non-reactive and a perfect anticipation. The third example compares all four types of anticipation.

2.5.1 Example 1: Make or Buy Decisions

Consider the following medium term production problem: For given capacities and given demand determine the amount of an item to be produced and to be purchased such that profit is maximized. This problem can easily be stated as a linear program. Define the following quantities:

x_j: produced amount of product j,
y_j: purchased amount of product j,
y_j^{max}: highest allowed amount to be purchased,
q_j: selling price for product j,
c_j: variable production cost for product j,
p_j: purchase price for product j,

d_j: demand of product j,

T_i: capacity of production facility i,

a_{ij}:   production coefficient (inverse productivity rate) of product j with respect to capacity i, which describes the amount of capacity i needed to produce one unit of product j.

Indices: $j = 1, \ldots, n$ and $i = 1, \ldots, m$.

With these notations, the make or buy problem can readily be stated as follows:

Maximize the contribution margin

$$CM = \sum_{j=1}^{n} q_j (x_j + y_j) - \sum_{j=1}^{n} c_j x_j - \sum_{j=1}^{n} p_j y_j \longrightarrow \max \qquad (2.6)$$

s.t. the capacity constraints

$$\sum_{j=1}^{n} a_{ij} x_j \leq T_i, \qquad\qquad i = 1, \ldots, m$$

the purchase constraints

$$y_j \leq y_j^{max}, \qquad\qquad j = 1, \ldots, n$$

the demand constraints

$$x_j + y_j \leq d_j, \qquad\qquad j = 1, \ldots, n$$

and the non-negativity constraints

$$x_j, y_j \geq 0, \qquad\qquad j = 1, \ldots, n.$$

This is the typical way a make or buy problem is traditionally stated. In reality, however, things are often more complicated.

In many cases, the buying decision y_j is made after the production decision x_j at a time when more information about demand d_j and sometimes also about the purchasing price p_j is available. Hence, the problem is to be split up into a sequence of decisions with a first (top-)decision made in $t = t_0$ and a second (base-) decision made in $t = t_1$. Let us therefore construct the following hierarchical model:

Top-level $(t = t_0)$

$$(2.7a) \quad CM^* = \max_{x \in X}\left\{\sum_{j=1}^{n}(q_j - c_j)x_j + \sum_{j=1}^{n}(q_j - \hat{p}_j)\hat{y}_j^0(x)\right\}$$

with $x := (x_1, \ldots, x_n)$, and $\hat{p}_j$ being the top-level's estimate at time t_0 of the purchasing price of product j in t_1. X denotes the top-decision space which is mainly restricted by the capacity constraints

$$X := \left\{x : \sum_{j=1}^{n}a_{ij}x_j \leq T_i, \, x \geq 0, \quad i = 1, \ldots, m\right\}.$$

The most interesting quantity in $(2.7a)$ certainly is $\hat{y}_j^0(x)$. As we know from the definition of equation $(2.5b)$, $\hat{y}^0(x)$ is the anticipation function of the purchasing problem and is given by

$$(2.7b) \quad \hat{y}^0(x) = \arg\max_{\hat{y} \in \hat{Y}_x}\sum_{j=1}^{n}(q_j - \hat{p}_j)\hat{y}_j$$

with $\hat{y} := (\hat{y}_1, \ldots, \hat{y}_n)$ and

$$\hat{Y}_x := \{\hat{y} : \hat{y}_j \leq y_j^{max}, \, \hat{y}_j \leq \hat{d}_j - x_j, \, \hat{y}_j \geq 0, \, j = 1, \ldots, n\}$$

with $\hat{d}_j$ denoting the top-level's demand forecast of product j in time $t = t_0$ for the demand situation in $t = t_1$.

The constraint

$$\hat{y}_j \leq \hat{d}_j - x_j$$

is called **coupling condition**. The reader will easily identify the internally produced amounts x_j $(j = 1, \ldots, n)$ as the instruction: $IN = IN(x) = x$. Hence, the coupling condition shows how the production model can influence the estimated purchasing model.

Base-level $(t = t_1)$

After the production decision $x = x^*$ has been made in $t = t_0$, the purchasing decision problem in $t = t_1$ can readily be formulated as

$$y^*(x^*) = \arg\max_{y \in Y_{x^*}} \sum_{j=1}^{n}(q_j - p_j)y_j. \qquad (2.7c)$$

Note that in $t = t_1$ the estimates $\hat{p}_j$ and $\hat{d}_j$ are replaced by their values p_j and d_j, respectively which, in time t_1, are assumed to be known.

Setting

$$C^{TT}(x) := \sum_{j=1}^{n}(q_j - c_j)x_j,$$

$$C^{B}(y) := \sum_{j=1}^{n}(q_j - p_j)y_j, \quad \text{and}$$

$$\hat{C}^{B}(y) := \sum_{j1}(q_j - \hat{p}_j)y_j,$$

one readily recognizes the coupling equations (2.5):

$$(2.8a) \qquad x^* = \arg \max_{x \in X} \left\{ C^{TT}(x) + \hat{C}^B(\hat{y}^0(x)) \right\}$$

$$(2.8b) \qquad AF(x) = \hat{y}^0(x) = \arg \max_{\hat{y} \in \hat{Y}_x} \hat{C}^B(\hat{y}(x))$$

$$(2.8c) \qquad y^* = \arg \max_{y \in Y_{x*}} C^B(y)$$

The system (2.8) is a special case of the general coupling equation (2.5): The criterion is additive (case (b)) and the top down criterion C^{TB} is identical to the estimated base-criterion $C^{TB} \equiv \hat{C}^B$. This particular case is typical of a situation in which there is just one decision maker so that, because of the absence of a conflict between the levels (conflict-free case in Fig. 2.3), there is no re-evaluation required. Furthermore, a trivial re-evaluation, simply because of the sheer fact that base- and top-criteria are measured in different dimensions, is not relevant either.

Which type of anticipation has been applied? Obviously, because of the existence of an anticipation function, we did not use a non-reactive anticipation. Furthermore, the anticipation is not implicit reactive (see Fig. 2.6), since $\hat{y}$ describes a possible (complete) decision of the base-level. Hence, we are left with an explicit reactive anticipation. The estimates $\hat{p}_j$ and $\hat{d}_j$ are assumed to be the *only* (stochastic) information available at $t = t_0$. Since no approximations are involved, this information is exactly processed by the anticipation relation (2.8b). Hence, Eq. (2.8b) is identified to be an exact explicit reactive anticipation (case (i), Sec. 2.4).

Remark: Generally, the solution of the non-hierarchically structured model, presented at the outset, is called a **simultaneous solution**. As was pointed out, such a solution, in its strict sense, does not exist, simply because the realizations of the random variables are not known.

It proves to be rewarding to study this simple example somewhat further. This will be done by simplifying the model even more and by comparing the exact explicit reactive anticipation with an unpretentious non-reactive top-down procedure. Let us therefore consider only one product and one production facility.

(1) Perfect anticipation

In this case of an exact explicit reactive anticipation, Eqs. (2.7a) and (2.7b) reduce to the **top-equation**

$$C^T = (q - c)x + (q - \hat{p})\hat{y}^0(x) = v^x x + \hat{v}^y \, \hat{y}^0(x) \longrightarrow \max$$

s.t.

$$ax \leq T$$

(using the abreviations $v^x := q - c$ and $\hat{v}^y := q - \hat{p}$).

The **anticipation function** is the optimizer of

$$\hat{C}^B = \hat{v}^y \hat{y} \longrightarrow \max$$

s.t.

$$0 \leq \hat{y} \leq y^{max}$$
$$\hat{y} + x \leq \hat{d}$$

yielding (for $\hat{v}^y > 0$)

$$\hat{y}^0(x) = \min \{y^{max}; \hat{d} - x\}.$$

Substituting $\hat{y}^0(x)$ in C^T and assuming $v^x > 0$ and $\hat{v}^y > 0$ yields the following result:

$$x^* = \begin{cases} \hat{d} \text{ if } \frac{T}{a} \geq \hat{d} \wedge v^x \geq \hat{v}^y & \text{nothing will be purchased} \\[2em] \frac{T}{a} \text{ if } \frac{T}{a} \leq \hat{d} \wedge v^x \geq \hat{v}^y & \text{production up to } \frac{t}{a}, \\ & \text{the remaining amount} \\ & \hat{d} - \frac{T}{a} \text{ will be} \\ & \text{purchased up to the} \\ & \text{highest possible amount} \\[2em] \min\{\frac{T}{a}; \hat{d} - y^{max}\} & \text{production of} \\ \text{if } y^{max} \leq \hat{d} \wedge v^x < \hat{v}^y & \hat{d} - y^{max} \text{ as far} \\ & \text{as possible; the} \\ & \text{remaining amount} \\ & y^{max} \text{ will be purchased} \\[2em] 0 \text{ if } y^{max} \geq \hat{d} \wedge v^x < \hat{v}^y & \text{everything will be} \\ & \text{purchased} \end{cases}$$

Let us now consider the case of a non-reactive anticipation.

(2) Non-reactive anticipation

Since in this strict top-down case an anticipation function does not exist, one simply has for the

Top-level

$$C^T = C^{TT} = v^x x \longrightarrow \max$$

s.t.

$$ax \leq T$$

$$0 \leq x \leq \hat{d}$$

resulting (for $v^x > 0$) in

$$x^* = \min\{\hat{d}; \frac{T}{a}\}.$$

Note that the only anticipation is through the estimate $\hat{d}$ of total demand. Since there is no anticipation function to be determined, the base-model can immediately be formulated yielding

$$C^B = v^y y \longrightarrow \max$$

s.t.
$$0 \leq y \leq y^{max}$$
$$y \leq d - x^*$$

with the optimal solution

$$y^*(x^*) = \min\{y^{max}; d - \min\{\hat{d}; \frac{T}{a}\}\}.$$

Obviously, this result differs considerably from the perfect anticipation which enables a far richer description of the base-level at the time when the top-decision has to be made.

Remark: The above decision models are formulated in the usual standard format of a linear program. Using the formulation of the coupling equations, one readily may write for the top equation

$$x^* = \arg\max_{x \in A^T} v^x x$$

with
$$A^T := \{x : ax \leq T, 0 \leq x \leq \hat{d}\}$$

and for the base-equation

$$y^* = \arg\max_{y \in A^B} v^y y$$

with
$$A^B := \{y : 0 \leq y \leq y^{max}, y \leq d - x^*\}.$$

2.5.2 Example 2: A Working Time Planning Model

As a second somewhat more detailed and comprehensive example, let us take a working time planning problem. This problem is typical for the important class of plain tactical-operational hierarchies defined by (i, b) in Section 2.4.

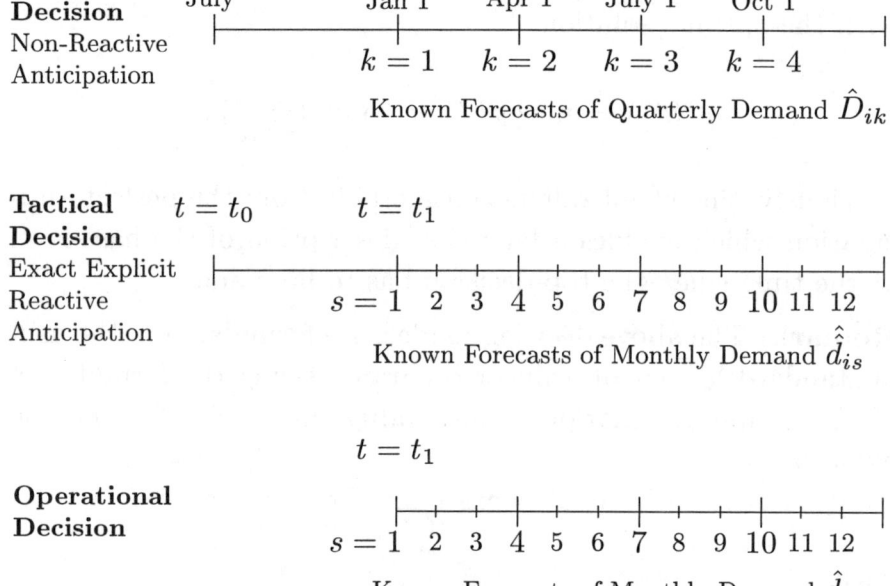

Fig. 2.7: Time Scales and Information Situation of the Example

Consider a company's department which, half a year in advance (in July), has to plan its manpower capacity Y_k ($k = 1, \ldots, 4$) for the quarters of the following year (see Fig. 2.7, tactical decision). Let us assume that, for the four quarters, there exist reliable demand forecasts $\hat{D}_{ik}$ of product i ($i = 1, \ldots, n$). The distribution of this demand over the 3 months of a quarter, however, is only known stochastically.

Half a year later, by the end of December, production has to be planned for the next 12 months (see Fig. 2.7, operational decision). At this time there exist reliable forecasts $\hat{d}_{is}$ ($s = 1, \ldots, 12$) for detailed monthly demand as well. In contrast to the tactical level, inventories x_{is}^I can be built up at the operational level, and one can increase capacity y_s by overtime o_s.

(a) The tactical problem (top-level, $t = t_0$) now is to make a hiring (Y_k^+) or firing (Y_k^-) decision such that the demand of the four quarters can be produced and (man power) capacity cost is minimized.

(b) The operational problem (base-level, $t = t_1$) is to minimize inventory and overtime costs while monthly demand must be met.

Let us now consider two possible hierarchical models. The first model describes a non-reactive anticipation whereas the second one illustrates a perfect anticipation.

(1) Non-reactive anticipation

In this situation the top-level does only take into account some general information about the base-level. It simply 'anticipates' (operational) monthly demands $\hat{d}_{is}$ by the aggregate quarterly forecasts $\hat{D}_{ik}$. Hence, the **top-equation** (2.5a) yields

$$a^{T^*} = \arg \min_{a^T \in A^T} \sum_{k=1}^{4} (c_k Y_k + c_k^+ Y_k^+ + c_k^- Y_k^-). \qquad (2.9a)$$

The top-decision is defined as $a^T := (Y, Y^+, Y^-)$ with $Y := (Y_1, \ldots, Y_4)$, $Y^+ := (Y_1^+, \ldots, Y_4^+)$, and $Y^- := (Y_1^-, \ldots, Y_4^-)$. Eq. (2.9a) minimizes the sum of manpower capacity cost as well as hiring and firing costs. Obviously, the top-criterion reduces to a private criterion

$$C^T = C^{TT} = \sum_{k=1}^{4} (c_k Y_k + c_k^+ Y_k^+ + c_k^- Y_k^-)$$

as it must be the case for a pure top-down planning situation. The top-decision space A^T is defined by

$$A^T := \{a^T : (I) \wedge (II) \wedge (III) \wedge (IV) \wedge (V)\}$$

(I) $Y_k = Y_{k-1} + Y_k^+ - Y_k^-$ $\forall k$: capacity balance equation

(II) $Y_0 = Y_0'$: initial capacity

(III) $Y_k^+ \leq Y^{+max}$,   : hiring and
       $Y_k^- \leq Y^{-max}$ $\forall k$ firing limitation

(IV) $\sum_{i=1}^{n} \bar{a}_i \hat{D}_{ik} \leq Y_k$ $\forall k$: fulfillment of demand,
                                  ($\bar{a}_i$: production coefficient)

(V) $a^T \geq 0$: non-negativity constraint

Notice that the non-reactive anticipation $\hat{D}_{ik}$ influences the top-level via the top-decision space $A^T = A^T(\hat{D}_{11}, \ldots, \hat{D}_{n,4})$. In fact, no anticipation function can be determined.

As a solution of (2.9a), one obtains the decision a^{T^*}. This decision is immediately executed, i.e., a^{T^*} is not only factual, but also *final*. As **instruction** for the base-level, one has

$$IN^* = \{IN_k^*, \quad k = 1, \ldots, 4\} \quad \text{with}$$

$$IN_k^* = IN_k(a_k^{T^*}) = Y_k^* \quad (k = 1, \ldots, 4)$$

which fixes the available amount of monthly working hours y_s^* ($s = 1, \ldots, 12$) for the 12 months of the next year, $y_s^* = \frac{1}{3} Y_k^*$ $\forall s \in M(k)$, with $M(1) = \{1, 2, 3\}$, $M(2) = \{4, 5, 6\}$, $M(3) = \{7, 8, 9\}$, $M(4) = \{10, 11, 12\}$. Note that, for this example, the instruction is *not* identical with the top-decision.

The **base-problem** at $t = t_1$ can now be stated as follows:

(2.9c) $$a^{B^*} = \arg \min_{a^B \in A_{IN^*}^B} \left\{ \sum_{s=1}^{12} \sum_{i=1}^{n} h_{is} x_{is}^I + \sum_{s=1}^{12} c_s^0 o_s \right\}.$$

Eq. (2.9c) minimizes inventory and overtime costs with h_{is} and c_s^0 being inventory and overtime cost parameters respectively.

(Variable production cost other than manpower capacity cost need not be considered.) The base-decision is given by

$$a^B := \big((x_{is}), (x_{is}^I), (o_s)\big), \quad \text{with} \quad (x_{is}) := (x_{11}, \ldots, x_{n,12})$$

being the production plan for all products; similarly

$$(x_{is}^I) := (x_{11}^I, \ldots, x_{n,12}^I) \quad \text{and} \quad (o_s) := (o_1, \ldots, o_{12}).$$

The base-decision space is defined by

$$A_{IN^*}^B := \{a^B : \text{(i)} \wedge \text{(ii)} \wedge \text{(iii)} \wedge \text{(iv)} \wedge \text{(v)}\}$$

(i) $x_{is}^I = x_{is-1}^I + x_{is} - \hat{d}_{is}$ $\forall i, s$: inventory balance equation

(ii) $x_{i0}^I = x_{io}^{I'}$ $\forall i$: initial condition

(iii) $\sum_{i=1}^{n} a_i x_{is} \leq y_s^* + o_s$ $\forall s$: capacity restriction

(iv) $o_s \leq o^{max}$ $\forall s$: overtime restriction

(v) $x_{is}, x_{is}^I, o_s \geq 0$ $\forall i, s$: non-negativity constraints

Note that the instruction Y_k^* implies $y_s^* = \frac{1}{3} Y_k^*$ and enters the base-level through the capacity constraint (iii). Eq. (iii) therefore turns out to be the **coupling condition**.

(2) Perfect anticipation

Consider now the case of an exact explicit reactive anticipation. Assume that all parameters h_{is} and c_s^0 are known at $t = t_0$ and, in addition, the top-level possesses, as the *only* information, monthly demand forecasts $\hat{\hat{d}}_{is}$. These might differ from the operational forecasts $\hat{d}_{is}$, i.e., $\hat{\hat{d}}_{is} \neq \hat{d}_{is}$ $\forall i, s$.

Since we assume the hierarchical system to build a team, no re-evaluation is necessary. Hence, the top-criterion is given by

$$C^T = C^{TT} + \hat{C}^B(AF)$$

resulting in the **top-equation**

$$a^{T^*} = \arg \min_{a^T \in A^T} \big\{ C^{TT}(a^T) + \hat{C}^B\big(AF(IN)\big) \big\} \qquad (2.10a)$$

with C^{TT} and $\hat{C}^B$ as given in case **(1)** of the non-reactive anticipation (see Eq. (2.9c)). The same holds for the decision space A^T. One can take the decision space equivalent to case **(1)** but without the non-reactive bottom-up influence (IV)

$$A^T := \{a^T : (\text{I}) \wedge (\text{II}) \wedge (\text{III}) \wedge (\text{V})\}.$$

Remark: Clearly, since all characteristics (i.e., h_{is} and c_s^0) are known exactly, $\hat{C}^B$ could in this particular case be replaced by C^B.

The **anticipation function** $AF(IN) = \hat{a}^{B^0}(IN)$ can be calculated from the anticipation relation which, except for $\hat{\hat{d}}_{is}$, is structurally identical with (2.9c):

$$(2.10b) \qquad \hat{a}^{B^0} = \arg\min_{\hat{a}^B \in \hat{A}^B_{IN}} \left\{ \sum_{s=1}^{12} \sum_{i=1}^{n} h_{is} \hat{x}^I_{is} + \sum_{s=1}^{12} c_s^0 \hat{o}_s \right\}$$

with

$$\hat{A}^B_{IN} := \{\hat{a}^B : (\text{i'}) \wedge (\text{ii'}) \wedge (\text{iii'}) \wedge (\text{iv'}) \wedge (\text{v'})\},$$

where, for example, (i) is replaced by

$$(\text{i'}) \quad \hat{x}^I_{is} = \hat{x}^I_{is-1} + \hat{x}_{is} - \hat{\hat{d}}_{is},$$

and the same replacement with anticipated variables holds for the remaining constraints. Finally, the base-equation is identical with (2.9c).

Remark: If the top-level does not only possess forecasts $\hat{\hat{d}}_{is}$, but has (subjective) probabilities for the occurrence of $\hat{d}_{is}$, Eq. (2.10a) could be written as

$$a^{T*} = \arg\min_{a^T \in A^T} \left\{ C^{TT}(a^T) + E\{\hat{C}^B(\hat{a}^{B^0}) | I^T_{t_0}\} \right\}$$

with $\hat{\hat{d}}_{is}$ being replaced with the random variables $\hat{d}_{is}$ and $I_{t_0}^T$ comprising the necessary probabilities (see also the general case of two-stage programming in Section 4.2.3).

2.5.3 Example 3: Supply Contracts

The third example illustrates different anticipations for a problem in supply chain management. Consider the following situation: A supplier negotiates with two customers I and II the conditions of a supply contract for a special mechanical part. The contract fixes the price of the part and binds the supplier to provide the customers with the number of parts they will order in the next year. This amount is not known in advance, i.e., d^I and d^{II} are random variables. However, the supplier knows that only the two scenarios shown in Table 2.1 can occur and that these scenarios will have equal probability. The price customer I is willing to pay is 6 EUR, and for customer II it is 7 EUR (see Table 2.1).

	Demand I d^I	Demand II d^{II}	Probability
Scenario 1	1000	10000	0.5
Scenario 2	5000	2000	0.5
Price (EUR)	6	7	

Table 2.1: Selling Conditions

The supplier is able to produce 8000 units at a cost of 5 EUR each. If, however, demand exceeds the amount of 8000 units, she has to switch to additional far more expensive capacity incurring a cost of 15 EUR per unit (see Table 2.2).

	Normal Production x	Excess Production y
Cost (EUR)	5	15

Table 2.2: Production Conditions

The question now arises *which customer might be the most attractive* to the supplier. Or, to be more specific, should there be a contract with customer I or with II, or possibly with both or none of them? Since the contract has to be fixed before the actual production and delivery starts, we have a typical hierarchical planning problem. In particular, one again has a decision time hierarchy (see Fig. 1.3). The top-level is defined by the decision about the contract, whereas the base-level determines, *for known demand*, the actual production decision.

Let us now derive the coupling equations and their solution for all four kinds of anticipation we introduced above.

(1) Perfect anticipation

Clearly, for the exact explicit reactive anticipation, one has, as in the previous examples, the typical case of a tactical-operational hierarchy with C^T being linear. The coupling equations (2.5) therefore yield

$$(2.11a) \quad a^{T^*} = \arg \max_{a^T \in A^T} E\{C^{TT}(a^T) - C^{TB}(AF(IN))|I_{t_0}^T\},$$

$$(2.11b) \quad AF(IN) = \hat{a}^{B^o}(IN) = \arg \min_{\hat{a}^B \in \hat{A}_{IN}^B} \hat{C}_{IN}^B(\hat{a}^B),$$

$$(2.11c) \quad a^{B^*} = \arg \min_{a^B \in A_{IN^*}^B} C_{IN^*}^B(a^B).$$

Note that because demand is assumed to be revealed at $t = t_1$, no expectations have to be taken in $(2.11b)$ and $(2.11c)$.

A contract is evaluated by its expected contribution margin. The private criterion is representing turnover

$$C^{TT} = 6d^I a_I^T + 7d^{II} a_{II}^T,$$

with

$$a_I^T := \begin{cases} 1 & \text{contract with I} \\ 0 & \text{no contract with I} \end{cases}$$

and

$$a_{II}^T := \begin{cases} 1 & \text{contract with II} \\ 0 & \text{no contract with II.} \end{cases}$$

The top-down criterion is yielding total production cost

$$C^{TB} = 5x + 15y.$$

Since there is no re-evaluation, one obviously has

$$C^{TB} = \hat{C}_{IN}^B.$$

Moreover, production unit costs do not depend on the contract and are known at $t = t_0$ to be 5 or 15, depending on whether one has normal production or not. Therefore one simply has

$$\hat{C}_{IN}^B \equiv \hat{C}^B \equiv C^B.$$

Hence, incorporating the anticipation relation $(2.11b)$ in Eq. $(2.11a)$, one obtains

$$a^{T*} = \arg \max_{a^T \in A^T} E\{6d^I a_I^T + 7d^{II} a_{II}^T - \min_{\hat{a}^B \in \hat{A}_{IN}^B} \{5x + 15y\}|I_{t_0}^T\}. \tag{2.12a}$$

Note that since no estimates need be taken, one has $\hat{A}^B = A^B$.

As further specifications, one easily verifies

a^T :   contract decision, implying a defined demand pattern (a_I^T, a_{II}^T)

A^T :   set of possible contracts

$A^T := \{$no contract $(a_I^T = a_{II}^T = 0),$

contract with I $(a_I^T = 1, a_{II}^T = 0),$

contract with II $(a_I^T = 0, a_{II}^T = 1),$

contract with I and II $(a_I^T = a_{II}^T = 1)\}$

$IN \equiv a^T$

a^B :   production decision, $a^B := (x, y)$

A_{IN}^B :   feasible set of production decisions, subject to a specific contract characterized by (a_I^T, a_{II}^T), i.e.,

$$A_{IN}^B := \{(x, y) : x + y \geq d^I a_I^T + d^{II} a_{II}^T, x \leq 8000\}$$

Finally, $I_{t_0}^T$ represents the probability distribution of the demand scenarios d^I and d^{II} at time t_0 when the contract decision has to be made. According to (2.11c), the base-model may therefore be stated as follows:

$$a^{B^*} = \arg\min_{a^B \in A_{IN^*}^B} (5x + 15y)$$

and

$$A_{IN^*}^B := \{(x, y) : x + y \geq d^{I'} a_I^{T^*} + d^{II'} a_{II}^{T^*}, x \leq 8000\}$$

with $d^{I'}$ and $d^{II'}$ denoting realizations of demand.

With these explanations, a solution to the top-equation (2.12a) is now straightforward. For each contract, the profit is calculated for scenario 1 and for scenario 2. As a next step, the mean value is calculated, and, finally, the contract yielding the best profit is chosen. The calculations presented in Table 2.3 result in the recommendation that a contract should be made with customer I, i.e., $a_I^T = 1$ and $a_{II}^T = 0$.

	No Contract	Contract with I	Contract with II	Contract with I and II
Scenario 1				
Turnover	0	6 · 1000 = **6000**	7 · 10000 = **70000**	**76000**
Low Prod. Cost	0	5 · 1000 = **5000**	5 · 8000 = **40000**	**40000**
High Prod. Cost	0	0	15 · 2000 = **30000**	**45000**
Profit	0	**1000**	0	**-9000**
Scenario 2				
Turnover	0	6 · 5000 = **30000**	7 · 2000 = **14000**	**44000**
Low Prod. Cost	0	5 · 5000 = **25000**	5 · 2000 = **10000**	**35000**
High Prod. Cost	0	0	0	0
Profit	0	**5000**	**4000**	**9000**
Exp. Profit	0	**3000**	**2000**	0

Table 2.3: Determination of the Contract Decision for the Exact Explicit Reactive Anticipation

(2) Approximate explicit reactive anticipation

There exist various approaches to determine an anticipation function approximately. One possibility that is often met in practice is simply a reduction of the information which might, in principle, be available. Thus, rather than taking the full probability distribution of demand, let us content ourselves with the mean values of the two scenarios:

$$\hat{d}^I = \frac{1}{2}(1000 + 5000) = 3000 \quad \text{and}$$

$$\hat{d}^{II} = \frac{1}{2}(10000 + 2000) = 6000$$

Consequently, the coupling equations (2.11) now take on the form

$$(2.13a) \quad a^{T^*} = \arg \max_{a^T \in A^T} \{C^{TT}(a^T) - C^B(AF(IN))\}$$

$$(2.13b) \quad AF(IN) = \arg \min_{\hat{a}^B \in \hat{A}^B_{IN}} C^B(\hat{a}^B)$$

$$(2.13c) \quad a^{B^*} = \arg \min_{a^B \in A^B_{IN^*}} C^B(a^B)$$

with

$$C^{TT}(a^T) = 6\hat{d}^I a^T_I + 7\hat{d}^{II} a^T_{II}$$

	No Contract	I	II	I and II
Turnover	0	6 · 3000= 18000	7 · 6000= 42000	60000
Low Prod. Cost	0	5 · 3000= 15000	5 · 6000= 30000	40000
High Prod. Cost	0	0	0	15000
Profit	0	3000	12000	5000

Table 2.4: Determination of the Contract Decision for the Approximate Explicit Reactive Anticipation

and

$$\hat{A}_{IN}^{B} = \{(x, y) : x + y \geq \hat{d}^{I} a_{I}^{T} + \hat{d}^{II} a_{II}^{T}, x \leq 8000\}.$$

The solution of (2.13a) is straightforward and is presented in detail in Table 2.4. As a result, the proposed approximate anticipation recommends a contract to be concluded with customer II, i.e., $a_{II}^{T} = 1$ and $a_{I}^{T} = 0$.

(3) Implicit reactive anticipation

For an implicit reactive anticipation, there still exists an anticipation function. This function, however, can no longer be identified with an anticipated behavior (x, y) of the base-level. There are only certain features that are taken into account. As an example, let us take an estimate of the supplier's unit production cost. Assume that from past experience the supplier has an idea how her production cost might depend on the type of contract she is going to conclude. Hence one has

$$\hat{c} = \hat{c}(IN),$$

and the top-equation now reads

$$a^{T*} = \arg \max_{a^{T} \in A^{T}} E\{C^{TT}(a^{T}) - C^{TB}(\hat{c}(IN)) | I_{t_0}^{T}\} \qquad (2.14a)$$

yielding the top-criterion

$$C^{T} = 6d^{I} a_{I}^{T} + 7d^{II} a_{II}^{T} - \hat{c}(IN)(d^{I} a_{I}^{T} + d^{II} a_{II}^{T}). \qquad (2.15)$$

The type of contract being recommended now depends, of course, on the specific estimates $\hat{c}(IN)$.

Remark: Rather than taking 'free' estimates from past experience, one could calculate $\hat{c}(IN)$ in an iterative way. Working with demand forecasts, as in the approximate explicit reactive anticipation case (2), one could start with an initial value for

$\hat{c}$. Using this value, one optimizes the top-level and obtains a certain contract. For this contract, one then determines an updated estimate of the cost parameter $\hat{c}$. Using this procedure, however, it is obviously necessary to calculate base-decisions and one would not have an implicit but an approximate explicit anticipation. In fact, the proposed procedure describes a specific (hierarchical) solution algorithm for Eq. (2.13a).

(4) Non-reactive anticipation

A non-reactive anticipation simply takes into account the base-level's behavior in a non-specific way. Thus there does no longer exist an anticipation function, and the top-equation (2.11a) reduces to

$$(2.16a) \qquad a^{T^*} = \arg \max_{a^T \in A^T} E\{C^{TT}(a^T)|I_{t_0}^T\}.$$

Hence, the private criterion has to incorporate the non-reactive anticipation. As for the approximate explicit case, a large number of possible approaches exist. Let us choose, like in the implicit case (3), mean production unit cost $\hat{c}$ as a suitable antici-pation. Relying on 'general experience', assume that *irrespective of the envisaged contract*, 8 % of the production requires excess capacity resulting in the non-reactive anticipation of

$$\hat{c} = 0.92 \cdot 5 + 0.08 \cdot 15 = 5.8.$$

Notice that we have now only one value $\hat{c}$, whereas in the implicit case (3) we had a complete function $\hat{c} = \hat{c}(IN)$. Substituting $\hat{c}$ in $C^{TT} = C^T$ (see Eq. (2.15)), one obtains

$$C^{TT} = 6d^I a_I^T + 7d^{II} a_{II}^T - \hat{c}(d^I a_I^T + d^{II} a_{II}^T)$$
$$= 0.2d^I a_I^T + 1.2d^{II} a_{II}^T.$$

Since all contribution margins are positive, the non-reactive antipation recommends a contract with both customers, i.e., $a_I^T = a_{II}^T = 1$.

Comparing the recommendations the different anticipation procedures are generating, one readily recognizes that the kind of anticipation can have a crucial impact on the solution to a hierarchical planning problem.

2.6 Some General Observations Concerning the Solution of the Coupling Equations

The solution to the coupling equations (2.5) can be understood as the solution to the top-equation (2.5a) subject to a constraint defined by the anticipation relation (2.5b). If the constraints exerted by the base-criterion had not to be taken into account, one simply had the problem to optimize

$$\bar{C}^T = E\left\{C^T\big(C^{TT}(a^T), C^{TB}(a^B)\big)|I^T\right\}$$

with respect to A^T and A^B. For a general discussion of this optimization problem let us first look for efficient solutions, i.e., let us first discuss the multi-criterion optimization problem

$$\{\bar{C}^{TT}(a^T), \bar{C}^{TB}(a^B)\} \longrightarrow \mathop{\mathrm{opt}}_{\substack{a^T \in A^T \\ a^B \in A^B}}$$

with the bar denoting expectations. The private criterion $\bar{C}^{TT}$ and the top-down criterion $\bar{C}^{TB}$ can reasonably be assumed to be competing criteria, so that the efficient border has a monotonously decreasing shape as depicted in Fig. 2.8. If, as an example, $\bar{C}^T$ is additive

$$\bar{C}^T = \bar{C}^{TT} + \bar{C}^{TB},$$

one could easily find the solution by drawing a tangent to the efficient border. Let us call the resulting point the **first-best** solution (see Fig. 2.8).

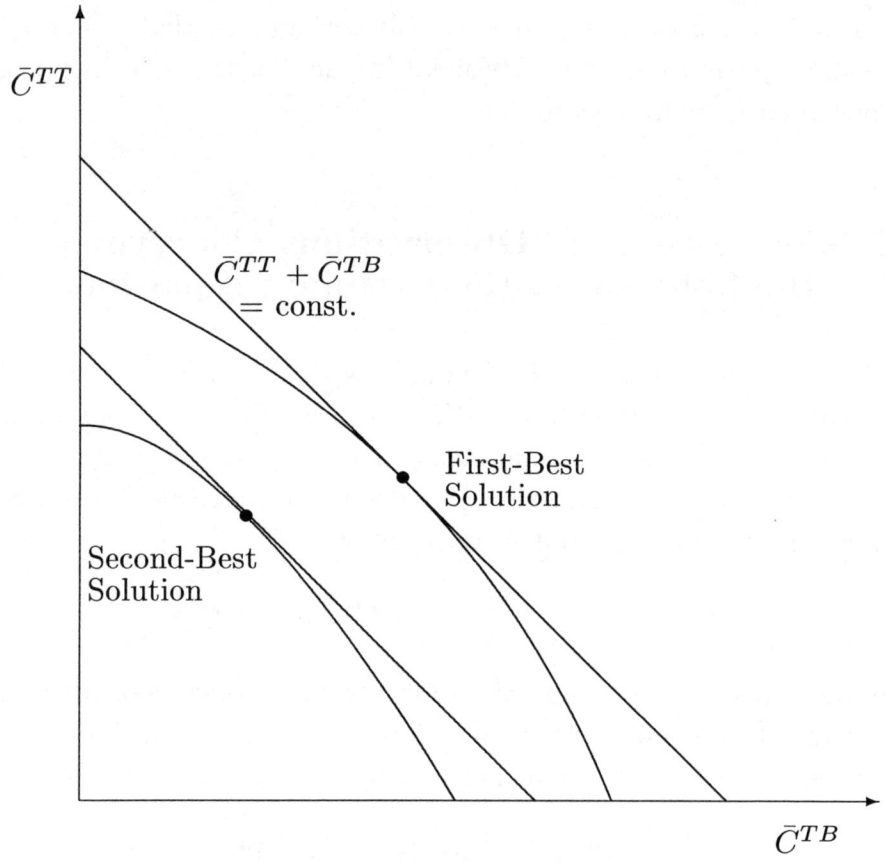

Fig. 2.8: Solution Aspects of the Coupling Equations

If an optimization problem has to be structured hierarchically because of an asymmetric information situation and/or a restricting base-criterion, one no longer has $C^{TB} = C^{TB}(a^B)$, but only $C^{TB} = C^{TB}(\hat{a}^{B^0})$. As a consequence, in general, this results in a restricted set of solutions yielding an efficient border which is dominated by the first-best efficient solutions. These solutions will be called **second-best**.

For the team-based hierarchical planning situation, mainly considered in this chapter, $\hat{C}^B$ and C^{TB} are complementary and, in particular, $C^{TB} = \hat{C}^B = C^B$. If, in addition, the top-criterion is additive and we have the case of an exact reactive anticipation, both efficient borders are identical, and there is no loss in optimality. Later, in Section 4.2, we will call this case a plain tactical-operational hierarchy. Obviously, because of the (additive) separability of the corresponding top-criterion, dynamic programming provides an optimal solution procedure. Hence, the only loss might be caused by a non-exact, that is, only approximate anticipation.

Chapter 3

Constructional Hierarchies

Constructional hierarchies were introduced in Chapter 1 (Sec. 1.1) as the result of a hierarchical structuring process. In contrast to organizational hierarchies, they are characterized by a conflict-free team situation (see Fig. 2.3) and by symmetric information. Thus constructional hierarchies are mainly constructed to reduce conceptual and/or computational complexity.

Differentiating somewhat further, let us define the term *real constructional hierarchy* in case the hierarchy is the result of an abstraction process. In case the structuring is only used to better manipulate a model, the result will be called a *formal constructional hierarchy*. It is these latter hierarchies on which we will mainly focus in this chapter.

The **real constructional hierarchy** results from a separation of a real-life problem into smaller hierarchically dependent parts. Often it can be considered as an operationalization of a complex planning problem. All decisions are made by one decision maker at the same time. As an example, think of buying a car. You might separate your decision by first reflecting on the purpose you need the car for, second by considering the money you would like to spend, and finally by choosing the car's color. Of course, though the decisions are hierarchically ranked, they intimitely depend on each other.

The **formal constructional hierarchy** also separates a complex system into simpler subsystems. In contrast to the real constructional hierarchy, however, the separation is not aimed at a better understanding or handling of the system but at improving its formal mathematical tractability. Discrete variables, for example, are separated from continuous ones. Or, as another example, consider a system being described in aggregate and disaggregate terms giving rise to an aggregation - disaggregation hierarchy. In contrast to real constructional hierarchies, formal hierarchies usually do not represent real-life objects. They are pure intellectual ('virtual') constructs to better manipulate a planning task.

Two main types of formal constructional hierarchies will be investigated (see Fig. 3.1)
– the *decomposition hierarchy* and
– the *relaxation hierarchy*.

The **decomposition hierarchy** is the result of decomposing a system into subsystems which can be manipulated more easily. The hierarchy's base-level consists of the submodels, while the top-level describes the coordination of these models.

The **relaxation hierarchy**, on the other hand, consists of two levels, each of them describing the *entire* decision problem. The levels differ from each other in that the top-level represents a model which, formally, does not allow an easy solution, while the base-level represents a relaxed version of the top-model for which a solution may more easily be obtained.

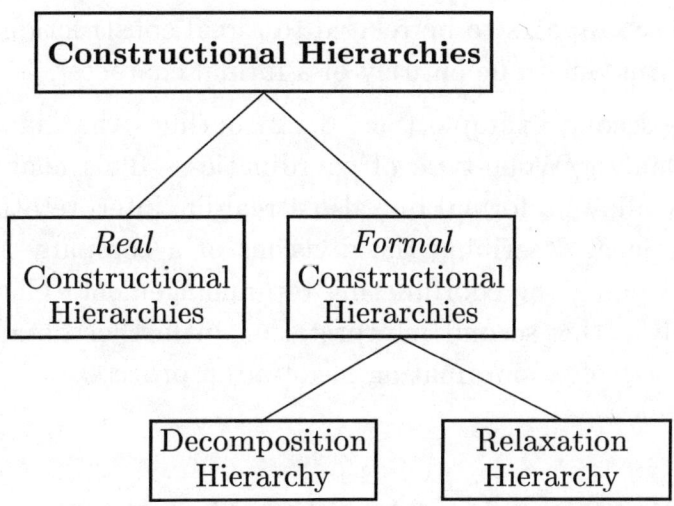

Fig. 3.1: Constructional Hierarchies

Decomposition hierarchies will be treated in Section 3.1, whereas relaxation hierarchies will be the subject of Section 3.2.

3.1 Decomposition Hierarchies

Decomposition hierarchies describe the separation and subsequent coordination of two or more formal subsystems. This coordination can be achieved through the subsystems themselves giving rise to a self-coordination, or it can be performed by a separate coordinating unit. Obviously, the coordinating unit represents the top-level, and the subsystems that are to be coordinated constitute the base-level.

Two prominent examples will be considered. The first example, Sec. 3.1.1, describes the coordination of the two levels of a production planning problem [Graves]. With this example the difference between a constructional and an organizational hierarchy can readily be shown. Though the problem, at a first glance, appears to be related to a real constructional hierarchy, it turns out to be entirely of a formal character.

The second example (Sec. 3.1.2) outlines the main features of a Dantzig/Wolfe-type of coordination. This coordination not only allows a formal but also a real-life interpretation, with the base-level describing the divisions of a company and the top-level being the coordinating top-management. Chapter 11 will analyze this second interpretation in further detail within the context of a coordinating negotiation process.

3.1.1 A Capacity Adaptation Model

The capacity adaptation model to be described in the following section will not only serve as an example of a formal constructional hierarchy but will also be used for later reference. Thus the problem will later be cast into the format of an organizational hierarchy (see Sec. 4.2.1).

(1) Problem statement

Consider a capacity adaptation problem for which the capacity is determined within an aggregate production planning model. The actual production, on the other hand, is scheduled at a detailed production scheduling level. Let us first state the entire model simultaneously for both aggregation levels:

$$(3.1) \qquad C = \sum_t \left[cK_t + \sum_i h_i x_{it}^L + \sum_j s_j \delta_{jt} \right] \longrightarrow \min$$

s.t.

$$(3.2) \qquad x_{it}^L = x_{i,t-1}^L + x_{it} - \bar{d}_{it} \qquad \forall i, t$$

$$\sum_i a_i x_{it} \leq K_t \qquad\qquad \forall t \qquad\qquad (3.3)$$

$$\sum_{j \in J^i} y_{jt}^L = x_{it}^L \qquad\qquad \forall i, t \qquad\qquad (3.4)$$

$$y_{jt}^L = y_{jt-1}^L + y_{jt} - d_{jt} \qquad\qquad \forall j, t \qquad\qquad (3.5)$$
$$y_{j0}^L = y_{j0}^{L'}$$

$$y_{jt} \leq M\delta_{jt} \qquad\qquad \forall j, t \qquad\qquad (3.6)$$
$$\delta_{jt} \in \{0, 1\} \qquad\qquad \forall j, t \qquad\qquad (3.7)$$
$$K_t, x_{it}, x_{it}^L, y_{jt}^L \geq 0, y_{jt} \geq 0 \qquad\qquad \forall j, t \qquad\qquad (3.8)$$

Indices

i : product group
j : individual item
J^i : set of item indices j belonging to product group i
t : period

Decision variables

x_{it} : aggregate production of product group i in period t
y_{jt} : production of item j in period t
δ_{jt} : setup indicator
x_{it}^L : aggregate inventory of group i in period t
y_{jt}^L : inventory of item j in period t
$y_{j0}^{L'}$: initial inventory (given)
K_t : capacity in period t

Data and parameters

$\bar{d}_{it}$: known aggregate demand of group i
d_{jt} : known detailed demand of item j
h_i : holding cost parameter of group i
s_j : setup cost for item j
c : capacity cost parameter

a_i : production coefficient (consumption rate) for group i

M : maximum production quantity of any item at any period

The criterion (3.1) minimizes capacity, holding, and setup costs, respectively. Holding costs are minimized on an aggregate basis, while setup costs are accounted for on the detailed item level. The constraints (3.2) and (3.5) describe the well-known inventory balance equations for aggregate and detailed variables, respectively. Relation (3.3) represents the capacity constraints, and (3.7) relates production to the setup indicator δ_{it}. The most interesting constraint is (3.4) which relates aggregate to disaggregate variables. It is therefore called the aggregation - disaggregation constraint or **consistency relation**.

(2) Solution procedure

In solving the model, one could think of a situation in which capacities K_t have to be determined at a medium term level, whereas production is scheduled at a lower level. Consequently, the information situation would usually improve in moving from the medium term decision to the short term decision. Thus one would have an asymmetric information situation. This, however, *is not the case* for a constructional hierarchy. In fact, the model at hand assumes short term (overtime) capacity adaptations, and *no increase of information* is taken into consideration. The hierarchy to be built is focusing solely on solution aspects. (For a model which reflects the interpretation as an organizational hierarchy, see Section 4.2.1.) These solution aspects may not be underestimated. Since the model consists of binary variables, it is not easy to solve, and structuring the problem hierarchically turns out to a possibility to overcome the considerable computational burden.

In solving the model (3.1) through (3.8), one is guided by separating some of the continuous variables from the discrete variables δ_{jt}. This is achieved by applying a Lagrangean relaxation to the consistency constraint (3.4) and in subsequently solving the

Lagrangean dual problem by a subgradient algorithm.

Relaxing constraints (3.4) results in the following Lagrangean function

$$L(\lambda) := C + \sum_{i,t} \lambda_{it} \left(\sum_{j \in J^i} y_{jt}^L - x_{it}^L \right)$$

with λ_{it} being the respective Lagrangean parameters. To solve the Lagrangean dual: $\max_\lambda \min L(\lambda)$ (e.g., see [Crowder], [Held et al.]), one substitutes C and conveniently separates $L(\lambda)$ into two terms

$$L(\lambda) = \sum_t \left[cK_t + \sum_i (h_i - \lambda_{it}) x_{it}^L \right]$$
$$+ \sum_t \sum_i \left[\sum_j \lambda_{it} y_{jt}^L + s_j \delta_{jt} \right]$$

giving rise to the following two subproblems:

(1) Aggregate Production Problem (AP)

$$\sum_t cK_t + \sum_i (h_i - \lambda_{it}) x_{it}^L \longrightarrow \min$$

s.t. (3.2), (3.3), and (3.8).

(2) Disaggregate Scheduling Problem (DS)

$$\sum_j \sum_t (\lambda_{it} y_{jt}^L + s_j \delta_{jt}) \longrightarrow \min \quad \forall i$$

s.t. (3.5), (3.6), (3.7), and (3.8), with i connected to j by $j \in J^i$.

Problem (AP) is a simple linear production program, while (DS), for each i, turns out to be an easy to solve Wagner/Whitin model [Wagner/Whitin].

In solving the Lagrangean dual, one can apply a subgradient algorithm with an updating procedure defined by

$$\lambda^{k+1} = \lambda^k + \alpha_k \gamma^k. \tag{3.9}$$

The constant $\alpha_k > 0$ denotes a suitable step size, and γ_k represents the subgradient with components

$$(3.10) \qquad \gamma_{it}^k = \sum_{j \in J^i} y_{jt}^{Lk} - x_{it}^{Lk} \quad \text{(step } k\text{)}.$$

The vector γ^k is a measure for the inconsistency of the two submodels. The larger γ^k, the larger λ^{k+1} will be, and since the Lagrangean parameter λ describes penalty costs for not keeping the relaxed constraint, it proves to be natural that for an enlarged discrepancy γ^k the penalty λ is increased.

Generally, solving the Lagrangean dual does not result in a feasible solution of the original (primal) optimization problem (i.e., it remains a duality gap). Since $L(\lambda)$ is maximized, however, one can expect the algorithm to converge to a high (non-feasible) lower bound. To obtain a feasible solution, a Lagrangean heuristic has to be applied which, in the present case, leads to acceptable results [Graves].

(3) Constructional hierarchy

Having found a solution one might again ask for the hierarchical nature of the procedure that has been applied. Obviously, from the outset the general production planning and scheduling problem has been formulated in the hierarchical framework of aggregate and detailed variables. This formulation, however, did not lead to a hierarchy but only to a separation into equally ranked submodels, which, in addition, was not motivated by the level of aggregation but by pure computational considerations. There is no self-coordination of the models (AP) and (DS) such that they are directly influencing each other by (hypothetical) instructions and reactions.

Eq. (3.9) together with (3.10) represents the top-equation while $(x_{jt}^{Lk}, y_{jt}^{Lk})$ corresponds to a value of the anticipation function. The resulting instruction is given by λ^{k+1}, and finally the (anticipated) base-level is composed of {(AP),(DS)}. Since the two submodels (AP) and (DS) are coordinated by the instruction, one may call the procedure described in Fig. 3.2 a coordinating **hierarchical algorithm**.

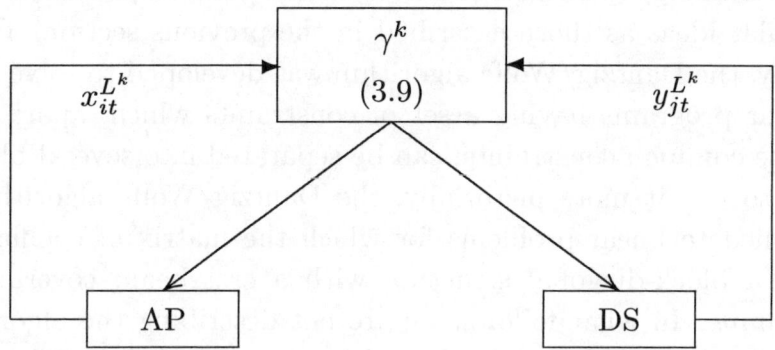

Fig. 3.2   Coordination Hierarchy

Leaving aside the refinement of a Lagrangean heuristic, one realizes that the hierarchy that has actually been employed is a coordination hierarchy activated by the subgradient algorithm. In fact, both submodels (AP) and (DS) are coordinated by a central DMU (top-level) through the Lagrangean parameter λ^{k+1} determined by the updating procedure (3.9) (see Fig. 3.2). The top-criterion is given by the discrepancy γ^k of the solutions of the submodels that are to be coordinated. The top-model can stop the coordination process after a sufficiently large number of iterations or after γ^k has fallen below a preset aspiration level AL^γ.

For completely different hierarchies associated with the general capacity adaptation problem see Sections 4.2.1 and 6.2.

Remark: Formal constructional hierarchies, particularly of the kind just described, can be met in various fields. As examples, see [Anandaligam/Friesz], [Dirickx/Jennergren], [Heinrich/Schneeweiss], [v. Houtem et al.], [Paulli], [Sawik], or [Sherali et al.].

3.1.2 A Coordination Hierarchy of the Dantzig/ Wolfe-Type

The Dantzig/Wolfe coordination scheme [Dantzig/Wolfe] follows similar ideas as those described in the previous section. Originally, the Dantzig/Wolfe algorithm was developed to solve large linear programs having a set of constraints which, apart from some common constraints, can be separated into several blocks, or, to put it more pictorially, the Dantzig/Wolfe algorithm is applied to linear problems for which the matrix of coefficients has a block-diagonal structure with a crossbeam covering all columns. In what follows, we are not describing the algorithm in all its refinements. In fact, we are mainly interested in the coordination aspect which later, in Section 11.2, will allow us to interpret the algorithm as a negotiation process between the divisions of a company and the central management.

To be more specific, let us illustrate the Dantzig/Wolfe coordination scheme with a simple budgeting problem which may be stated as follows:

$$(3.11) \qquad C^T = C^{TB} = \sum_{s=1}^{S} d_s^{TB} x_s \longrightarrow \max$$

s.t.

$$(3.12) \qquad \sum_{s=1}^{S} A_s^{TB} x_s \leq b^T$$

$$(3.13) \qquad A_s^B x_s \leq b_s^B \qquad s = 1, \ldots, S$$

$$(3.14) \qquad x_1, \ldots, x_S \geq 0$$

Indices

$s = 1, \ldots, S$: division

Decision variables

x_s : decision vector (production plan) of division s

Parameters

d_s^{TB} : criterion vector (unit contribution margins) evaluating decision x_s of division s,

b_s^B : vector of local resources of division s,

A_s^B : matrix of consumption rates of local resources,

b^T : common resources,

A_s^{TB}: matrix of consumption rates of common resources used by division s.

Criterion (3.11) maximizes a contribution margin subject to two types of constraints: Inequality (3.13) describes local constraints for each division s, whereas (3.12) represents the constraints caused by the common use of resources b^T.

In solving the above linear program with its partially block diagonal structure, one separates it into a top- and a base-level. The base-level consists of all local (divisional) programs, while the top-level represents the central unit which coordinates the utilization of the common resources. The coordination is performed in adjusting the criteria of the local programs. Hence, in iteration k, one has the following decision model for division s:

model $(B_s(k))$

$$C_s^{TB} = d_s^{TB}(k)\, x_s \longrightarrow \max \qquad (3.15)$$

s.t.

$$A_s^B x_s \leq b_s^B \qquad (3.16)$$

$$x_s \geq 0$$

with $d_s^{TB}(k)$ being the vector of criterion coefficients prescribed by the coordinator in iteration k. All divisional models $(B_s), (s = 1, \ldots, S)$ make up the **base-level**.

The coordination mechanism now proceeds as follows. Starting with the isolated divisional models $B_s(k)$, suppose the algorithm has reached iteration k, and up to k the base-level has communicated solution vectors $x_s^0(l)(l = 1, \ldots, k$ and $s = 1, \ldots, S)$ to the top-level. The general idea of the algorithm is to iteratively adapt these divisional solutions to account for the common resources. In doing so, the top-level considers all past solutions and calculates new better adapted solutions for the divisions. These solutions are simply taken to be convex combinations

$$(3.17) \quad x_s = \sum_{l=1}^{k} \lambda_s(l) x_s^0(l), \sum_{l=1}^{k} \lambda_s(l) = 1 \text{ and } \lambda_s(l) \geq 0 \qquad \forall s, l$$

of all past optimal decision vectors of the divisions $x_s^0(l), l = 1, \ldots, k$. Note that, because of its construction, (3.17) constitutes a feasible solution for the divisions.

Before imposing this new suggestion for an overall solution on the divisional model, the parameters $\lambda_s(l)$ of (3.17) must first be specified. This is performed in optimizing $\lambda_s(l)$ with respect to criterion (3.11) (see (3.18)), particularly taking into account the restriction caused by the common resources b^T (see (3.19)). Hence, one may state, at iteration k, the following
top-model ($T(k)$)

$$(3.18) \qquad C^T = \sum_{s=1}^{S} d_s^{TB} \sum_{l=1}^{k} \lambda_s(l) x_s^0(l) \longrightarrow \max$$

s.t.

$$(3.19) \qquad \sum_{s=1}^{S} A_s^{TB} \sum_{l=1}^{k} \lambda_s(l) x_s^0(l) \leq b^T$$

$$(3.20) \qquad \sum_{l=1}^{k} \lambda_s(l) = 1 \qquad \forall s$$

$$\lambda_s(l) \geq 0 \qquad \forall s, l$$

The top-model is representing the top-equation (2.5a) (for iteration k) which is also known as the **master problem** of the Dantzig/Wolfe algorithm. The optimal solution

$$\boldsymbol{x}_s^* := \sum_{l=1}^{k} \lambda_s^*(l)\boldsymbol{x}_s^0(l) \quad (s = 1, \ldots, S)$$

may now be used to calculate the correction for the divisions' criteria coefficients d_s^{TB}. This may be seen as follows: The optimal solution $\boldsymbol{x}_s^*(l)$ is associated with the shadow prices $\boldsymbol{\pi}(k)$ of the common resources which are known to represent the improvement of the objective function if the common constraints are relaxed by one unit. Hence, it turns out to be appropriate to adapt the criteria coefficients by

$$\boldsymbol{d}_s^{TB}(k+1) := \boldsymbol{d}_s^{TB} - \boldsymbol{\pi}(k)\boldsymbol{A}_s^{TB} \qquad \forall s \qquad (3.21)$$

Eq. (3.21) clearly shows that if the actual optimal decision $\boldsymbol{x}_s^*(k)$ of division s exceeds the available common resources, its contribution margin should be reduced, resulting in a decreased amount of production. This reduction is given by $\boldsymbol{\pi}(k)\boldsymbol{A}_s^{TB}$ and describes the value of the exceeded common resources evaluated with respect to the top-level's objective function.

The diagram of Fig. 3.3 summarizes the described coordination algorithm: At iteration k, the base-level informs the top-level (by the 'algorithmic reaction' $\boldsymbol{x}_s^0(k)$) of its optimal solutions which explicitly consider local constraints, whereas the common constraints are only implicitly taken into account through the *coefficients* of the local criteria. Using the solutions $\boldsymbol{x}_s^0(k)$, the top-model calculates new 'algorithmic instructions' in form of revised base-criteria coefficients reflecting the optimization of the overall criterion (3.18) and the scarceness of common resources (3.19). The algorithm can be shown to converge after a finite number of iterations to the optimal value of the criterion

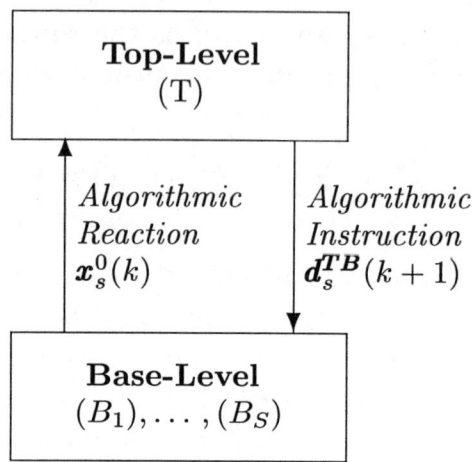

Fig. 3.3: Information Exchange in the Dantzig/Wolfe Algorithm

(3.11). Having optimally coordinated the production decisions of the divisions, the top-level then allocates, as an ultimate result of the algorithm, the necessary common resources.

As mentioned at the outset, the Dantzig/Wolfe algorithm was originally constructed to solve a large linear program with a special block diagonal structure. Hence, as for constructional hierarchies, there is just one decision maker possessing all information necessary to solve the top- and the base-models. It turns out, however, that this comprehensive state of information is not necessary for successfully solving the coordination task. In fact, if there existed local decision makers, they would only need the knowledge necessary to solve their own problems and similarly the top-level decision maker needed only to know the utilization of the common constraints by the divisions.

It is this observation which readily leads to a multi-person interpretation of the coordination scheme in which the divisions and the central unit have different decision makers. In this context the divisions are coordinated through their criteria (management by objectives) and in particular through affecting their costs by transfer prices. We postpone this interpretation of the Dantzig/Wolfe algorithm until Chapter 11 which will be devoted to multi-person coordination problems.

For further and more recent references on coordination schemes, see, e.g., [Benders], [Bogetoft et al.], [Burton et al.], [Burton/ Obel 1984 and 1995], [Flippo/Rinnooy Kan], [Holmberg], [Jörnsten/ Leisten], [Meijboom], [v.d. Panne], [Ten Kate], [Tind].

3.2 Relaxation Hierarchies

A relaxation hierarchy, as previously explained (Fig. 3.1), consists of a complex model described by the top-level, and of some simplified version of that model represented by the base-level. Let us call the complex model the **real** or **master model** and a simplified version a **decision generator**. This latter expression is used to indicate that the relaxed model is only considered to find an acceptable decision for the (real) model one is actually interested in. Distinguishing the decision generator DG_p by a parameter $p \in P$, let DG be the set of possible decision generators

$$DG := \{DG_p : p \in P\}.$$

Obviously, the optimal solution of the decision generator DG_p, $a^{B^o}(p)$, represents, as a function of p, the anticipation function $AF(p) = a^{B^o}(p)$. In analogy to Fig. 2.4, one has the solution hierarchy within the top-level as depicted in Fig. 3.4. The parameter p turns out to be the instruction $IN = p$, and the decision generator has to be interpreted as an anticipated base-model. It is interesting to see that no proper base-model exists. This is in accordance with our previous explanation that for a constructional hierarchy and, a fortiori, for a relaxation hierarchy no increase of information at a later point of time $(t = t_1)$ is taken into consideration. Furthermore, the optimal decision a^{B^0} of the best decision generator $a^{B^*} = a^{B^0}(p^*)$ defines the (constraint) optimal decision of the top-model.

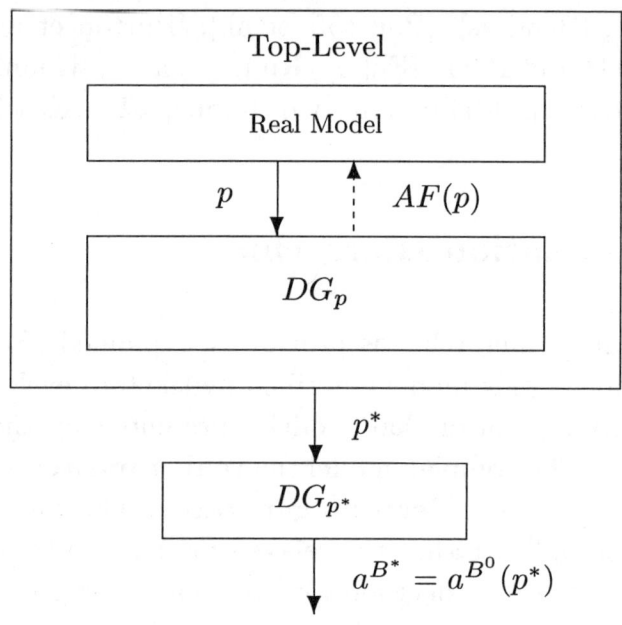

Fig. 3.4: Relaxation Hierarchy

(1) Formal description of a relaxation hierarchy

With these preliminary considerations, a formal description of a relaxation hierarchy is now straightforward. In view of $(2.5a)$ and $(2.5b)$, one obtains the following specification

$$(3.22a) \qquad p^* = \arg \operatorname*{opt}_{p \in P} E\{C^{TB}(AF(p))|I^T\}$$

$$(3.22b) \qquad AF(p) = \arg \operatorname*{opt}_{a^B \in A_p^B} E\{C_p^B(a^B)|I_p^B\}$$

with the final top-model solution

$$a^{T^*} \equiv a^{B^*} = a^{B^0}(p^*) = AF(p^*).$$

The set P contains all those parameters that imply solutions of decision generators which, in view of A^T, result in (*feasible*) solutions a^T of the master model. Note that C_p^B, A_p^B, and I_p^B are relaxations of C^{TB}, A^T, and I^T respectively. The algorithmic procedure indicated in very general terms by Eqs. (3.22a) and (3.22b) will be called **parameter adaptation**. In fact, it describes a parametric optimization.

To be somewhat more specific, a parameter adaptation may work as follows. Starting with a parameter value p^1, the decision generator calculates the value $AF(p^1)$ of the anticipation function resulting in the value $E\{C^{TB}(AF(p^1))|I^T\}$ of the master model's criterion. If this value is not acceptable to the decision maker, a new parameter value p^2 is chosen (hopefully) resulting in a better value $AF(p^2)$. Continuing this search procedure, one ideally ends up in the value p^*. (For an example, see Section 9.2.) Note that the updating procedure is not described in the Eqs. (3.22) and, of course, the search algorithm might end up in a suboptimal parameter value.

(2) Solution aspects

Obviously, because of the use of a decision generator, the solution of Eq. (3.22a) will usually be only of a second best character as introduced in Section 2.5. This can neatly be illustrated for the case when the master model criterion C^{TB} consists of two conflicting components, one, for example, being quantitative: C_q^{TB}, and the other one being qualitative: C_r^{TB} (see Fig. 3.5). As a relaxation, let us drop the qualitative component so that only the quantitative criterion is optimized: $C^B = C_q^{TB}$. The new efficient border, subject to the considered decision generator DG_p, i.e., subject to the anticipation function $AF(p)$, represents the (*feasible*) second best solutions (see Fig. 3.5).

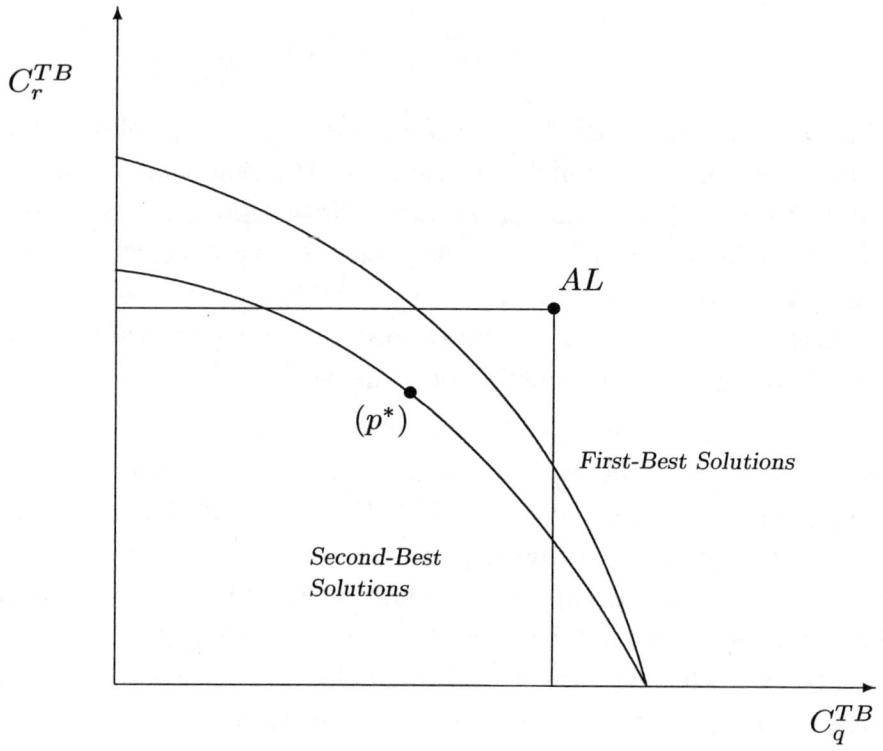

Fig. 3.5: Solution Aspects of the Relaxation Hierarchy

The gap between the first- and the second-best solution is called the **modeling gap**. It measures the loss of optimality one has to sacrifice in obtaining a solution. Generally, this gap is not known exactly (otherwise one would look for an approximate solution). In most cases, however, one can calculate bounds, or one can try to minimize a suitably defined distance DIS with respect to certain aspiration levels AL (see the points (p^*) and AL in Fig. 3.5):

$$(3.23) \quad DIS\{[C_r^{TB}(AF(p)), C_q^{TB}(AF(p)]; AL\} \longrightarrow \min_p.$$

(Note that the expression (3.23) represents a general parametric optimization problem.)

(3) General remark

In the discussion thus far, we more or less tacitly restricted ourselves to just one class of decision generators induced by the variation of some possibly rather complex parameter p. This restriction is of course not essential. In fact, one can consider several classes of decision generators and can look for the best solution out of this richer class of models (see [Schneeweiss (1987)]).

Relaxation hierarchies play an important role in the modeling task of Operations Research. They allow the construction of formal models and their validation with respect to a model which provides a richer description of reality. In fact, relaxation hierarchies are at the very heart of Operations Research. All too often, however, one does not recognize this two-step character of the modeling task, and hence does not question enough the correct choice of the parameter p. We will return to this essential problem in Chapter 11.

In Chapter 9 we are going to discuss another important aspect related to a relaxation hierarchy: the evaluation of cost parameters. In fact, the derivation of parameters p^* turns out to be a very general way of deriving certain opportunity costs. Thus, from a practical and theoretical point of view, relaxation hierarchies are of particular importance.

Chapter 4

Organizational Hierarchies

In contrast to constructional hierarchies, planning organizational hierarchies is not just a computational task. Indeed, forecasting and modeling problems play a predominant role taking into account the fact that the base-decision is made under a different state of information than the top-decision. Hence, the conceptual problem of how to anticipate the base-level is of major significance.

The preceding chapter focused on constructional hierarchies which were mainly characterized by a team situation and by symmetric information. We will now relax this condition and investigate levels with asymmetric information. Furthermore, the levels will, in principle, be allowed to be in a non-team situation though most of the hierarchies to be considered will be team-based. In Section 3.1, these hierarchies were called organizational hierarchies (see also Fig 2.3). Antagonistic behavior will not be analyzed but will be left for the next chapter. Our aim is to provide the reader with some additional examples of organizational hierarchies and to report on some real-life cases.

Therefore, the main focus of this chapter will be on the nature of the anticipation. Hence, in Section 4.1, we first give examples for pure top-down planning procedures, and, in Section 4.2, we will discuss the important tactical-operational hierarchy.

4.1 Top-Down Hierarchies

For top-down hierarchies, the general coupling equations (2.5) reduce to

$$(4.1a) \qquad a^{T^*} = \arg \operatorname*{opt}_{a^T \in A^T} E\{C^{TT}(a^T)|I_{t_0}^T\}$$

$$(4.1c) \qquad a^{B^*} = \arg \operatorname*{opt}_{a^B \in A_{IN*}^B} E\{C_{IN*}^B(a^B)|I_{IN*,t_1}^B\}.$$

There is no reactive anticipation in that the top-decision depends on a *reaction* of the base-level. Therefore, as has already been explained in Section 2.4, no anticipation function exists, and hence there is no top-down criterion. There remains, however, a non-reactive anticipation which still allows the base-level to be taken into account in various ways.

The reader is already acquainted with a considerable number of pure top-down planning hierarchies. One may think of the strict top-down hierarchy of PPC-systems (see Fig. 1.8) or, as part of it, of the successive structure of the well-known MRP-system [Vollmann et al.]. For the introductory examples in Section 2.5 we derived top-down planning hierarchies and compared them with reactive anticipations. Furthermore, top-down hierarchies will be discussed within the classical approach of hierarchical production planning (HPP), so that the reader will encounter further 'top-down examples' in Chapter 6.

Let us therefore, in this section, restrict ourselves to just one additional example which is typical of an application of hierarchical planning in practice. Let us briefly outline the planning model of the Deutsche Lufthansa AG for their repair shops of electronic parts [Schneeweiss/Schröder].

4.1.1 A Hierarchical Planning Model for the Repair Shops of the Deutsche Lufthansa AG

(1) General description

The repair process for electronic parts at the Deutsche Lufthansa AG can be described as follows (see Fig. 4.1). Electronic parts can break down at random and must be replaced immediately. These parts are then sent to the repair shop in Hamburg where they are repaired. They are then sent to one of the main warehouses, usually either in Frankfurt or in Hamburg. Once in the warehouse, the parts are again available to replace identical defective parts. Hence, the inflow of parts entering the repair shop is identical to the outflow ('demand') of parts leaving the warehouse. In short, the parts rotate in a circuit and may be in one of three states: in use, under repair (or in transport), or in stock. The number S_i of parts of a special type i that are under repair (in transport) or in stock (framed area in Fig. 4.1) is of particular importance. It will be called 'provision' of part i. It represents the portion of tied-up capital that can be influenced by planning and scheduling the repair shop.

Because repairable parts are often expensive (up to EUR 300,000), it is important to minimize their number in the repair

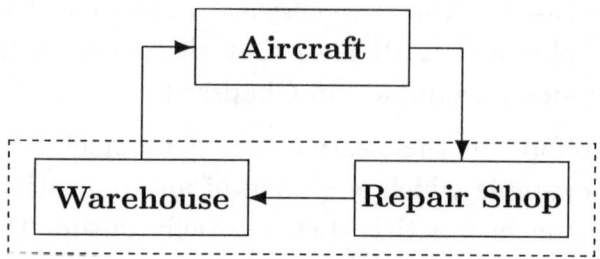

Fig. 4.1: Logistic Circuit of Recoverable Parts

shop and the warehouse. That is, work in process (WIP) and in stock should be minimized. On the other hand, the high service level Lufthansa requires cannot be maintained with too few parts in the repair system. Hence, the problem that has to be solved may be stated as follows: Minimize tied-up capital, while an overall service level must be maintained.

For a repair shop, the provision, i.e., WIP and in stock, can be determined (and changed) only at certain time periods (usually every 6 months). This means that the described problem has the character of a decision time hierarchy: first one has to decide upon the provision and later, on a daily basis, the scheduling decision has to be made. Or, stated differently, the problem has to be separated into a medium-term provision decision and a short-term scheduling decision.

The medium-term decision determines the economically best provision for the system with respect to an overall service level. Given this provision, the short-term decision problem must then guarantee a specified service level for each type of parts, taking into account the actual state of the repair process. Fig. 4.2 depicts the two planning levels showing the appropriate performance measures on the left hand side and, on the right, the information which the planning level relies on. In fact, the decisions at each level rely on the information that is available when the decision is made. Further, separating cost criteria from the more technical (stock-out) criteria simplifies the problem for the shop floor worker.

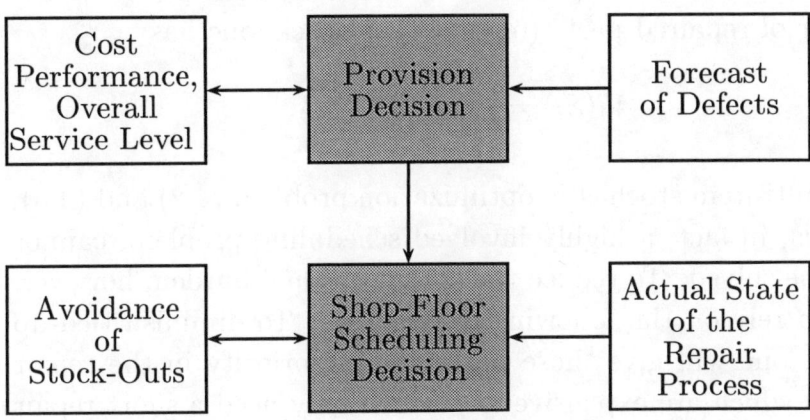

Fig. 4.2: The Planning Hierarchy of the Repair System

Obviously, Fig. 4.2 essentially represents two operational planning levels of a general PPC-system as depicted in Fig. 1.8.

(2) Provision decision

For the provision decision, the following model can be stated: For part type $i = 1, \ldots, N$ having purchase price c_i, minimize total tied up capital

$$\sum_{i=1}^{N} c_i S_i \longrightarrow \min \tag{4.2}$$

s.t. an overall service level $\bar{V}$

$$\sum_{i=1}^{N} g_i V_i(S_i) \geq \bar{V} \tag{4.3}$$

with $V_i(S_i)$ $(i = 1, \ldots, N)$ denoting the individual service level and g_i being a suitably chosen weight.

$V_i(S_i)$ describes an α-service level, that is, $V_i(S_i)$ represents the probability of not being out of stock. Thus, with W_i being the number of repaired parts (of type i) in stock, one has

$$(4.4) \qquad\qquad V_i(S_i) = Prob\{W_i \geq 1\}.$$

The multi-item stochastic optimization problem (4.2) and (4.3), which is, in fact, a highly involved scheduling problem, cannot easily be solved. To reduce the computational burden, however, one can rely on the following observation: To diminish tied-up capital, one will give those parts highest priority in the repair process which are expensive and which only need a short repair time (b_i). Hence, that part of type $i = i^*$ is receiving highest priority for which

$$R_{i^*} := \frac{c_{i^*}}{b_{i^*}} = \max_i \frac{c_i}{b_i}.$$

With this particular scheduling rule, called R-rule, the above optimization problem can be solved resulting for each part type in an optimal provision S_i^* $(i = 1, \ldots, N)$.

(3) Scheduling decision

For given provisions S_i^*, the scheduling level now has to guarantee the overall service level prescribed by the higher level. To achieve this aim, we once again use a priority rule. However, this rule no longer takes into account economic considerations. Instead it concentrates on avoiding stock-outs. Hence, that part i is given highest priority for which the 'danger of running out of stock' is greatest. Or, more technically stated, let $\Delta RISK$ be the increase in risk for type i of being out of stock, if its repair is postponed by a specified time period Δt. We then assign highest priority to that part of type i for which $\Delta RISK$ has the greatest value. This rule is called the $\Delta RISK$-rule. It depends on the echelon stock e_i, i.e., on the total inventory of parts i being in the pipeline ahead of the item considered.

Hence, in contrast to the R-rule, the $\Delta RISK$-rule is an on-line rule. It uses short-term information, and it turns out to keep the overall service level better than the R-rule, which was originally used on the medium-term level.

(4) Top-down hierarchy

The formulation of the optimization problem as a top-down planning hierarchy is now straightforward (see also Fig. 4.3).

The **top-level** is characterized by

$$C^T = C^{TT} = \sum_{i=1}^{N} c_i S_i \longrightarrow \min_{A^T},$$

$$A^T = \big\{(S_1, \ldots, S_N) : \sum_{i=1}^{N} g_i V_i(S_i) \geq \bar{V}, R\text{-rule}\big\},$$

I^T : probabilities of demand.

Instruction: $IN^* = (S_1^*, \ldots, S_N^*)$

The **base-level** is characterized by

C^B : no stock-out for each $i(i = 1, \ldots, N)$,

$A^B = A^B\big((S_1^*, \ldots, S_N^*), \Delta RISK\big),$

I^B : given (realized) demand.

In conclusion, let us stress again the information situation. The top-level has only probabilities, whereas the base-level can work with realizations, i.e., it can rely on online information. The two priority rules are adapted to this difference in information. It is interesting that the R-rule is only used to calculate optimal provisions S_i^* and is never applied physically. According to the medium-term type of decision, the R-rule, with the purchasing price c_i, takes into account economic aspects. For the short-term decision, on the other hand, economic considerations are no longer of importance. Here the physical criterion of a stock-out has to be observed. In addition, the $\Delta RISK$-rule has to consider the information available at the base-level. Hence, it is not surprising that the priority rule being used to calculate the provision is not employed for the short-term decision.

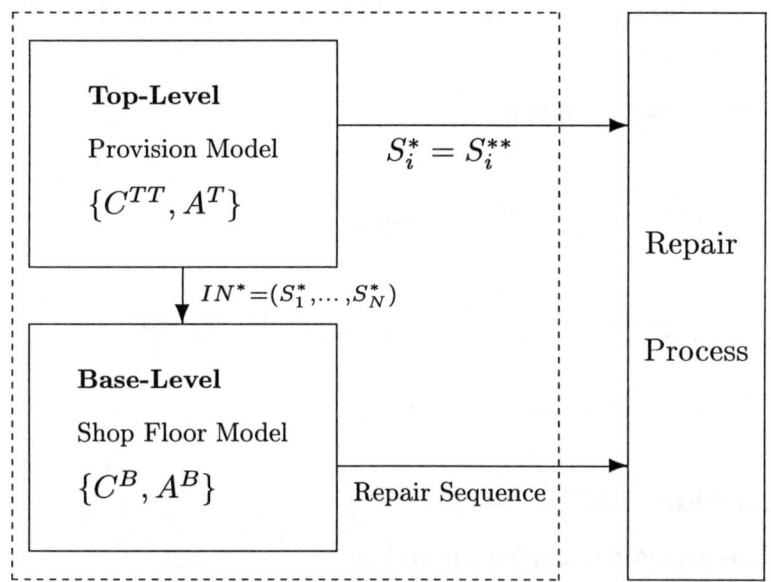

Fig. 4.3: The Formal Planning Hierarchy

4.2 Tactical-Operational Hierarchies

One of the most prominent planning hierarchies is the **tactical-operational hierarchy**. This hierarchy describes the (tactical) provision of the operational level with resources.   Hence, it is a decision time hierarchy. Furthermore, tactical-operational hierarchies are team-based (see Fig. 2.3) and possess an additive top-criterion $C^T = C^{TT} + C^{TB}$. This criterion evaluates the tactical level by some monetary criterion C^{TT}, while the operational level is taken into account by the top-down criterion C^{TB} which, because of the team situation, is complementary to $\hat{C}^B$. Examples of such a hierarchy will be given in Section 4.2.2 and in Section 6.2 within the context of hierarchical production planning.

A rich subclass of tactical-operational hierarchies constitute the so-called **plain tactical-operational hierarchies**. This class is characterized by the further specification in that the base-criterion is known to the tactical level ($\hat{C}^B = C^B$) and is taken into account without any amendment, hence

$$C^{TB} = \hat{C}^B = C^B. \qquad (4.5)$$

Examples of this type of hierarchy have already been given in Section 2.5. We are now investigating general and plain tactical-operational hierarchies somewhat further and examine four prominent subtypes, three of them being of the plain tactical character. The first is the **capacity adaptation hierarchy** which, in particular, will allow us to discuss more deeply the formal decomposition hierarchy described in Section 3.1.1. As a second type, we investigate **two-stage stochastic linear programming**, and the third hierarchy to be considered is the **strategic-tactical-operational planning hierarchy**. As an example of a proper tactical-operational hierarchy let us take the investment production hierarchy to be described in Section 4.2.2.

First, however, let us derive, for the plain tactical subtypes, the specification of the general coupling equations (2.5).

Because of (4.5), one has

(4.6)
$$E\{C^{TB}(AF)|\hat{I}^B\} = E\{C^B(\hat{a}^{B^0})|\hat{I}^B\} = \operatorname*{opt}_{\hat{a}^B \in \hat{A}^B_{IN}} E\{C^B(\hat{a}^B)|\hat{I}^B\}$$

such that Eqs. (2.5) readily reduce to

(4.7a)
$$a^{T^*} = \arg \operatorname*{opt}_{a^T \in A^T} E\{[C^{TT}(a^T) + \operatorname*{opt}_{\hat{a} \in \hat{A}^B_{IN}} E\{C^B(\hat{a}^B)|\hat{I}^B\}]|I^T_{t_0}\}$$

(4.7c)
$$a^{B^*} = \arg \operatorname*{opt}_{a^B \in A^B_{IN*}} E\{C^B(a^B)|I^B_{t_1}\}$$

For a perfect anticipation, Eqs. (4.7) simply describe the functional equation of dynamic programming (e.g., see [Nemhauser]) with (4.7c) representing the last stage and (4.7a) the second last stage of the backward recursion. This observation clearly shows that, if separability is guaranteed, hierarchical planning can be considered as a dynamic program yielding (of course, only in case of an exact reactive anticipation) an optimal solution. If, on the other hand, separability is enforced by a hierarchy, then, obviously, hierarchical planning results in a loss of optimality (see again the discussion in Section 2.6, Fig. 2.7).

Remark: Note that it is not only the additive form of the top-criterion that is responsible for the separability. It is also the assumption that the levels have no private information so that a re-evaluation of the base-information status is obsolete. This resulted in (4.5) and allowed to separate the information $\hat{I}^B$

from the overall top-information $I_{t_0}^T$ guaranteeing separability as a prerequisite for applying dynamic programming.

4.2.1 Capacity Adaptation Hierarchy

In contrast to an ordinary investment problem, which will be treated in the next section, a capacity adaptation hierarchy considers a comparatively short-term capacity increase or decrease. As an example, one may think of an increase of personal capacity for the next 12 months as described in Section 2.5.2. Clearly, the adaptation decision makes up the tactical level, and the usage of the additional capacity defines the operational level.

Let us illustrate this type of a tactical-operational hierarchy with a problem related to the capacity adaptation model of Section 3.1.1. In applying Eqs. (4.7), let us assume that the state of information is restricted to demand forecasts. Hence, at the tactical level, one has forecast variables denoted by a double hat ' $\hat{\hat{}}$ ', whereas for the operational forecasts we are using a single hat ' $\hat{}$ '. All other variables and parameters are assumed to be the same at both levels. In particular, for both levels we take the same degree of aggregation. Consider the following variables and data:

Decision variables

K_t : capacity in month t $(t = 1, \ldots, 12)$

K $= (K_1, \ldots, K_{12})$

K^{max} : maximal capacity

y_{jt} : production quantity of product j $(j = 1, \ldots, n)$ in t

(y_{jt}) : $\{y_{jt} : j = 1, \ldots, n; t = 1, \ldots, 12\}$: production program

$\delta(y_{jt}) = \begin{cases} 1 & \text{if } y_{jt} > 0 \\ 0 & \text{if } y_{jt} = 0 \end{cases}$

y_{jt}^L : inventory of product j at the end of period t

$y_{j0}^{L'}$: initial inventory (given)

Data and parameters

$\hat{\hat{d}}_{jt}$: forecast of demand at the tactical level

$\hat{d}_{jt}$: forecast of demand at the operational level

c : cost per capacity unit

h_j : inventory holding cost per unit

s_j : cost per setup

a_j : production coefficient (consumption rate)

At the tactical level at time t_0, capacities K_t and anticipated production lot sizes $\hat{y}_{jt}$ are determined in optimizing capacity cost as well as inventory holding and setup costs. Hence, the top-equation (4.7a) becomes

(4.8a)

$$K^* = \arg \min_{K \in A^T} \left\{ \sum_{t=1}^{12} cK_t + \min_{(\hat{y}_{jt}) \in \hat{A}_K^B} \sum_{t=1}^{12} \sum_{j=1}^{n} \left[h_j \hat{y}_{jt}^L + s_j \delta(\hat{y}_{jt}) \right] \right\}$$

with

$$A^T := \left\{ K_t : 0 \le K_t \le K^{max}, t = 1, \ldots, 12 \right\}$$

and

$$\hat{A}_K^B := \begin{pmatrix} \sum_{j=1}^{n} a_j \hat{y}_{jt} \le K_t \\ \hat{y}_{jt}^L = \hat{y}_{j,t-1}^L + \hat{y}_{jt} - \hat{\hat{d}}_{jt} \\ \hat{y}_{j0}^L = \hat{y}_{j0}^{L'} \\ \hat{y}_{jt}^L, \hat{y}_{jt} \ge 0 \end{pmatrix} .$$

After being provided with the optimal capacity K^*, the operational level (at time t_1) determines actual production quantities using the base-equation (4.7c)

(4.8c) $$(y_{jt}^*) = \arg \min_{(y_{jt}) \in A_{K^*}^B} \sum_{t=1}^{12} \sum_{j=1}^{n} \left[h_j y_{jt}^L + s_j \delta(y_{jt}) \right]$$

with

$$A_{K^*}^B := \left(\begin{array}{c} \sum_{j=1}^n a_j y_{jt} \leq K_t^* \\[2mm] y_{jt}^L = y_{j,t-1}^L + y_{jt} - \hat{d}_{jt} \\[2mm] y_{j0}^L = y_{j0}^{L'} \\[2mm] y_{jt}^L, y_{jt} \geq 0 \end{array} \right).$$

Comparing the tactical-operational model with the constructional hierarchy of Section 3.1.1 clearly shows the distinctly different aims one has in mind in building a hierarchy. For the constructional hierarchy, the levels were built according to computational arguments. For the tactical-operational hierarchy, on the other hand, the points in time when a decision has to be made, and hence the information status, are of primary importance.

Both aspects could be combined. The top-equation (4.8a) could be solved using the decomposition hierarchy of Section 3.1.1 yielding a result which is then processed to the operational level. This clearly demonstrates that constructional hierarchies may be employed to solve the anticipation problem within the top-level.

Later, in Section 6.2, we will consider a more realistic and comprehensive model which will be constructed along the aggregation-disaggregation framework of the so-called Hax/Meal model giving additional insight into the relationship between constructional and organizational hierarchies.

4.2.2 Investment-Production Hierarchies

As a second example of a tactical-operational hierarchy let us consider an investment-production problem. Again, the investment level can be identified with the top-level, while the base-level is given by the subsequent production activities. Investments $a^T \in A^T$ are usually evaluated by the net present value which typically consists of an investment expenditure term and a discounted sequence of future inflow terms. The investment expenditure term can be identified with the private criterion $C^{TT}(a^T)$. The future incoming cash flow, on the other hand, (via $AF_k(IN)$) is determined by the anticipated base-criterion $\hat{C}^B$ which, for example, describes production revenues. Hence,

$$(4.9a) \quad C^{T^*} = \underset{a^T \in A^T}{\mathrm{opt}} \left\{ C^{TT}(a^T) + \sum_{k=1}^{N} C_k^{TB}(AF_k(IN))\rho^k \right\}$$

with $\rho < 1$ denoting the discount factor and N being the planning horizon of the investment model. The investment is just the instruction $IN(a^T) = a^T$ which is providing the production level with the necessary production capacities.

The anticipation function $AF = (AF_1, \dots, AF_N)$ turns out to be a vector, each component of which representing the optimal twelve month production plan of a particular year k. Hence, one has the usual anticipation relation

$$(4.9b) \quad AF_k(IN) = \hat{a}_k^{B^0}(IN) = \arg \underset{\hat{a}_k^B \in \hat{A}_k^B(IN)}{\mathrm{opt}} \hat{C}_k^B(\hat{a}_k^B).$$

The criterion $\hat{C}_k^B$ usually represents a contribution margin, and $\hat{A}_k^B$ describes the operational decision field in year k which is typically defined by four categories of constraints:

(1) capacity constraints,
(2) sales constraints,
(3) sub-yearly transition equations, like the inventory balance equation, and
(4) initial values for the state variable, in particular, initial inventory.

As an example, take a capacity investment model with a base-model being composed of a sequence of N yearly linear production programs. The top-criterion (4.9a) stands for a net present value with capacity investment cost cK and an incoming cash flow $C_k^{TB} = C_k^{TB}(\hat{a}_k^{B^0})$ $(k = 1, \ldots, N)$.

The anticipated production plan is calculated by the anticipation relation (4.9b) for year k. With $\hat{C}_k^B$ denoting a (medium term) contribution margin let us be content with formulating only the decision field $\hat{A}_k^B$ $(k = 1, \ldots, N)$. First we define the following indices and variables

Indices

j	: product, $j = 1, \ldots, n$
t	: month, $t = 1, \ldots, 12$
k	: year, $k = 1, \ldots, N$
t, k	: month t in year k

Decision variables

K	: capacity investment
$y_{jt,k}$	: production of product j in month t of year k
$y_{jt,k}^L$	: inventory of product j at the end of month t of year k
$(y_{jt})_k$	: production plan of year k, $(y_{jt})_k = a_k^B$

Data

a_{jk}	: production coefficient (consumption rate) of product j in year k
$\hat{\hat{d}}_{jt,k}$	: demand forecast in t_0

Hence, the anticipated decision field $(\hat{A}_k^B(K))$ of year k as a function of the investment K is given by

$$
\hat{A}^B_k(K) := \left(
\begin{array}{ll}
\sum_{j=1}^{n} a_{jk} \cdot \hat{y}_{jt,k} \leq K & \forall t \\[2mm]
\hat{y}^L_{j1,k} = \hat{y}^L_{j12,k-1} + \hat{y}_{j1,k} - \hat{\hat{d}}_{j1,k} & \forall j \\[2mm]
\hat{y}^L_{jt,k} = \hat{y}^L_{jt-1,k} + \hat{y}_{jt,k} - \hat{\hat{d}}_{jt,k} \ (t = 2, \ldots, 12)\ \forall j \\[2mm]
\hat{y}^L_{jt,k}, \hat{y}_{jt,k} \geq 0 & \forall j, t
\end{array}
\right).
$$

The initial value of the inventory balance equation for January $(t = 1)$ of year k is given by the amount of stock at the end of December $(t = 12)$ of the previous year $(k - 1) : \hat{y}^L_{j12,k-1}$. The amount describes the coupling of subsequent years. Hence, the overall anticipated base-decision space is given by

$$
\hat{A}^B(K) = \{\hat{y}^L_{j12,0} = \hat{y}^{L'}_{j12,0} \ \forall j;\ \hat{A}^B_k,\ k = 1, \ldots, N\}
$$

with the overall anticipated initial inventory $\hat{y}^{L'}_{j12,0}$.

Later, in Section 9.3.1, the main features of this model will be used to discuss the relationship between cost accounting and investment calculus which, in addition, will give us the opportunity to deeper discuss the relationship between the criteria C^{TB} and $\hat{C}^B$.

4.2.3 Two-Stage Linear Programming

Two-stage linear programming describes a linear optimization problem for which the second-stage parameters defining the linear constraints and the linear objective function are random (e.g., see [Wagner]). It owes its two-stage character to the particular way stochastics is realizing. In fact, special examples of two-stage programs have already been studied in previous chapters.

Two-stage programming can easily be understood considering the case of a two-period production plan. For the first period all variables of that period are deterministically known, whereas (some of) the variables of the second period are still random. These latter variables, however, become known prior to the decision of the second period. The situation is typical of dynamic decisions made within a rolling horizon scheme for which always the first period is 'frozen'. A simple example of the general problem is given by the make-or-buy model which has been explained in Section 2.5.1 in great detail. Generally, two-stage linear programming can be viewed as a specific stochastic dynamic program. Hence, it is obvious that it can be described within the framework of hierarchical planning.

The general problem may be stated as follows. In accordance with the make-or-buy example of Section 2.5.1, let $x := \{x_j, j = 1, \dots, n_1\}$ be the variables of stage 1 and $y := \{y_j, j = 1, \dots, n_2\}$ of stage 2, then two-stage linear programming can be formulated by the functional equation

$$C(x^*) = \max_{x \in X} \left\{ \sum_{j=1}^{n_1} d_j^x x_j + E\{\max_{y \in Y} \sum_{j=1}^{n_2} d_j^y y_j\} \right\}$$

with d_j^x $(j = 1, \dots, n_1)$ and d_j^y $(j = 1, \dots, n_2)$ being deterministically known coefficients of the objective functions, and X and Y denoting linear decision spaces:

$$X := \{(\mathrm{i}) \wedge (\mathrm{ii})\}$$

$$(\mathrm{i}) : \sum_{j=1}^{n_1} a_{ij} x_j \le c_i, \quad i = 1, \dots, m_1$$

$$(\mathrm{ii}) : x_j \ge 0, \quad \forall j$$

and

$$Y := \{(\text{iii}) \wedge (\text{iv})\}$$

$$(\text{iii}) : \sum_{j=1}^{n_1} \tilde{g}_{ij} x_j + \sum_{j=1}^{n_2} \tilde{b}_{ij} y_j \leq \tilde{h}_i, \quad i = 1, \dots, m_2$$

$$(\text{iv}) : x_j \geq 0, \quad \forall j.$$

The parameters a_{ij} and c_i denote (deterministic) first-stage coefficients, whereas $\tilde{g}_{ij}, \tilde{b}_{ij},$ and $\tilde{h}_i$ define (stochastic) second-stage quantities. The stochastic parameters may be understood to possess a common probability distribution such that only certain parameter constellations may occur (in [Wagner] a finite number of 'scenarios' is considered).

A formulation of the coupling Eqs. (2.5) is now straightforward

$$a^{T*} = \arg \max_{a^T \in A^T} \{C^{TT}(a^T) + E \max_{\hat{a}^B \in \hat{A}_{IN}^B} \hat{C}^B(\hat{a}^B)\}.$$

Clearly, one has the following correspondence

$$a^T = x$$
$$A^T = X$$
$$C^{TT} = \sum_{j=1}^{n_1} d_j^x x_j$$
$$\hat{a}^B = y$$
$$\hat{A}^B = Y$$
$$\hat{C}^B = C^B = \sum_{j=1}^{n_2} d_j^y y_j.$$

The optimal instruction is $IN^* = x^*$. In optimizing a^T, the second maximization has to be performed for each of the realizations of the triple $\tilde{g}_{ij}, \tilde{h}_{ij}, \tilde{k}_i$. The results of the optimization are then weighted with the probabilities of $\tilde{g}_{ij}, \tilde{h}_{ij}, \tilde{k}_i$ and added up to yield the expectation value. (For a similar kind of procedure, see Section 2.5.3.)

4.2.4 Strategic-Tactical-Operational Hierarchy

(1) Preliminary remarks

As a third type of a tactical-operational hierarchy, let us consider the so-called strategic-tactical-operational hierarchy (STO hierarchy). In fact, STO hierarchies are just an extension of the tactical-operational hierarchy in that an additional strategic level is taken into account. Having in mind the introductory examples in Chapter 1 (Figs. 1.6 and 1.8), STO hierarchies are rather important so that they justify a separate treatment. In addition, STO hierarchies give us the opportunity to extend our discussion to more than two hierarchical levels.

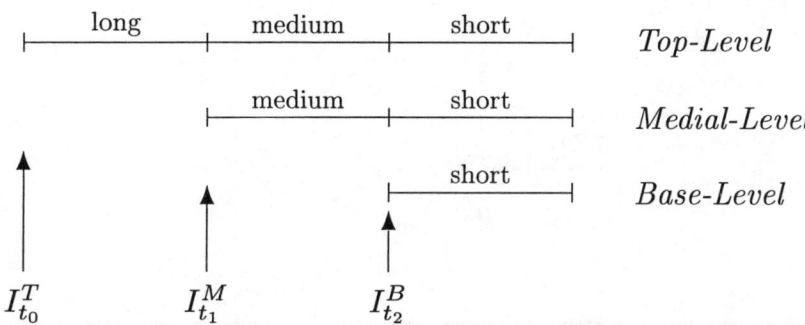

Fig. 4.4: Long Term, Medium Term, and Short Term Decision Stages

Thus, let us consider three-stage hierarchies with a top-, a medial-, and a base-level having three decision points: t_0, t_1, t_2, and three information states $I_{t_0}^T$, $I_{t_1}^M$, $I_{t_2}^B$ with M denoting 'medial'. Fig. 4.4 shows the general relationship of long term, medium term, and short term planning activities.

Generally, an STO hierarchy can be represented by a decision tree in which the higher level influences the decision field and the criteria of the lower levels. Fig. 4.5 illustrates this situation: The strategic level (A^T) influences the tactical and the operational level. The tactical level $A^M(a^T)$, on its part, exerts its influence on the operational level resulting in the decision field $A^B(a^T, a^M)$.

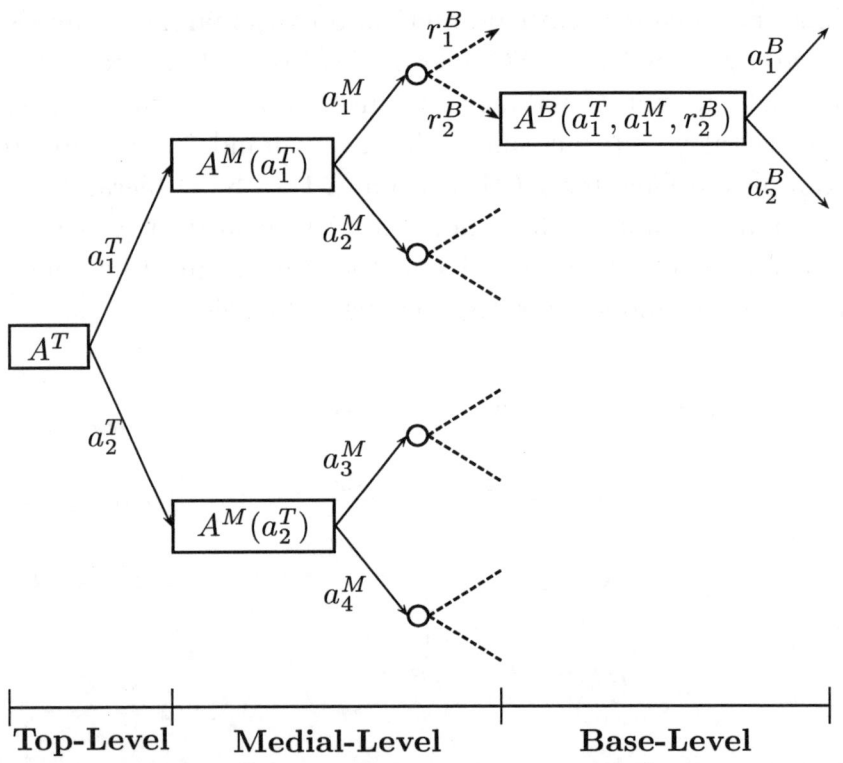

Fig. 4.5: Decision Tree of the Corporate Planning Hierarchy

Without loss of generality, the decision tree in Fig. 4.5 illustrates a specific situation. We suppose uncertainty (broken arrows in Fig. 4.5) to enter the system at the operational level with the assumption that this external stochastics is realized at time t_2 when the operational decision has to be made.

Finding a solution for a three-stage hierarchy, one must, for the top-level, anticipate the medial- and the base-level, and again, for the medial-level, it is the base-level that has to be considered. In fact, one has a rolling planning schedule which will subsequently be described in general terms. First, however, let us illustrate the three-stage planning hierarchy with an instructive real-life example.

(2) Example: Planning personal capacity and working time

The task of planning personal capacity and working time may be split up into three planning levels as indicated in Fig. 4.6 [Wild/Schneeweiss].

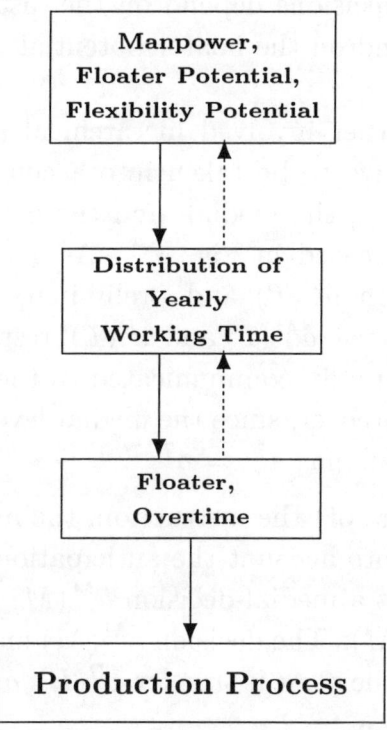

Fig. 4.6: Planning Levels of Personal Capacity and Working Time

1. The **top-level** determines total manpower, the number of workers being capable to work at variable working places (so-called floaters), and the flexibility potential. This potential is defined as the corridor within which weekly working time may fluctuate.

2. The **medial-level** distributes yearly working time over the months or the weeks of the year. In particular, this distribution allows a company to adapt to seasonalities. This distribution, of course, depends on the manpower capacity and the flexibility potential determined at the top-level.

3. The **base-level** actually executes the usage of floaters which were provided by the strategic (top-level) decision. In addition, overtime is ordered at this operational stage. Again, the base-level decisions depend on the distribution of yearly working time and on the floater potential.

In solving this rather involved hierarchical planning problem, the lower levels have to be taken into account. Thus, in optimizing the top-level, the medial- and the base-level have to be anticipated as indicated in Fig. 4.7. As a result, one obtains a top-level decision $a^T(T)$ and preliminary decisions for the medial- and base-level, $\hat{a}^M(T)$ and $\hat{a}^B(T)$, respectively. The top-level decision is directly communicated to the medial-level, i.e., $a^T = IN(a^T)$. Moreover, since the medial-level cannot interfere, a^{T^*} is final, and one has $a^{T^*} = a^{T^{**}}$.

Using (at least part of) the instruction, the medial-level is optimized by taking into account the anticipation of the base-level. Again, one obtains a medial-decision $a^M(M)$ and a preliminary base-decision $\hat{a}^B(M)$. The decision $a^M(M)$ may, of course, differ from $\hat{a}^M(T)$, and the same is true for $a^B(B)$, $\hat{a}^B(M)$, and $\hat{a}^B(T)$.

Fig. 4.7 clearly exhibits the typical structure of a rolling horizon scheme. The anticipated optimal decisions $\hat{a}^{M^*}(T)$, $\hat{a}^{B^*}(T)$, and $\hat{a}^{B^*}(M)$ are only preliminary and are executed at the latest

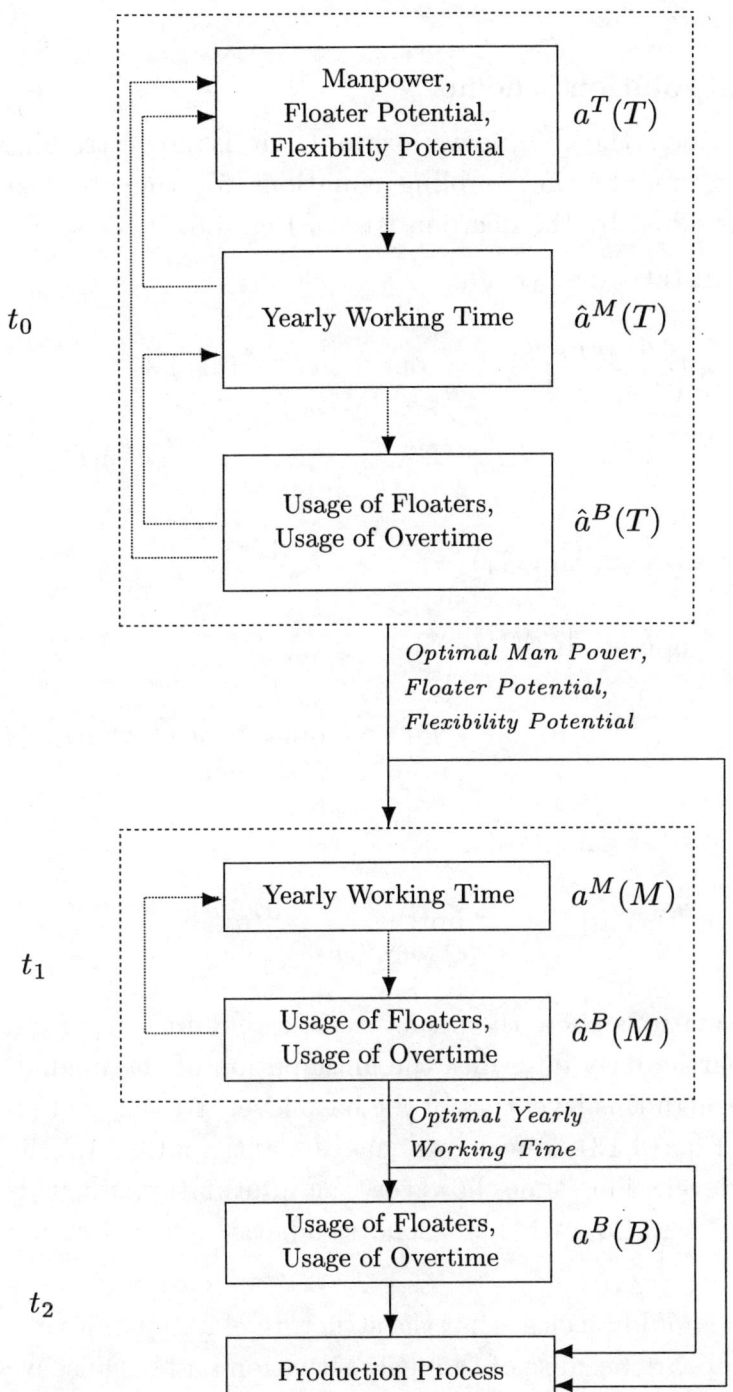

t_0

Manpower,
Floater Potential,
Flexibility Potential $a^T(T)$

Yearly Working Time $\hat{a}^M(T)$

Usage of Floaters,
Usage of Overtime $\hat{a}^B(T)$

Optimal Man Power,
Floater Potential,
Flexibility Potential

t_1

Yearly Working Time $a^M(M)$

Usage of Floaters,
Usage of Overtime $\hat{a}^B(M)$

Optimal Yearly
Working Time

t_2

Usage of Floaters,
Usage of Overtime $a^B(B)$

Production Process

Fig. 4.7: Manpower Capacity Planning as a Rolling Schedule

possible point in time.

(3) General solution scheme

Having described the manpower example, it is now straightforward to formulate the coupling equations for the abstract situation described by the decision tree of Fig. 4.5.

Top-decision (at time t_0)

$$a^{T^*} = \arg \operatorname*{opt}_{a^T \in A^T} \left[C^{TT}(a^T) + \operatorname*{opt}_{\hat{a}^M \in \hat{A}^M(a^T)} [C^{MM}(\hat{a}^M) + \right.$$

$$(4.12) \qquad\qquad\qquad + E\{ \operatorname*{opt}_{\hat{a}^B \in \hat{A}^B(a^T, \hat{a}^M)} C^B(\hat{a}^B) | I_{t_0}^T \}] \Big]$$

Medial-decision (at time t_1)

$$a^{M^*} = \arg \operatorname*{opt}_{a^M \in A^M(a^{T^*})} \left[C^{MM}(a^M) + \right.$$

$$(4.13) \qquad\qquad\qquad + E\{ \operatorname*{opt}_{\hat{a}^B \in \hat{A}^B(a^{T^*}, a^M)} C^B(\hat{a}^B) | I_{t_1}^M \} \Big]$$

Base-decision (at time t_2)

$$(4.14) \qquad a^{B^*} = \arg \operatorname*{opt}_{a^B \in A^B(a^{T^*}, a^{M^*}, r^B)} C^B(a^B).$$

The three equations show the structure of a dynamic program. Eq. (4.12) particularly describes the anticipation of the medial-level and through this level that of the base-level. At the medial-decision of Eq. (4.13), one again has an anticipation of the operational level. This time, however, the information status is not I^T but I^M. In Eq. (4.14), r^B denotes a particular realization of $\tilde{r}^B$.

Remark: It should be clear that the structure of a dynamic program only appears because of the team situation and because we assumed an exact explicit reactive anticipation. In Sections 6.3.1

and 6.3.2, we will compare a dynamic programming solution with an approximation which realistically grants the levels more autonomy. Hence, in reality, a dynamic programming solution to STO problems as proposed here will, in most cases, have to be replaced by a structure which guarentees the different levels a higher degree of independence.

Chapter 5

Principal Agent Hierarchies

Up to now we have investigated the situation of one or more decision makers taking decisions within the framework of a team or an enforced team situation. (See the definition of constructional and organizational hierarchies in Fig. 2.3.) The levels were allowed to possess different states of information; an antagonistic behavior, however, was not assumed to be present or effective. That is to say, the levels did not exploit their information in an opportunistic way.

We are now ready to examine the antagonistic case in some detail. Let us focus on (antagonistic) principal agent settings taking the top-level to be the principal and the base-level the agent. It is interesting to see how the general theory on hierarchical planning can be adapted to the antagonistic situation, showing that it is comprehensive enough to incorporate the important and well-established principal agent theory. With antagonistic levels, it is necessary to discuss in far more detail the different states of information and, in particular, the way how information is communicated. Up to now, the gathering of information was assumed to be the usual activity of statistical data analysis. In the case, however, when human decision makers are involved, information is often not obtained in simply screening the environment. Instead, it is the environment itself that is revealing and producing (right or wrong) information actively.

Hence, the next section will examine the different information states and the particular way of gaining information during the hierarchical decision process. In Section 5.2, we then analyze the so-called standard problem of principal agent theory and show its close relationship to classical hierarchical planning procedures. Section 5.3 will provide an illustrative example, and Section 5.4 is devoted to a general discussion of solution aspects. Finally, Section 5.5 introduces, as a fairly general representation of the standard problem, the LEN-model which will help the reader to deeper understand the basic concepts of principal agent theory.

5.1 Information Situation in the Principal Agent Theory

The principal agent setting can briefly be described as follows. The principal (top-level) concludes a contract with an agent (base-level) who is providing her with certain services. The problem is that the principal cannot achieve to be fully informed about the agent's behavior. In order to overcome this lack of knowledge, the principal can at least try to improve her state of information, or she can try to moderate the consequences of not being informed. This latter strategy will result in offering the agent suitable incentives.

To characterize the information state, three points in time are of particular interest (see Fig. 5.1): The state of information

(1) **before** the contract is completed ($t \leq t_0$),
(2) **between** the conclusion of the contract and the executional (base-) decision of the agent ($t_0 \leq t \leq t_1$), and
(3) **after** the agent's activity ($t_1 \leq t$).

Ad (1) The principal's lack of information before the completion of the contract is called **hidden characteristics**. As in team-based hierarchical planning, the principal is providing herself with estimates $\hat{A}^B, \hat{C}^B, \widehat{\text{opt}}$, and $\hat{I}^B$ of all characteristics of the agent, i.e. she is anticipating the agent. What is different, however, is the way how information is gained. The base-level now plays a far more active role. In addition to the anticipated base-model, the diagram of Fig. 5.1 therefore depicts the base-level in time t_0 (and before) as an active party in finding a contract.

The less well-known the agent is, the higher is the risk of selecting a less favorable contract, hence one has a **risk of adverse selection**.

To avoid or, at least, to reduce a situation of hidden characteristics, the contracting parties have three major strategies:
- screening,
- signaling, and
- self selection.

Screening denotes the traditional passive way of information gathering, as has been explained before.
Signaling describes an active revelation of information by the agent. As an example, consider the application for a job at which the candidate is providing the employer with additional certificates she at first did not ask for.
Self-selection characterizes a situation in which the principal works at her low state of information, but offers different contracts so that in choosing one of them the agent reveals at least some of his characteristics.

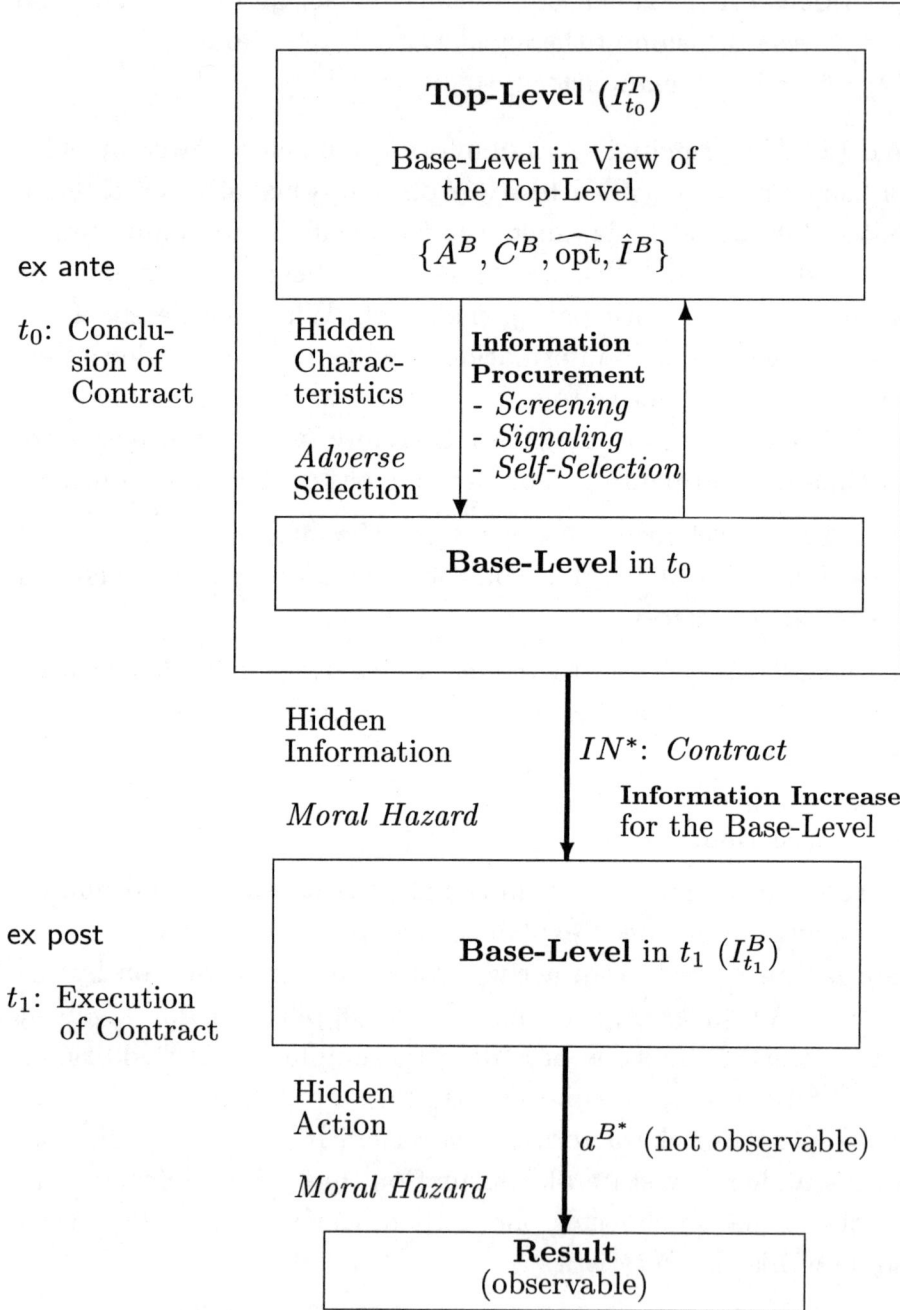

Fig. 5.1: Information Situation in a Principal Agent System

Ad (2) The asymmetry of information between the contract and its execution is called **hidden information**. Having made the contract, it might happen that the agent obtains further information which is not communicated to the principal and is thus increasing the information asymmetry. This increase often concerns the stochastic information I^B. The agent can try to exploit the new situation to his favor. One therefore calls this attitude **moral hazard**.

To counteract moral hazard, the principal can try to anticipate the agent's possible behavior after his increase of information. Moreover, she can offer incentives so that the agent is acting at least partly in her direction. In addition, control mechanisms could be agreed upon along with the conclusion of the contract.

Ad (3) In many cases, one has to face the situation that at the executional level (in $t = t_1$) only the result of the agent's activity can be observed but not the activity itself. This lack of information is called **hidden action**. In fact, if the agent is facing uncertainty, the result he obtains allows no conclusion as to the activity he actually exerted. Hence, the principal has to be aware of a **moral hazard** situation. As a prevention, in completing the contract, the principal can offer incentives so that both, the principal and the agent, support each other. Note that in this pure hidden action case, i.e., no hidden characteristics and hidden information being present, one has common information until t_1. The following section will examine this type of problem somewhat further.

5.2 The Standard Problem of Principal Agent Theory

The so-called standard problem of principal agent theory is characterized exclusively by the hidden action situation; hidden characteristics and hidden information are assumed not to be present. To cope with this situation, the principal tries to offer incentives. Identifying, as usual, the principal with the top-level and the agent with the base-level, a contract turns out to be just the instruction IN. Moreover, the actions a^T the principal has at her disposal are the various incentive schemes, and the optimal incentive a^{T^*} defines the contract, and hence the final instruction $IN^* = IN(a^{T^*})$.

Having in mind this correspondence, the standard problem can now be stated as follows: With his activity a^B the agent earns a profit $P(a^B)$ which he is handing over to the principal. The principal on her part offers an incentive ϕ which depends on the profit and hence on the activity of the agent: $\phi = \phi(P)$. Thus, the principal obtains the net profit $P - \phi(P)$ and the agent gets the incentive diminished by the effort going along with his activity a^B.

We are now using the general coupling Eqs. (2.5) of hierarchical planning to precisely formulate the standard problem of the principal agent theory. In doing so, one simultaneously will recognize that the structural properties of agency theory, as mentioned earlier, just turn out to be a particular specification of the comprehensive theory of hierarchical planning.

As a general characteristic, C^{TB} and C^B are now no longer complementary as in the team case but competitive and antagonistic with the important consequence that the case of hidden action needs a special treatment. Because of the antagonistic behavior, offering incentives comes to be a coupling strategy.

Hidden characteristics and hidden information not being present implies that $\hat{C}^B = C^B$ and $\hat{A}^B = A^B$ are deterministically known to the principal at time t_0. Furthermore, $\hat{I}^B = I^B = I^B_{t_1}$, is known and, for the hidden action case, I^B describes a probability distribution. In particular, $I^B = I^B_{t_1}$ says that there is no information increase for the base-level.

With these preliminary remarks the coupling equations (2.5) can now be stated as follows

$$a^{T*} = \arg \operatorname*{opt}_{a^T \in A^T} E\{C^{TB}(AF(a^T))|I_{t_0}^T\} \qquad (5.1a)$$

$$AF(a^T) = \arg \operatorname*{opt}_{\hat{a}^B \in A_{IN}^B} E\{C_{IN}^B(\hat{a}^B)|I^B\} \qquad (5.1b)$$

$$a^{B*} = \arg \operatorname*{opt}_{a^B \in A_{IN*}^B} E\{C_{IN*}^B(a^B)|I^B\} \qquad (5.1c)$$

According to the explanation given above, one has the following correspondence

$a^T := \phi(P)$: incentive
A^T : function space of all feasible incentive schemes
a^B : agent's activity
A^B : agent's activity space
P : profit
$P - \phi(P)$: net profit

The top-criterion C^T fully depends on the agent's activity. Hence, there exists no private criterion, and one has $C^T = C^{TB}$. Moreover, since the principal's utility u^T is a function of her net profit, one obtains

$$C^{TB} = u^T(P - \phi(P)). \qquad (5.2)$$

For the agent, one has

$$C^B = u^B(\phi(P(a^B)), a^B) \qquad (5.3)$$

indicating that his utility u^B depends on the premium (incentive) ϕ and the disutility incurred by his effort a^B.

Obviously, there will be no contract if the incentive is not substantial enough to guarantee the agent a certain aspiration level AL^B. Hence, the principal has to consider the so-called **participation condition**

$$(5.4) \qquad E\{u^B\} \geq AL^B.$$

In fact, the participation condition restricts and hence defines the base-action space and can alternatively be formalized as

$$(5.5) \qquad A_\phi^B := \{a^B : E\{u^B\} \geq AL^B\}.$$

With these explanations, the coupling equations (5.1) take on the more explicit form

$$(5.6a) \quad \phi^* = \arg \max_{\phi \in A^T} E\{u^T[P(AF(\phi)) - \phi(P(AF(\phi)))]|I_{t_0}^T\}$$

$$(5.6b) \qquad AF(\phi) = \arg \max_{\hat{a}^B \in A_\phi^B} E\{u^B[\phi(P(\hat{a}^B)), \hat{a}^B]|I^B\}.$$

As a result, the anticipated optimal decision $\hat{a}^{B^*}$ of the agent is given by

$$(5.6c) \qquad \hat{a}^{B^*} = \hat{a}^{B^0}(\phi^*).$$

Note that the instruction ϕ^* is only specified up to the random influence I^B.

Before discussing general solution aspects of the Eqs. (5.6a) and (5.6b), let us consider, as a first step, a simple example in which the antagonists are assumed to be risk-neutral. Later, in Section 5.6, we will solve Eqs. (5.6) under fairly general assumptions (LEN-model) which will allow us to illustrate and carefully discuss the significance of the antagonists' behavior towards risk.

5.3 An Illustrative Example with Risk-Neutral Antagonists

5.3.1 Problem Statement and Problem Formulation

Consider a company that is planning to start a new activity. In doing so, new machines must be bought and a specialist has to be hired. The company intends to pay the specialist a fixed salary (fixum) and a premium depending on the profit he is contributing through good management. This is because the company can only control the *profit* the specialist will contribute. A payment according to his *activities* seems not to be possible since in view of non-observable random influences the company is not able to evaluate the new employee's efforts. Thus we have the following payment (incentive) to the employee

$$\phi(P) = F + fP$$

with F being a fixum (fixed salary or rent) and fP a premium which is a percentage f of profit P.

Defining a^B to be the specialist's activity level, one has

$$P = P(a^B).$$

As for the standard model, a^T has to be identified with the working contract, i.e., with the payment to be offered. Hence, $a^T = \phi(P)$, and A^T defines the set of all feasible compensation schemes. Again, the company's criterion C^{TB} is defined as the utility u^T of net profit

$$C^{TB} = u^T(P - \phi(P)) = u^T[(1 - f)P - F].$$

The employee's criterion C^B can be assumed to be the sum of the utility $u^B(\phi)$ of the payment ϕ and the disutility $V(a^B)$ (or costs) going along with his efforts:

$$C^B = u^B(\phi) - V(a^B).$$

Clearly, the new candidate will not accept a contract if his expected utility is lower than a certain aspiration level AL^B. This aspiration level could be the expected utility of the salary of the applicant's present job.

Let us assume that AL^B is known to the company. Hence, the participation condition reads

$$(5.7) \qquad E\{u^B(\phi) - V(a^B)|I^B\} \geq AL^B$$

giving rise to the base-decision space A_ϕ^B (see Eq. (5.5)).

With these specifications, the optimal payment can now be determined using the adapted coupling equations (5.6)

$$(5.8a) \qquad \phi^* = \arg\max_{\phi \in A^T} E\{u^T[(1-f)P(AF(\phi)) - F]|I_{t_0}^T\},$$

$$(5.8b) \qquad AF(\phi) = \arg\max_{\hat{a}^B \in A_\phi^B} E\{u^B(\phi) - V(\hat{a}^B)|I^B\}.$$

What still remains to be discussed, however, is the uncertainty aspect which is constitutive for problems of asymmetric information and, in particular, for the hidden action case.

Let us assume the profit $P(a^B)$ of activity a^B to be a random variable. As usual, its probability distribution is described by I^B. Since there is symmetric information up to $t = t_1$, I^B is assumed to be known to the company and the applicant. Together with the information situation, we can now discuss somewhat deeper, risk and incentive aspects.

If the company only pays a fixum: $\phi = F$, then there is no incentive and the company has to carry all the risk. If, on the other hand, no fixed salary is paid but exclusively a premium: $\phi = fP$, one has a maximum incentive but full risk for the employee. Consequently, the contract to be chosen will depend on the respective attitudes u^T and u^B of employer and applicant with respect to risk. If, for instance, the applicant is highly risk-averse, he needs, supplementary to his incentive, a higher compensation than some one who is less risk-averse, so that the participation condition (5.7) can less easily be satisfied. Clearly, if the employer is highly risk-averse, no incentive could be better than a risky one. We return to this point in Section 5.5 and in the general discussion on the solution properties of Eqs. (5.6) in the following Section 5.4.

5.3.2 Problem Solution

In order to easily determine the optimal contract for the problem stated in the previous section let us assume that both parties are *risk-neutral* and that the applicant has only a high (a_1^B) and a low (a_2^B) activity level. Furthermore, there are only two scenarios $S_i (i = 1, 2)$ of equal probability that have to be considered. Depending on the applicant's activity, these scenarios imply the profit listed in Table 5.1.

	S_1	S_2	$V(a^B)$
a_1^B	12 000	18 000	500
a_2^B	18 000	22 000	3 000

Table 5.1: Profit Depending on Activity and Scenario

As further dates one has the disutilities $V(a^B)$ (see Table 5.1), the aspiration level $AL^B = 6000$, and the fixum $F = 5000$. With a given fixum the only task that still remains is to determine the employee's share f of the profit.

In solving the Eqs. (5.8), let us start with the anticipation relation (5.8b). For a risk-neutral base-decision maker, one obtains

(5.9)
$$\bar{C}^B(\hat{a}^B) = E\{\phi(\hat{a}^B)|I_{t_1}^B\} - V(\hat{a}^B)$$
$$= fE\{P(\hat{a}^B)|I_{t_1}^B\} + F - V(\hat{a}^B).$$

This function has the two branches, $\bar{C}^B(\hat{a}_1^B)$ and $\bar{C}^B(\hat{a}_2^B)$.

1. Low level of activity: $\hat{a}_1^B$

(5.10)
$$\bar{C}^B(\hat{a}_1^B) = f\frac{1}{2}(12000 + 18000) + 5000 - 500$$
$$= 4500 + 15000f.$$

Hence, the participation condition $\bar{C}^B(\hat{a}_1^B) \geq 6000$ is fulfilled for $f \geq 0.1$.

2. High level of activity: $\hat{a}_2^B$

(5.11)
$$\bar{C}^B(\hat{a}_2^B) = f\frac{1}{2}(18000 + 22000) + 5000 - 3000$$
$$= 2000 + 20000f.$$

The participation condition $\bar{C}^B(\hat{a}_2^B) \geq 6000$ is fulfilled for $f \geq 0.2$.

Fig. 5.2 shows the low level and the high level expected utility as a function of the premium rate f. Obviously, for a premium rate $f < 0.5$ the agent employs his low level activity, whereas for $f \geq 0.5$ he switches to his high level activity. Hence, the anticipation function (5.8b) turns out to be

(5.12)
$$AF(f) = \hat{a}^{B^0}(f)$$

$$= \arg \max_{\hat{a}^B \in \{\hat{a}_1^B, \hat{a}_2^B\}} \bar{C}^B(\hat{a}^B) = \begin{cases} \hat{a}_1^B & \text{for } 0.1 \leq f < 0.5 \\ \hat{a}_2^B & \text{for } 0.5 \leq f \leq 1.0 \end{cases}$$

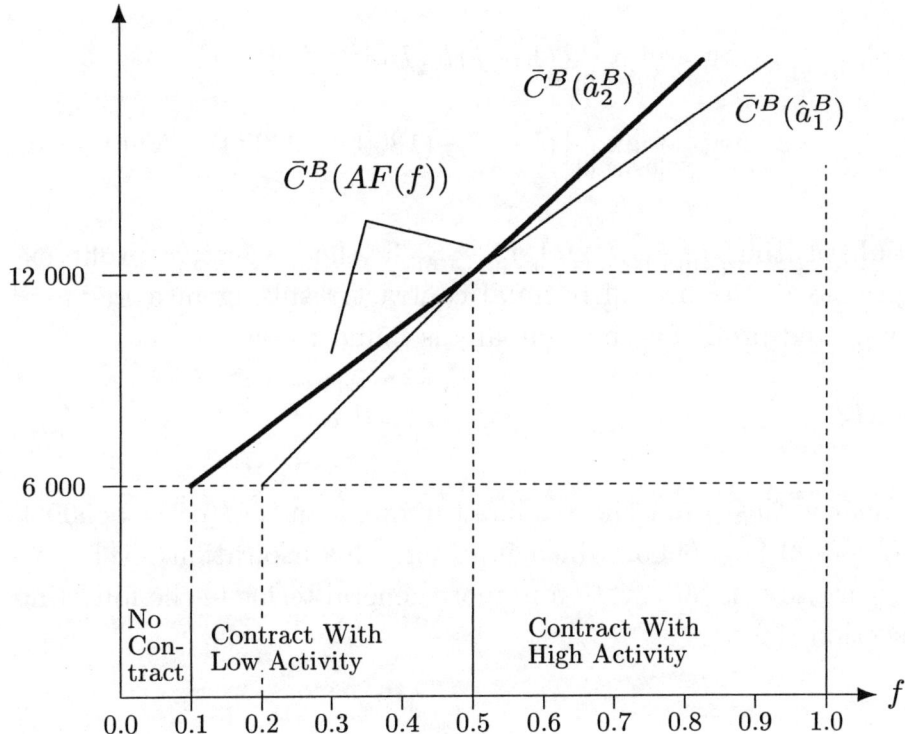

Fig. 5.2: Calculation of the Anticipation Function

Note that in (5.12) it is assumed that in case of $f = 0.5$ the principal can expect the agent to choose that activity level ($\hat{a}_2^B$) which is the more favorable to him.

With $AF(f)$ one can now solve (5.8a) to obtain the optimal contract $f = f^*$. Substituting the piecewise linear function (5.12) in (5.8a) we consider the two branches $0.1 \leq f < 0.5$ and $0.5 \leq f \leq 1$.

1. Branch $0.1 \leq f < 0.5$

$$f_{[0.1,0.5)}^* = \arg \max_{f \in [0.1,0.5)} \left\{ (1-f)E\{P(\hat{a}_1^B)|I_{t_0}^T\} - F \right\}$$

$$= \arg \max_{f \in [0.1,0.5)} \left\{ (1-f)\frac{1}{2}(12000 + 18000) - 5000 \right\} = 0.1$$

2. Branch $0.5 \le f \le 1.0$

$$f^*_{[0.5,1.0]} = \arg \max_{f \in [0.5,1.0]} \{(1-f)E\{P(\hat{a}_2^B)|I_{t_0}^T\} - F\}$$

$$= \arg \max_{f \in [0.5,1.0]} \{(1-f)\frac{1}{2}(18000 + 22000) - 5000\} = 0.5.$$

Substituting $f^*_{[0.1,0.5)}$ and $f^*_{[0.5,1.0]}$ in the respective profit expressions, the overall optimal contract resulting in a maximal expected profit for the company is found to be

$$(5.13) \qquad\qquad f^* = f^*_{[0.1,1.0]} = 0.1.$$

Clearly, this profit share offers the applicant $\bar{C}^B(a^B) = 4500 + 15000 \cdot 0.1 = 6000$, which is exactly his aspiration level. We return to this observation in more general terms in the following section.

5.4 Some General Observations Concerning the Solution of the Principal Agent Coupling Equations

In analogy to the discussion of the team-based case in Sections 2.6 and 3.2, let us now summarize some observations as to the nature of the solution of Eqs. (5.6) of the standard model.

Clearly, C^{TB} and C^B are conflicting criteria. Thus, the solution of Eqs. (5.1a) and (5.1b) (or equivalently (5.6a) and (5.6b)) for a decision space A^B, which is not restricted by the participation condition (5.4), amounts to solving the vector maximum problem

$$(5.14) \qquad\qquad \{\bar{C}^{TB}, \bar{C}^B\} \Longrightarrow \operatorname*{opt}_{a^T \in A^T, a^B \in A^B}.$$

If there is no hidden action, one has the case of information symmetry and no profit-dependent incentives have to be paid. The solution of this vector maximum problem is represented by the (outer) efficient boarder depicted in Fig. 5.3 and is called **first-best**.

In case of an information asymmetry (i.e., the hidden action case) these first-best solutions, however, cannot be reached. Formally, this is due to the restricting anticipation relation. Hence, one can only reach a dominated efficient border and the according solutions are called **second-best** solutions (see Fig. 5.3). There is, however, one important exception. If the agent is risk-neutral, it can be shown [Milgrom/Roberts] that the anticipation relation does not restrict the solution of the top-equation.

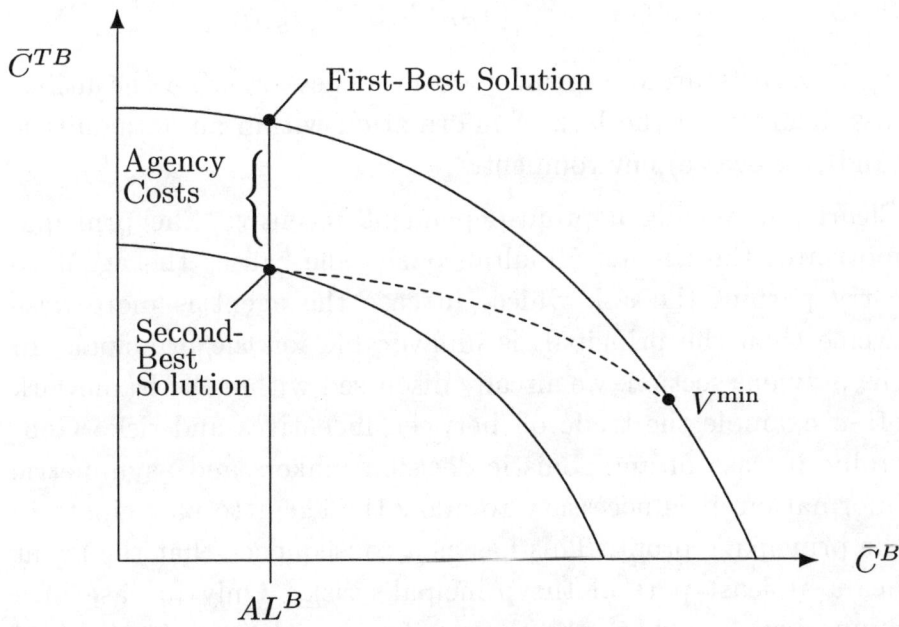

Fig. 5.3: General Solution of the Principal Agent Problem

Strictly speaking, Eq. (5.6b) contains not one but two constraints. The second one is given by the participation condition which is depicted in Fig. 5.3 as well. This constraint says that solutions only on the right hand side of the vertical line are feasible. For antagonistic partners, however, the solution must be on the border $\bar{C}^B = AL^B$. All other solutions would be less favorable for the principal (see again the result of the previous example). That is, the principal will (and can) offer the agent a premium such that the second-best solution, as indicated in Fig. 5.3, is reached. Hence, there exists only one second-best (a_{SB}^{T*}) and one first-best (a_{FB}^{T*}) solution. (Note that, with the assumption of a participation condition, a discussion of a multi-criterion optimization problem is excluded from principal agent theory. Or, to put it differently, in economic theory the discussion is replaced with market equilibrium considerations [Tirole].) The difference in the expected value of the top-criterion is called **agency costs**

$$(5.15) \qquad AC := \bar{C}^{TB}(a_{FB}^{T*}) - \bar{C}^{TB}(a_{SB}^{T*}).$$

Agency costs are opportunity costs. They describe the utility loss incurred by the lack of information within an antagonistic (and risk-averse) environment.

Clearly, in paying a profit-dependent incentive, the principal motivates the agent. Simultaneously, she causes the agent to carry part of the risk which, in case the agent is more risk-averse than the principal, is unfavorable for the principal. In the previous section, we already discussed within the framework of an example the trade off between incentives and risk. Generally, in case of antagonistic decision makers and asymmetric information, it is necessary to allow the agent to participate in the principal's profit. This has as a consequence that the agent bears at least part of the principal's risk. Only in case of a fixum, i.e., $F = AL^B$, the agent is free of risk (and deprived, of course, of any chances). Hence, the attitude against risk plays an important role in allocating risk to both parties. In fact, the solution of the standard model, for defined risk and utility functions, provides a solution which, with its offered incentive, optimally balances risk and incentive aspects.

One may ask why the principal does not pay a fixum which would guarantee her the first-best solution, and hence a higher profit. Unfortunately, such a solution is not realizable. If the principal is paying a fixum, there is no incentive for the agent to apply a high activity level a^B. He therefore chooses that feasible value a^B which minimizes his disutility which might result in the point V^{min} depicted in Fig. 5.3. Obviously, this point is less favorable for the principal than her first-best solution she intended to achieve and even less favorable than the second-best solution, which can be guaranteed. Clearly, because the principal cannot observe and control the action of the agent, she cannot prevent him from taking an action leading to V^{min}. Hence, the principal is forced to pay an incentive that is not a fixum but is profit dependent.

The following fairly general specification of the agency coupling equations (5.1) and (5.6) for the hidden action case will serve as a further illustration and, in addition, will provide an increased insight into the general solution properties.

5.5 The LEN-Model

To obtain further insight into the general nature of the agency coupling equations (5.6), let us now solve Eqs. (5.6a) and (5.6b) for a more general setting than that of the preceding example. In particular, we are interested in a solution which allows us to gain further insight into the effect of an agent being risk-averse. To this end let us introduce the so-called Linear-Exponential-Normal (LEN)-model.

(1) Definition of the LEN-model

The LEN-model (e.g., see [Spremann]) specifies the general Eqs. (5.6) such that

(1) profit P is assumed to depend *linearly* on the action a^B and the external stochastics $\tilde{r}$,

(2) the incentive $\phi^{(P)}$ is assumed to be a *linear* function of P, and

(3) the utility function u^B of the agent is assumed to be *exponential* and the external stochastics is taken to be *normally* distributed.

To be more specific, let us assume

$$(5.16) \qquad P = a^B + \tilde{r}$$

$$(5.17) \qquad \tilde{r} \sim N(0, \sigma^2)$$

$$(5.18) \qquad \phi(P) = F + fP = F + fa^B + f\tilde{r}$$

$$(5.19) \qquad C^{TB} = u^T(x) = x$$

$$(5.20) \qquad C^B = u^B(\phi, a^B) := u^B(\phi) - (a^B)^2$$

$$(5.21) \qquad u^B(\phi) = -exp\{-\alpha\phi\}, \alpha > 0$$

(Note that, as for the general equations (5.6), the quantities $P, \phi(P)$, and u^B are of course random.)

Using the measure of risk aversion of Pratt [Pratt/Zeckhauser], the agent is characterized by his risk aversion

$$(5.22) \qquad -\frac{u^{B''}}{u^{B'}} = \alpha > 0$$

and for the risk-neutral principal, one has

$$(5.23) \qquad -\frac{u^{T''}}{u^{T'}} = 0$$

with the prime denoting the differentiation with respect to the argument. Furthermore, the agent is assumed to suffer an increasing marginal disutility $V(a^B) = (a^B)^2$. With the specifications

(5.16) through (5.21) of the LEN-model, the general equations (5.6a) and (5.6b) (see also (5.8a) and (5.8b)) can be written

$$\phi^* = \arg \max_{\phi \in A^T} E\{(1-f)(a^B + \tilde{r}) - F\}, \qquad (5.24a)$$

$$\hat{a}^{B^0} = \arg \max_{\hat{a}^B \in A_\phi^B} \left[E\{-exp(-\alpha\phi)\} - (\hat{a}^B)^2 \right] \qquad (5.24b)$$

with

$$A_\phi^B := \left\{ \hat{a}^B : E\{-exp(-\alpha\phi)\} - (\hat{a}^B)^2 \geq AL^B \right\}. \qquad (5.25)$$

(2) Solution of the LEN-model

Solving the system (5.24), we start with Eq. (5.24b). Rather than optimizing expected utility, one can equally well optimize the adjoint certainty equivalent S which is known to be

$$S := u^{-1}\left(E\{u(x)\}\right) \qquad (5.26)$$

with $u(x)$ being a (monotonous) utility function. For an exponential utility function $u(\phi)$ (having risk aversion α and normally distributed risk), one has the well-known relation

$$S = E(\phi) - \frac{\alpha}{2} Var(\phi). \qquad (5.27)$$

Substituting (5.18) and taking into account (5.17), one obtains

$$S = F + f\hat{a}^B - \frac{\alpha}{2} f^2 \sigma^2. \qquad (5.28)$$

Hence, the maximizer of (5.24b) is the maximizer of

$$\bar{S} := S - (\hat{a}^B)^2. \qquad (5.29)$$

Thus, for a given ϕ, i.e., for given F and f, and leaving aside the participation constraint (5.25), Eq. (5.24b) is solved by

$$\hat{a}^{B^0} = \hat{a}^{B^0}(\phi) = \frac{f}{2}. \qquad (5.30)$$

Considering, in a second step, the participation constraint, one first calculates the optimal revenue of the agent

(5.31) $$\bar{S}^0 = F + \frac{f^2}{4}(1 - 2\alpha\sigma^2)$$

which (in view of the principal) is accepted by the agent if the fixum has at least the value

(5.32) $$F = AL^B - \frac{f^2}{4}(1 - 2\alpha\sigma^2).$$

Formally, Eq. (5.32) relates the fixum F to the share f so that only f remains to be determined by the top-equation. Taking the expectation in (5.24a) and substituting (5.32) and (5.30), the following expression for the expected utility of the principal's revenue

(5.33) $$\bar{C}^{TB} = (1 - f)\frac{f}{2} - AL^B + \frac{f^2}{4}(1 - 2\alpha\sigma^2)$$

is to be maximized with respect to f, resulting in the final optimal values

(5.34) $$f^* = \frac{1}{1 + 2\alpha\sigma^2},$$

(5.35) $$F^* = AL^B - \frac{1 - 2\alpha\sigma^2}{4(1 + 2\alpha\sigma^2)^2},$$

(5.36) $$a^{B*} = \frac{1}{2(1 + 2\alpha\sigma^2)} = \frac{f^x}{2}, \qquad \text{and}$$

(5.37) $$\bar{C}^{TB*} = \frac{1}{4(1 + 2\alpha\sigma^2)} - AL^B$$

$$= \frac{1}{4}f^* - AL^B.$$

(3) Solution properties of the LEN-model

Let us now interpret the solution of the LEN-model. As mentioned earlier, we are particularly interested in the influences of the external uncertainty (σ^2) and the risk aversion (α) of the agent. To this end, let us introduce the notion of a **risk premium** RP which is defined as the deviation of the certainty equivalent $S_u = u^{-1}E\{U(X)\}$ of a random variable X from its mean value $E(X)$

$$RP_u := E(X) - S_u. \tag{5.38}$$

For the agent, considering (5.28), the (optimal) risk premium is found to be

$$RP_{u^B} = \frac{\alpha}{2}f^{*^2}\sigma^2. \tag{5.39}$$

This is an interesting result. It shows that, because of the risk premium, for a given fixum F the revenue of the agent (see (5.31)) will be lower the higher his risk aversion α is, and the same is true for an increased environmental uncertainty σ^2. Moreover, the risk premium the agent might ask for in participating in the contract (see (5.32)) depends on the share f (or f^*), which clearly shows that, for a risk-averse agent, an output-dependent incentive (fP) does not only have a positive effect. Indeed, the higher the share f, the more the principal must compensate the agent's risk aversion. Obviously, there is no dependence of RP_{u^B} on the fixum F but, of course, as can readily be seen from $\hat{a}^{B^0} = \frac{f}{2}$ (see (5.30) or (5.36)), F has no effect on the activity level (effort) of the agent. It is only needed to support the participation of the agent in the contract.

As Eq. (5.37) shows, the principal's expected revenue depends on the percentage share f^*. This share will be near $f^* = 0$ (see (5.34)) for a high risk aversion α and/or a high uncertainty σ^2. On the other hand, it will take on its largest value $f^* = 1$ if the environment is deterministic ($\sigma^2 = 0$), or, if the agent is risk-neutral, i.e., $\alpha = 0$. Hence, though the principal's revenue depends proportionally on f, she is not free to take the extreme value $f = 1$. This can easily be seen from (5.32) which may be rewritten in the more convenient form

$$(5.40) \qquad AL^B = F + \frac{1 - 2\alpha\sigma^2}{4} f^2.$$

Obviously, for $1 - 2\alpha\sigma^2 < 0$, i.e., if α and/or σ^2 are large ($\alpha\sigma^2 > \frac{1}{2}$), an increasing share f has to be compensated by an increased F. Otherwise the principal is not able to meet the agent's (preset) aspiration level AL^B. This result, which can also be seen from the optimal value (5.35), seems, at a first glance, counter-intuitive. It again shows, however, the negative effect of the environmental uncertainty and of the risk aversion which overcompensates the positive incentives of profit sharing.

(4) Agency costs

Agency costs were defined in Eq. (5.15) by the difference of the principal's revenues $\bar{C}^{TB}$ in case of a first-best and a second-best solution. For the LEN-model, the second-best solution $\bar{C}_{SB}^{TB*}$ is given by (5.37).

The first-best solution is obtained by solving equation (5.24a) subject to (5.25). Substituting

$$AL^B = F + f\hat{a}^B - \frac{\alpha}{2} f^2 \sigma^2 - (\hat{a}^B)^2$$

into the principal's expected revenues (see Eq. (5.24a))

$$\bar{C}^{TB} = (1 - f)\hat{a}^B - F$$

results in

$$(5.41) \qquad \bar{C}^{TB}(AL^B) = \hat{a}^B - AL^B - \frac{\alpha}{2} f^2 \sigma^2 - (\hat{a}^B)^2.$$

Optimizing this expression with respect to $\hat{a}^B$ and f, one obtains the first-best values

$$a_{FB}^{B^*} = \frac{1}{2}, \tag{5.42}$$

$$f_{FB}^* = 0, \tag{5.43}$$

$$F_{FB}^* = AL^B + \frac{1}{4}, \tag{5.44}$$

$$\text{and} \quad \bar{C}_{FB}^{TB^*} = \frac{1}{4} - AL^B. \tag{5.45}$$

With (5.45) and the second-best revenue (5.37), one finally has for the **agency costs**

$$AC = \bar{C}_{FB}^{TB^*} - \bar{C}_{SB}^{TB^*} = \frac{\alpha\sigma^2}{2(1 + 2\alpha\sigma^2)}. \tag{5.46}$$

Eq. (5.46) represents an important result. It shows that

(1) for the assumptions of the LEN-model, agency costs do not depend on the aspiration level AL^B,
(2) the higher the risk aversion and/or the environmental uncertainty σ^2, the higher will be the agency costs,
(3) for a risk-neutral agent ($\alpha = 0$) or, in case of no stochastics ($\sigma = 0$), the first-best and the second-best solution coincide, and hence $AC = 0$.

The last observation is in accordance with our general comment in Section 5.5 where we stated this fact for more general settings than those defining the LEN-model. Reversely, this again shows that both, the non-observability of the agent's action and his risk aversion, are responsible for not reaching the first-best solution.

Remark: For further references concerning more general aspects of principal agent theory see, e.g., [Bamberg/Spremann], [Grossman/Hart], [Harris/Raviv], [Holmström], [Milgrom/Roberts], [Mirrless], [Tirole], [Varian].

PART II

General Applications

With the foundations being laid in the first part of this treatise particularly on general planning hierarchies, we are now in a position to apply the general theory to important problem classes. Consequently, the general theory is no longer illustrated by simple well-defined toy models but is used to conceptualize important areas in management science. Thus hierarchical planning provides an important contribution to the theoretical understanding of many general management areas.

Four of these general problems will be considered: Production planning, design, implementation, and costs. Not surprisingly, all four problem areas are connected to each other. Thus a production planning problem, e.g., can be considered under the heading of a design problem, an implementation problem, or even as a cost problem, and similarly the same is true for any other of the above four problem types. What is important, however, is the special angle of investigation. Thus, for production planning the problem of aggregation-disaggregation will play an important role. In fact, the general theory of hierarchical planning, expounded in part I, will it make possible to considerably extend the traditional theory on hierarchical production planning (Chapter 6). For design problems (Chapter 7) the concept of explicit anticipations will be of considerable significance and for the implementation problem (Chapter 8) planning itself turns out to be of a hierarchical character.

Of particular theoretical interest is a possible foundation of modern cost accounting by the theory of hierarchical planning (Chapter 9). In fact, hierarchical planning seems to be able to replace traditional cost theory. At least three reasons can be made out for this observation: First, hierarchical planning solves the important problem of connecting the cost accounting level with the level of investment calculus. Second, the cost evaluation problem is typically a hierarchical problem, and third, the modern concept of behavioral costs involves a multi-person setting which again is described in hierarchical planning but not in traditional cost theory.

Chapter 6

Hierarchical Production Planning

Hierarchical production planning (HPP) comprises a considerable number of models which originated from the seminal work of A. Hax, H. Meal, and G. Bitran. In fact, most of the models were developed at the Massachussetts Institute of Technology so that the entire theory is often called MIT-theory of HPP.

Of course, hierarchical production planning did not just start with the paper of Hax and Meal [Hax/Meal] on a hierarchical integration of production planning and scheduling for a tire production process. Indeed, hierarchical planning in the production area has a long tradition. This is because production planning is a highly complex task and, as mentioned in the introductory chapter, hierarchical planning is a way to reduce complexity. What was really quite a novelty, however, was the careful analysis of the hierarchical nature of the production problem, particularly the discussion of the aggregation problem as well as the coupling of the different levels.

In the sequel we shall not present the MIT-theory in every detail.

For a comprehensive presentation see [Hax/Candea]. Our main concern is the description of the most essential features of the standard model (Sec. 6.1) and the discussion of its hierarchical nature. This discussion will extensively make use of the theory of hierarchical planning being developed so far. In Section 6.2, we shall then present a new approach which particularly tries to overcome part of the difficulties arising from the aggregation procedure used in the MIT type of theory. Finally, in Section 6.3, we apply the new approach to a problem in the process industry showing its suitability in a real-life setting.

6.1 Standard Model of Hierarchical Production Planning

Hierarchical production planning was first developed for a tire production problem. Instead of tires, let us illustrate HPP with the typical process of flat glass production. This production starts with melting the raw material in a melting furnace yielding, e.g., white, yellow, and bronze coloured glass. Leaving the furnace, a pattern is applied and after a cooling process the glass is cut into various formats and packagings. Hence, one has the three aggregation levels of final products: colours, patterns, and formats which, in the following, will be used for illustrative purposes. It should be clear, however, that the glass production provides only a very special interpretation. More generally, think of product groups and families to be pure planning quantities which solely exist in abstract terms.

6.1.1 The Structure of the Model

The product groupings can be depicted by the three-stage hierarchy as illustrated in Fig. 6.1. The lowest level consists of final products (items (α, β, γ)) which are aggregated to families. These families (a, b, c) are then further aggregated yielding product groups (A, B, C). Obviously, for the glass example, one can identify groups with a specific glass smelting (white, yellow, or bronze), families with patterns, and a product item with a particular packaging format.

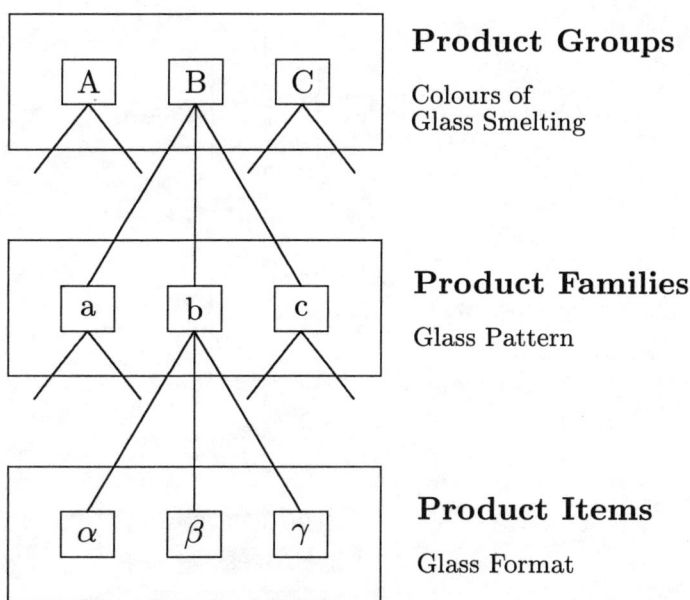

Fig. 6.1: Structure of Aggregation

The aggregation rule in the MIT model is simple: Families are items which share the same setup cost. Groups, on the other hand, are families possessing the same, or at least similar, cost parameters, production coefficients, and demand pattern (e.g., the same seasonality). Obviously, to find such families (and hence, items) will restrict the application of the standard model to only but the simplest settings. As will be shown later, the similarity assumption is crucial in order to guarantee a simple aggregation and disaggregation procedure and cannot easily be relaxed.

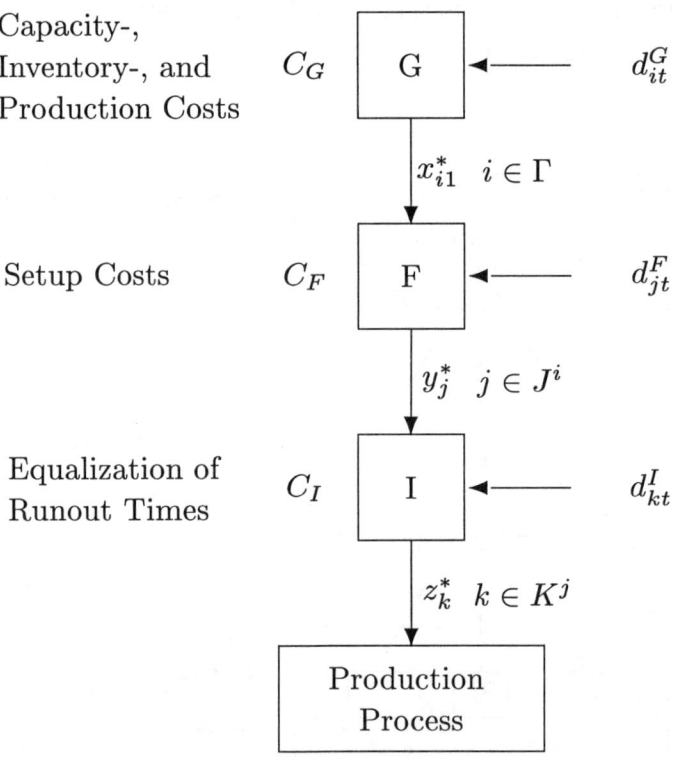

Fig. 6.2: General Structure of the Hierarchical Production Model

To be specific, let us now describe the production hierarchy somewhat more closely. As depicted in Fig. 6.2, the model describes three levels of increasing aggregation. The base-level

(I) considers single items k, the medial-level (F) aggregates these items resulting in product families j, and the top-level (G) consists of product groups i which are aggregates of families. Thus, a family j comprises $k \in K^j$ items, and a group i consists of $j \in J^i$ families.

The exogenous information each level works with is
- for the base-level the forecast of item demand d_{kt}^I of period t
- for the medial-level the forecast of family demand d_{jt}^F of period t aggregated over all items belonging to family j, and
- for the top-level the forecast of group demand d_{it}^G of period t aggregated over all families belonging to group i. (Note that the length of the period and, in particular, the time horizon can differ for the different levels.)

Primarily, the aim of the model is to optimize item lot sizes z_k^*. To achieve this aim, not only the decision field is split up, but also the criterion. Thus, one has at the top-level capacity cost as well as inventory and production costs, at the medial-level (family) one has to consider setup costs, and at the base-level, to guarantee a mutual setup, runout times are equalized (see Fig. 6.2).

6.1.2 Mathematical Formulation of the Decision Models for the Three Levels

Having introduced the general structure of the hierarchical production problem, let us now formulate for each level an appropriate model and let us show how these models are interrelated.

(1) Top-Level

At the aggregate planning level, the medium term production program for product groups is determined by a traditional linear optimization model

$$(6.1) \quad C_G = \sum_{t=1}^{T} \left(\sum_{i \in \Gamma} \left(c_{it} x_{it} + h_{it} x_{it}^L \right) + c_t^r r_t + c_t^0 o_t \right) \longrightarrow \min$$

s. t.

$$(6.2) \qquad\qquad x_{it}^L = x_{i,t-1}^L + x_{it} - d_{it}^G \qquad \forall i, t$$
$$x_{i0}^L = x_{i0}^{L'} \qquad\qquad \forall i$$

$$(6.3) \qquad\qquad \sum_{i \in \Gamma} a_i x_{it} \leq r_t + o_t \qquad \forall t$$

$$r_t \leq r_t^{max} \qquad \forall t$$
$$o_t \leq o_t^{max} \qquad \forall t$$
$$x_{it}^L \geq 0 \qquad \forall i, t$$
$$x_{it} \geq 0 \qquad \forall i, t$$

Indices, variables, and constants

a_i: aggregate production coefficient (consumption rate) of product group i

Γ: set of product groups $i, i \in \Gamma$

t: aggregate period (e.g., 1 month)

T: planning horizon (e.g., 1 year)

x_{it}:   aggregate production of product group i in period t [in man-hours]

x_{it}^L: aggregate inventory of product group i in period t [in man-hours]

r_t: regular working time in t, r_t^{max}: upper limit

o_t: overtime in t, o_t^{max}: upper limit

$c_{it}, h_{it}, c_t^r, c_t^o$: adjoint cost parameters ($c_t^r < c_t^0$)

To hold the discussion simple, no lead time is taken into consideration.

Note that, because of the specific (somewhat non-realistic) assumption concerning the parameters of the family models to be considered, the aggregation is trivial. For the aggregated group parameter, one just takes the parameter that is common for all families. The aggregation is becoming a problem, however, if the parameters were allowed not to be equal. Similarly, initial inventory $x_{io}^{L'}$ is, in principle, aggregated from initial single product inventories. Most of the discussion to follow will be concerned with the problems related to these aggregation devices.

The resulting optimal medium term production plan $\{x_{it}^* | 1 \leq t \leq T, i \in \Gamma\}$ is communicated to the family model. Since this plan is recalculated in a rolling horizon fashion, the production amount of only the first period, x_{i1}^*, will serve as an instruction for the family level.

(2) Medial-Level

In allocating x_{i1}^* to family lot sizes y_j, one has only to consider those families that have to be set up in the actual period (month), i.e. , having a runout time smaller than one period. The runout time ROT_j is defined by

$$ROT_j := \frac{y_{j0}^L}{d_{j1}^F} \tag{6.4}$$

with y_{jo}^L being the initial inventory of family j, and d_{j1}^F denoting family demand of (the aggregate) period 1. Hence, the index set SJ^i of 'setup families' is given by

$$SJ^i := \{j \in J^i : ROT_j < 1\}. \tag{6.5}$$

Optimal family lot sizes y_j^* can now be obtained by minimizing stationary setup cost

$$C_F = \sum_{j \in SJ^i} \frac{D_j^F(T)}{y_j} c_j^s \longrightarrow \min, \tag{6.6}$$

s. t. the **consistency constraint**

$$(6.7) \qquad \sum_{j \in SJ^i} y_j = x_{i1}^*$$

with

$c_j^s:$ being setup cost of family j, and

$D_j^F(T):$ denoting the cumulated demand of family j over horizon T.

The criterion (6.6) describes the setup cost part of the ordinary EOQ model. Holding costs are already accounted for by the aggregate cost optimization and enter the family model through the instruction (6.7). The 'look-ahead' horizon in (6.6) is assumed to be the same as in the aggregate model. This need not necessarily be the case. Often one will use the first macro-period as the medial-level horizon. Any device of the horizon, however, has to be justified carefully.

Solving the continuous knapsack problem (6.6) and (6.7), one obtains optimal family lot sizes y_j^* which are communicated to the item model (base-level).

Remark:

For simplicity, the family disaggregation model (6.6) and (6.7) describes only the most important features. One could easily consider lead times, safety stocks, and family lot size constraints (see [Hax/Candea]). Moreover, the simple EOQ-lot size type of model could be replaced, e.g., with a Silver-Meal heuristic [Silver/Meal], [Silver/Peterson]. In addition, one should analyze the cases of too low and too high values of x_{i1}^*. If, for instance, a too high amount of aggregate production, and hence too much capacity is provided, one should try to enlarge the set SJ^i which consequently leads to produce some families earlier than necessary. Using a look-ahead rule [Bitran et al.], one produces those families first which will be critical in the next aggregate period and which do not incur too many holding costs.

(3) Base-Level

At this level, all costs have already been determined. What still remains to be done, however, is to equalize the runout time of the items belonging to a family. This has the desirable consequence that all items of a family trigger simultaneously. Hence, the 'item problem' can be stated as follows:

$$C_J = \sum_{k \in K^j} \left(\frac{y_j^* + y_{j0}^{L'}}{D_j^F(T)} - \frac{z_k + z_{k0}^{L'}}{D_k^I(T)} \right)^2 \longrightarrow \min \qquad (6.8)$$

s. t. the consistency constraint

$$\sum_{k \in K^j} z_k = y_j^* \qquad (6.9)$$

with $D_k^I(T)$ denoting cumulated demand of item k over horizon T and $z_{k0}^{L'}$ being the initial inventory of k with $\sum_{k \in K^j} z_{k0}^{L'} = y_{j0}^{L'}$.

Criterion (6.8) equalizes the runout time of the items (measured in units of T) in minimizing their quadratic deviation from the family runout time. Equalizing the runout time is not only economically reasonable but also allows items to be aggregated into families.

Like the family problem, the item model represents a non-linear continuous knapsack problem which can be solved by an appropriate algorithm (e.g., see [Hax/Candea] or [Steven]) resulting in the desired optimal item lot sizes z_k^* (see Fig. (6.2)).

Remark:

Like in the family case, one can consider lead times and safety stocks, and one can impose upper and lower bounds on the item lot size. These additional aspects, however, are not crucial for the general concept of the described hierarchical approach.

6.1.3 General Discussion of Hierarchical Production Planning

The standard model together with its obvious extensions describes a three-stage hierarchy with levels having a decreasing degree of aggregation. According to the general framework given by the coupling equations (2.5), the model (6.1) through (6.9) turns out to be of the strict top-down type. Consequently, there does not exist an anticipation function and all criteria only possess a private component. The non-reactive anticipation is brought about by the demand and parameter aggregation for families and groups. For an *exact non-reactive* anticipation one would have $d_{jt}^F = \sum_{k \in K^j} d_{kt}^I$ and $d_{it}^G = \sum_{j \in J^i} d_{jt}^F$. Furthermore, estimates for the cost parameters and particularly for the production coefficients a_i must be provided. As described earlier, these parameters are trivially obtained by the simple aggregation device that only families with identical parameters are being aggregated. If one did not have this (severe) restriction, the aggregation procedure would not be obvious at all. One possibility would be to aggregate with respect to mean demand as suggested in (6.22) below. We return to this serious problem in the next section.

The instructions, as a further important concept, can easily be identified with the results x_{i1}^* and y_j^*. They influence the respective lower level through their decision field via the disaggregation equations (6.7) and (6.9).

Let us now discuss the hierarchical character of HPP more closely. With the general framework of hierarchical planning structures presented in Chapter 2, we are now in a position to analyze the type of hierarchy HPP is based on. This is important because it sheds new light on the general usefulness of the approach. Does HPP, one might for instance ask, describe an organizational hierarchy, or is it just a constructional hierarchy which merely reduces the complexity of a problem? Are families or groups independent physical quantities, or are they mere intellectual constructs?

In fact, the standard model allows two distinct interpretations:

1. For the first interpretation, the standard model can be understood as a **constructional hierarchy** (see Fig. 3.1). Complexity is reduced by an abstraction and/or relaxation procedure, and there is no increase in information in going from one level to the other. In addition, the aggregate quantities can be pure modeling constructs without any physical meaning. The instructions x_{i1}^* and y_j^* are intermediate quantities which are only calculated to determine the final decision of the item lot size z_k^*. The decisions x_{i1}^*, y_i^*, and z_k^* are made by just *one party at the same point in time*. Using the model within a rolling horizon regime, all three decisions are repeated in each month simultaneously.

2. The second interpretation of the standard model differs radically from the first one. For this interpretation, the structuring of the model goes along with an existing **organizational hierarchy**. The instructions x_{i1}^*, y_j^*, and z_k^* are well-defined physical quantities (like glass smelt, pattern, and format), and at least x_{i1}^* and y_j^* are not fixed simultaneously and, in general, are therefore based on different information.

For this second interpretation, the standard model needs some adaptation. Since one usually has to decide on x_{i1}^* well in advance, the (demand) *information* used in the three models *will no longer be the same*. It would be necessary to allow for some deviations in the consistency equations. Furthermore, thinking of a real-life situation, it usually is not the amount x_{i1}^* which is fixed. Instead (or at least in addition), it is the capacities one has to provide in order to guarantee the production of x_{i1}^*, and hence of $\sum_{j \in SJ^i} y_j$. Therefore, a more adequate and natural procedure would be to calculate the optimal capacities $r_t = r_t^*$ and $o_t = o_t^*$, and to take these quantities as instructions for the medial-model. Hence, one would not have a product disaggregation problem but, as with the model in Section 4.2.1, a capacity allocation problem. As an example, rather than using the consistency relation (6.7), take $\sum y_j \leq r_1^*$ with y_j being measured in capacity units. Particularly, in the case of not being able to rely on an exact aggregation-disaggregation scheme the transition from a disaggregation to a capacity allocation procedure is significant. This is the usual way of treating a hierarchical production problem and will be the starting point for a deeper discussion of HPP in the next section.

Finally, let us consider the initial inventory condition in (6.2). Initial group inventory $x_{i0}^{L'}$ is calculated from initial product values $z_{k0}^{L'}$. If, however, the top-decision is made earlier than the family decision, as being assumed in the second interpretation, such a calculation is meaningless in a strict top-down procedure. But even if one had the initial values of the lower levels, this would indirectly encumber general medium term considerations with short term casualities. Hence, for a decision time hierarchy one should treat initial inventories as decision variables. As an example, take $x_{i0}^L = x_{iT}^L$. In optimizing x_{iT}^L, one would simultaneously optimize x_{i0}^L. Moreover, one would introduce a cyclic coupling which, at the medium term level, contributes to a desired stable behavior. The next section will discuss this important aspect somewhat further.

Remark: There exists an extensive amount of **literature on HPP**. Most of the references concerning the MIT-approach are summarized in [Hax/Candea] and [Bitran/Tirupati] and will not be repeated here. Applications are reported, e.g., in [Axsäter et al.], [Barbarosoglu], [Carravilla], [Chen Chuan et al.], [Corbett et al.], [Gelders/van Wassenhove (1982)], [Günther], [Lasserre et al.], [Mehra et al.], [Stadtler], [Van Wassenhove/Vanderhenst]. As discussed above, one of the severe problems of classical HPP is its strict top-down character causing feasibility problems. Within the framework of a constructional hierarchy, the paper of [Mehra et al.] tries to avoid this problem by a particular implicit reactive anticipation. Stochastics, for instance, is considered in [Ari/Axsäter], [Fransoo et al.], [Gfrerer/Zäpfel], and [Lasserre/Mercé].

For a more general treatment of hierarchies in the production area see, e.g., [Bertrand et al.], [Dempster et al.], [Gelders/Van Wassenhove (1981)], and [Kistner/Steven]. In [Gershwin] and particularly in [Sethi/Zhang] the separation of the levels by the coarseness of the time grid plays a dominant role, in particular the question of the loss of optimality in applying a hierarchical approximation that separates the levels by the degree of period aggregation.

As we have seen, aggregation-disaggregation problems play an important role in HPP. For further references see, e.g., [Axsäter (1981)], [Axsäter (1986)], [Axsäter/Jönsson], [Erschler et al.], [Gabbay], [Jörnsten/Leisten], [Lasserre/Mercé], [Leisten/Jörnsten], [Rogers et al.].

6.2 Integrative Hierarchical Production Planning

One of the most serious drawbacks of traditional HPP is its strict top-down character which merely considers a non-reactive anticipation. Such an anticipation is achieved by simply aggregating production and demand characteristics of the family level without taking into account the specific decision model at that level. Furthermore, in order to guarantee feasibility on the family level, the aggregation is restricted to families having the same demand characteristics as well as production, and cost characteristics.

Both, the top-down character and the impeding aggregation condition, restrict the application of HPP to only but the simplest settings. Let us therefore design a new, more integrative approach to HPP which is based on the far richer and more realistic concept of tactical-operational hierarchies as described in Section 4.2. These decision time hierarchies are not constructional but organizational hierarchies. Decisions at the different levels are no longer made simultaneously but at different points in time under different information conditions. Moreover, the non-reactive anticipation is replaced, at least partly, with a reactive anticipation procedure. Typically, in better anticipating the lower level, both levels can be permitted to be more self-contained, and hence, in general, allow for a more realistic description of actually practiced HPP.

Considering the group and the family level as the two crucial levels of HPP, the tactical level mainly represents an aggregated operational level. In contrast to traditional HPP, however, it is not the aggregate production quantity which is of interest, but rather the capacity that has to be decided upon at the aggregate level and which must be fixed well in advance. Hence, the aggregate model will not be concerned with the optimization of aggregate production quantities but, as it is the case for a tactical-operational hierarchy, it will explicitly calculate the medium-term production resources.

6.2.1 A Model to Illustrate the Integrative Approach to HPP

Let us illustrate the concept of a more realistic and comprehensive theory of HPP with a fairly extensive example which, in its generality, is comparable with the standard model of Section 6.1.2 and which is detailed enough to explain the main features of the integrative approach. In fact, the model describes the typical relationship between the aggregate production level and the MRP level of a PPC system (see Fig. 1.8). An even richer model which is able to capture the main features of important industrial manufacturing processes will be presented in Section 6.3.

Let us consider just one product group which represents a suitable aggregation of families. No assumptions as to the equality of cost and production parameters have to be incurred. Think of a tactical-operational planning hierarchy for which the capacity decision has to be made some time in advance of the operational production decision. Furthermore, as for the manpower model of Section 2.5.2, assume the time grid of the operational level to be more refined than that of the tactical level. Fig. 6.3 may serve as an illustration.

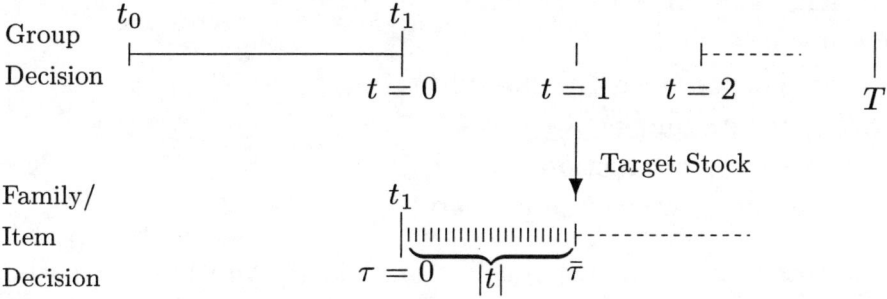

Fig. 6.3   Time Grids and Horizons

Let the **top-level** be described by the following decision model for resources K_t $(t = 1, \dots, T)$, which, as in the HPP standard model, can be regular working time (i.e., man power) and overtime:

$$C_G = \sum_{t=1}^{T} \{\kappa_t K_t + \bar{h} x_t^L\} \longrightarrow \min \qquad (6.10)$$

s.t.

$$x_t^L = x_{t-1}^L + x_t - \hat{d}_t \qquad \forall t \qquad (6.11)$$

$$x_0^L = x_T^L \qquad (6.12)$$

(6.13) $$\bar{a}x_t + \bar{s}\,\frac{x_t}{\bar{x}} \leq K_t \qquad \forall t$$

(6.14) $$K_t, x_t^L, x_t \geq 0 \qquad \forall t$$

Indices

$t:$ macro period $t = 1, \ldots, T$

Decision variables

K_t: capacity for group production at $t = 1, \ldots, T$
x_t^L: group inventory at $t = 0, 1, \ldots, T$
x_t: group lot size at $t = 1, \ldots, T$

Parameters

$\hat{d}_t$:   aggregate forecast of demand in period t
$\bar{x}$:   mean lot size
κ_t: unit capacity cost in period t
$\bar{h}$:   aggregate unit holding cost
$\bar{a}$:   aggregate production coefficient
$\bar{s}$:   aggregate setup time per setup

The top-criterion (6.10) consists of capacity and holding costs, respectively, and the top-decision field is given by (6.11) through (6.14). Obviously, the top-model is a linear model which explicitly does not take into account setup costs, but only setup times (according to the linear expression (6.13)). Note that for convenience of presentation, we restrict the analysis to just one product group so that we can drop the index i.

Capacities K_t are exclusively used for operations on the lower level. No capacity consumption takes place on the tactical level. Hence, the parameters $\bar{a}$, $\bar{s}$, and $\bar{h}$ will exclusively be determined by the operational level. Furthermore, they are assumed to be time independent. If, as in the flat glass example, the medium term (smelting) level needs some production capacity by its own, the model may easily be adapted to capture this more general situation as well. The same holds for the consideration of the capacity and the costs of top-level specific setups, like change-over from one color to the other (see Sec. 6.3).

In contrast to the Hax/Meal approach, initial inventory is now not provided by the lower level but is treated as a decision variable. This allows for a cyclic coupling as postulated in (6.12) and permits to consider stability requirements. (We return to this point on a later occasion. In particular, see the extensive discussion in Section 6.3.)

The **base-model** describes the operational part of the envisaged capacity-production problem. For the $\bar{j} = |J|$ families that comprise the group J under consideration, a detailed description is given as follows:

$$\sum_{\tau=1}^{\bar{\tau}}\sum_{j=1}^{\bar{j}} h_j x_{j\tau}^L + c_j^s \delta_{j\tau} \longrightarrow \min \tag{6.15}$$

s.t.

$$x_{j\tau}^L = x_{j,\tau-1}^L + x_{j\tau} - d_{j\tau} \quad \forall j, \tau \tag{6.16}$$

$$x_{j0}^L = x_{j0}^{L'} \quad \forall j \tag{6.17a}$$

$$\sum_j x_{j\bar{\tau}}^L = x_1^{L^*} \tag{6.17b}$$

$$\sum_j a_j x_{j\tau} + s_j \delta_{j\tau} \leq K_\tau^*, \quad \forall \tau \tag{6.18}$$

$$K_\tau^* = \frac{1}{|t|} K_1^* \quad \forall \tau$$
$$x_{j\tau} \leq M \delta_{j\tau} \quad \forall j; \tau \tag{6.19}$$

$$x_{j\tau}^L, x_{j\tau} \geq 0, \quad \delta_{j\tau} \in \{0,1\}, \quad M := \max_{j\tau} x_{j\tau} \quad \forall j, \tau \tag{6.20}$$

Indices

τ: micro period, $\tau = 1, \dots, \bar{\tau}$
j: family, $j = 1, \dots, \bar{j}$

Decision variables

$x_{j\tau}^L$:   family inventory for the detailed period τ
$x_{j\tau}$:   family lot size at the detailed period τ
$\delta_{j\tau}$:   family setup point of time

Parameters and preset quantities

$d_{j\tau}$:   revealed family demand in period τ
h_j: family unit holding cost
c_j^s: family unit setup cost
s_j: family setup time per setup
a_j: family production coefficient (consumption rate)
$x_{j0}^{L'}$:   initial stock (of family j)

As depicted in Fig. 6.3, the length of period τ is assumed to
be shorter than that of period t such that the macro interval
$\{t\}$ consists of $|t|$ detailed periods $\tau \in \{t\}$. Moreover, the short
term horizon $\bar{\tau}$ will usually not be equal to T. Depending on
the specific situation, one might take $\bar{\tau}$ equal to the length of
one aggregate period or, what would be more adequate for the
subsequent analysis, one could choose the duration given by the
interval between two setups of the group model within its rolling
horizon scheme. In that case the instruction would not only be
given by the resources K_1^* calculated for the first macro-period
but by later periods as well.

Compared with the aggregate top-model, setups are now described in full detail, which formally has as a consequence that
one no longer has a continous linear model.

The top-down coupling of the two models is accomplished by
the provided capacity and the target stock $x_1^{L^*}$ in (6.17b). The
capacity K_1^* for the first (or possibly further) macro period is a
result of the aggregate optimization. For convenience, we simply

took $K_\tau^* = \frac{1}{|t|}K_1^*$ in (6.18). In that case one has, of course, $|t| = \bar\tau$. As postulated by Eq. (6.17b), the operational model has to guarantee, at its horizon $\bar\tau$ (see Fig. 6.3), a stock level which is optimal for the medium term model. Without this instruction, optimal short term stocks would become $x_{j\bar\tau}^{L^0} = 0 \quad \forall j$ which would not be acceptable for the medium term level. (For a more profound discussion of this point see the following section.)

The bottom-up coupling, on the other hand, is exerted through the parameters $\bar h, \bar a, \bar s$, and $\bar x$. Demand $d_{j\tau}$ is assumed to be deterministically known, and initial inventories are no longer decision variables but actually given data.

(1) Non-reactive anticipation

If the bottom-up coupling parameters do not depend on the performance of the detailed model, one has the typical case of a non-reactive anticipation. For example, one could take 'demand weights'

$$\bar g_j := \frac{\hat D_j}{\sum\limits_j \hat D_j} \quad \forall j \tag{6.21}$$

as aggregation weights with $\hat D_j$ being the top-level's total demand forecast for family j:

$$\hat D_j := \sum_{t=1}^{T} \hat d_{jt}.$$

The weight $\bar g_j$ describes the percentage of total demand of family j. Hence, for a non-reactive anticipation one may take

$$\bar h := \sum_j \bar g_j\, h_j|t|, \quad \bar a := \sum_j \bar g_j a_j \tag{6.22}$$

which simply assumes that the contribution of individual holding cost h_j and capacity usage (consumption) a_j is proportional to the family's demand.

For $\bar{x}$, and $\bar{s}$ one could take estimates from past data, since no non-reactive ex ante data are available (s. Eq. (6.27) below).

(2) Reactive anticipation

Let us now consider the important case of a reactive anticipation. In that case, to obtain its anticipated version, the base-model (6.15) through (6.20) is replaced with its estimate, i.e., demand and initial inventory are substituted by their (medium term detailed) family forecasts $\hat{d}_{j\tau}$ and $\hat{x}_{j0}^{L'}$, respectively. The resulting optimal (family) stock $\hat{x}_{j\tau}^{L^o}$ is then used to define aggregation weights for the holding cost parameter $\bar{h}$

$$(6.23) \qquad g_j^L := \frac{\sum\limits_{\tau}^{\bar{\tau}} \hat{x}_{j\tau}^{L^o}}{\sum\limits_{j}\sum\limits_{\tau}^{\bar{\tau}} \hat{x}_{j\tau}^{L^o}} \quad \forall j.$$

Similarly, for the production coefficient $\bar{a}$ one can take the weights

$$(6.24) \qquad g_j^a := \frac{\sum\limits_{\tau}^{\bar{\tau}} \hat{x}_{j\tau}^{0}}{\sum\limits_{j}\sum\limits_{\tau}^{\bar{\tau}} \hat{x}_{j\tau}^{0}} \quad \forall j$$

yielding

$$(6.25) \qquad \bar{h} = \bar{h}(\hat{\boldsymbol{x}}^{\boldsymbol{L^o}}) := \sum_j g_j^L h_j |t|$$

and

$$(6.26) \qquad \bar{a} = \bar{a}(\hat{\boldsymbol{x}}^{\boldsymbol{0}}) := \sum_j g_j^a a_j,$$

respectively ($\hat{\boldsymbol{x}}^{\boldsymbol{0}}$, e.g., being the vector $\hat{\boldsymbol{x}}^{\boldsymbol{0}} := (\hat{x}_{11}^0, \dots, \hat{x}_{j,\bar{\tau}}^0)$).

Using (6.23) or (6.24) as aggregation weights seems to be more justified than taking the simple weights (6.21) which, moreover, were used for both, holding cost $\bar{h}$ and production coefficient $\bar{a}$. On the other hand, they need more detailed information and, of course, an explicit solution of the base-model. Furthermore, the parameters are used over the total medium term horizon T, even though they are gained only from the short term horizon $\bar{\tau}$. They are updated, however, at each setup of the aggregate model within its rolling horizon scheme.

For $\bar{x}$ one reasonably defines

$$\bar{x} := \frac{\sum_j \sum_\tau^{\bar{\tau}} \hat{x}_{j\tau}^0}{\sum_j \sum_\tau^{\bar{\tau}} \hat{\delta}_{j\tau}^0} \tag{6.27}$$

which can be interpreted as a mean lotsize of those families that are set up during the horizon $\bar{\tau}$.

Similarly, one defines for the setup time of one 'virtual' group setup

$$\bar{s} = \frac{\sum_j \sum_\tau^{\bar{\tau}} s_j \hat{\delta}_{j\tau}^0}{\sum_j \sum_\tau^{\bar{\tau}} \hat{\delta}_{j\tau}^0}. \tag{6.28}$$

With these parameters, applying (as usual) a hierarchical algorithm between the top- and the anticipated base-model, the final instruction is determined as

$$F^* = F^*(\hat{x}^*, \hat{x}^{L^*}, \hat{\delta}^*) \tag{6.29}$$

with

$$\begin{pmatrix} \hat{x}^* \\ \hat{x}^{L^*} \\ \hat{\delta}^* \end{pmatrix} = \begin{pmatrix} \hat{x}^0 \ (F^*) \\ \hat{x}^{L^0} \ (F^*) \\ \hat{\delta}^0 \ (F^*) \end{pmatrix}. \tag{6.30}$$

6.2.2 Interpretation of the Integrative Model in Terms of a Tactical-Operational Hierarchy

Obviously, the exact reactive anticipation (see **(2)** of the previous section) describes a tactical-operational hierarchy consisting of an additive top-criterion

$$(6.31) \qquad\qquad C^T = C^{TT} + C^{TB},$$

with the private criterion representing capacity cost

$$(6.32) \qquad\qquad C^{TT} := \sum_{t=1}^{T} \kappa_t K_t$$

and the top-down criterion describing holding cost

$$(6.33) \qquad\qquad C^{TB} := \sum_{t=1}^{T} \bar{h} x_t^L.$$

The top-decision field A^T is represented by Eqs. (6.11) through (6.14). The anticipation results in the anticipation function

$$(6.34) \qquad\qquad AF = \begin{pmatrix} \hat{x}^0 \ (IN) \\ \hat{x}^{L^0}(IN) \\ \hat{\delta}^0 \ (IN) \end{pmatrix}$$

and affects the top-model through the criterion by influencing the cost parameter

$$\bar{h} = \bar{h}(\hat{x}^{L^0}).$$

Moreover, it exerts its influence on the top-decision field via the production coefficients

$$\bar{a} = \bar{a}(\hat{x}^0),$$

the mean setup time
$$\bar{s} = \bar{s}(\hat{\boldsymbol{\delta}}^0),$$

and the mean lotsize
$$\bar{x} = \bar{x}(\hat{\boldsymbol{\delta}}^0).$$

The instruction is given by the capacity $K_1 = K_1(\bar{h}, \bar{a}, \bar{s}, \bar{x})$ and the target stock x_1^L
$$IN = (K_1, x_1^L)$$

with the final instruction

$$IN^* = (K_1^*, x_1^{L^*}). \tag{6.35}$$

Finally, base-criterion C^B and decision field A^B are given by Eqs. (6.15) through (6.20).

It is interesting to observe that, for calculating the aggregation weights, an exact reactive explicit anticipation is necessary. Hence, assuming the functional form of Eqs. (6.23) and (6.24) to be given, aggregation is performed in an optimal way. Or, to put it differently, aggregation and optimization are carried out simultaneously such that the aggregation is determined together with the overall optimum.

The top-down criterion C^{TB} of Eq. (6.33) is not identical with $\hat{C}^B$ (given by the forecast version of (6.15)). Hence, one has the case of a tactical-operational hierarchy in which a team-based re-evaluation of the base-criterion is performed. Moreover, the top-decision field is influenced by an anticipation function: $A^T = A_{AF(IN)}^T$.

For the anticipation described in the example, we assumed that, at the base-level, demand is known with certainty and that at the top-level demand can be forecast.

The situation is slightly different, if not only forecasts can be obtained but full probability distributions. In that case, one optimizes detailed production and inventory values and takes as aggregation weights mean values over a sufficient number of simulated results. Formally, one obtains $\bar{g}_j^L$ and $\bar{g}_j^a$ by replacing in (6.23) and (6.24) the variables $\hat{x}^L$ and $\hat{x}$ with their mean values $\bar{\hat{x}}^L$ and $\bar{\hat{x}}$, respectively.

6.2.3 General Discussion of the Integrative HPP

Compared with traditional HPP, the integrative approach (IHPP) clearly represents an organizational hierarchy and is not vague as to its organizational or constructional character. The main focus is on the information aspect and particularly on the fact that capacity decisions have to be made earlier than detailed production decisions.

Taking the initial inventory as an additional decision variable has the advantage of a less tight integration, leaving the levels some freedom. Thus, for our top-model we postulated $x_0^L = x_T^L$ (see Eq. (6.12)), which supports a cyclic behavior, and hence allows the top-level to conform to stability requirements. Such requirements on the medium term level are often of vital importance and should not adversely be effected by short term disturbances at the operational level. We return to this important point in the next section.

Because of the better anticipation compared with the top-down approach of traditional HPP, feasibility problems can be anticipated without relying on unrealistic equality assumptions concerning cost and production parameters. In addition, short term initial inventories do not unduly effect the medium term level. Through the anticipative aggregation of medium term parameters, however, their influence is not totally neglected.

In aggregating the short term production coefficients a_j and cost parameters h_j (see Eq. (6.25)), we used the aggregation weights g_j^a and g_j^L, respectively. These weights account for the impact an item has within the aggregate production type as to its capacity usage (consumption) and cost contribution. Besides these capacity and cost-oriented aggregations, we had to determine aggregate demand (see Eq. (6.11)) which required an aggregation relying on the number of items or on another quantity by which demand might be measured. As a consequence, x_t and x_t^L, and, in particular, the target stocks (see Eq. (6.17b)) depend on the way how demand is quantified, and the same holds for the weights (6.23) and (6.24).

To evaluate the impact of this type of elementary market-oriented aggregation, one has to consider the entire hierarchical system. Firstly, a particular aggregation might affect the individual service level, and one would need to introduce safety stocks in order to avoid stock outs caused by an insufficient production which, on its part, is a consequence of wrongly determined aggregate production coefficients. Since the introduction of safety stocks is left for the more comprehensive model of Section 6.3, let us postpone the discussion of using safety stocks to amend aggregation errors. In this discussion, lead times will play an important role, which are not considered in the present model.

Secondly, even if one does not provide for safety stocks, the effect of an unbalanced market-oriented aggregation will not be dramatic. Due to the explicit anticipation, the instruction being determined in the medium term model, relying on the aggregation $\hat{d}_t$ of demand, must guarantee feasibility on the operational level. Hence, applying a parameter adaptation procedure (see Sec. 3.2), the aggregate parameters $\bar{h}, \bar{a}, \bar{x}$ and $\bar{s}$ will be adjusted such that medium term optimality and short term feasibility will be realized.

The speed of convergence and the value of the medium term optimum C^{T^*}, however, might depend on the specific market-oriented aggregation device. One might conjecture that the results will improve the better 'balanced' the aggregate is, that is, the more the items' demand patterns are comparable.

The integrative model has to be calibrated carefully. The longer the short term horizon $\bar{\tau}$ is, the more stable the aggregate parameters will be. On the other hand, the computational burden will increase considerably with $\bar{\tau}$. Clearly, in fixing $\bar{\tau}$, one has to keep in view the time interval between two setups of the aggregate model within the rolling horizon scheme. The shorter this interval is, the shorter $\bar{\tau}$ can be chosen and, in general, the less important will be a reactive anticipation. In fact, if, e.g., non-feasibilities on the family level can immediately be removed by the group-level, a top-down approach turns out to be appropriate. Such a tight coupling over the time horizon, however, is not consistent with the general idea of having separate planning tasks on the tactical and operational levels. The following section will illustrate how the general ideas of the integrative approach can be applied to the realistic and highly important case of medium and short term decisions for process production.

6.3 Process Production

Process production can be considered as one of the most important types of production. Many processes in the chemical, pharmaceutical and the nourishment industries are of this kind. As an example, think of the flat glass production mentioned in Section 6.1 or the production of washing powder described in [Günther]. In fact, the tire production case, used by Hax and Meal in illustrating and applying HPP, can be considered to be typical for the process industry.

Process production may formally be characterized by a small number of product types (like white, yellow, and bronze colored glass) to be produced on just one production facility. Often without any intermediate buffering, these types are then, in a second step, further processed to result in a variety of final products. Hence, as it is the case for many other kinds of production, process production has a hierarchical structure.

This hierarchical structure is particularly evident in the case that types have to be planned on a medium term level and products on a short term level. In that case process production cannot simply be described as a mere two-step loading problem but one has to account for the particular information one has at the different levels. In general terms, one has to describe the hierarchical relationship between the MPS and the MRP level (e.g., see [Vollman et al.]). What is specific, however, is the particular situation at the upper level. Due to the single production facility available, the order in which the product types are to be processed turns out to be of crucial importance. Moreover, for practical reasons, in most industrial situations, this sequence has to be of a stable cyclic character. Thus, stability is a main prerequisite for many planning procedures in process production and does not only have consequences for the medium term top-level but, in fact, for the whole structuring of the hierarchical approach. Not taking into account the sequencing problem, and hence the stability aspect, as it is done in applying classical HPP to the 'tire problem', one misses one of the main features hierarchical production planning should capture.

As a consequence, compared to the basic model treated in the preceding section, the medium term level will now no longer be a simple linear model but a (discrete) lot sizing and sequencing model which, in addition, takes into account stability aspects. Moreover, safety stocks will now be considered in order to guarantee a desired service level. Hence, the overall (top-) criterion (C^T) does not only have to consider financial aspects (C^{TF}) but must take into account robustness (C^{TR}) and service level

(C^{TSL}) considerations as well,

$$(6.36) \qquad\qquad C^T := \left(C^{TF}, C^{TSL}, C^{TR}\right).$$

Service level considerations will be taken into account by an α-service degree while robustness aspects will be operationalized by the stability of the sequence in which the different product types are produced. This stability will be maintained by various means to be described in the sequel.

To gain a deeper insight into the nature of process production and, more generally, into essential features of hierarchical production planning, let us first, in Section 6.3.1, formulate a comprehensive model being based on a stochastic dynamic program. This model is trying to exploit all available information in an optimal way. In particular, medium term decisions are based on short term information about the initial inventory level of single items.

As discussed earlier (see previous section), such a tight coupling does not leave the levels enough freedom to assess particular level-specific goals. Hence, a hierarchical approach, which separates the levels, is the only appropriate way to optimize the comprehensive criterion (6.36). This approach, however, should not be of the simple top-down nature as the traditional Hax/Meal model. In fact, it should be far more sophisticated using the general ideas of an integrative hierarchical model, as described in Section 6.2. The subsequent Section 6.3.2 will give the details.

6.3.1 A Dynamic Programming Formulation for Medium and Short Term Process Production

As a first step, leaving aside an explicit consideration of stability aspects, process production may be described with a two-stage stochastic dynamic program. The first stage defines the medium term product type level while the second stage stands for the (operational) family or item level. With this structure in mind, the formulation of a dynamic program is now straightforward.

Top-criterion

$$
C^{TF^*} = \min_{(T, \Delta K_\tau, \beta_{i,\tau}) \in A^T} \sum_{i=1}^{m} E\Big\{ \frac{1}{T} \sum_{\tau=1}^{T} \Big[\kappa \Delta K_\tau + c_i^T \beta_{i\tau}
$$
$$
+ \min_{(\delta_{j\tau}, y_{jt}^L) \in A^B} E\{ \sum_{j \in J^i} (c_j^B \delta_{j\tau} + h_j^B y_{j\tau}^L) | I_{t_1}^B \} \Big] \mid I_{t_0}^T \Big\}
\tag{6.37}
$$

subject to the following constraints:

Decision field A^T
Setup and sequencing conditions:

$$
\alpha_{i0} = \alpha_{iT} \qquad \forall i \tag{6.38}
$$

$$
\sum_{i=1}^{m} \alpha_{i\tau} \leq 2 \qquad \forall \tau \tag{6.39}
$$

$$
\sum_{i=1}^{m} \beta_{i\tau} \leq 1 \qquad \forall \tau \tag{6.40}
$$

$$
\sum_{i=1}^{m} \alpha_{i\tau} - \sum_{i=1}^{m} \beta_{i\tau} \leq 1 \; \forall \tau \tag{6.41}
$$

$$
\beta_{i\tau} \geq \alpha_{i\tau} - \alpha_{i,\tau-1} \qquad \forall i, \tau \tag{6.42}
$$

Technical conditions:

$$
\alpha_{i\tau} \in \{0, 1\}, \quad \beta_{i\tau} \in \{0, 1\}, \quad \Delta K_\tau \geq 0, \quad T > 0 \quad \forall i, \tau \tag{6.43}
$$

Decision field A^B
Material relation:

$$
y_{j\tau+1}^L = \max\{ y_{j\tau}^L + y_{j\tau} - d_{j\tau}; 0 \} \quad \forall j, \tau \tag{6.44}
$$
$$
y_{j0}^L = y_{j0}^{L'} \qquad \forall j
$$

Setup and sequencing conditions:

$$(6.45) \qquad y_{j\tau} \leq M\gamma_{j\tau} \qquad \forall j, \tau$$

$$(6.46) \qquad \sum_{j \in J^i} \gamma_{j\tau} \leq 2 \qquad \forall \tau$$

$$(6.47) \qquad \sum_{j \in J^i} \delta_{j\tau} \leq 1 \qquad \forall \tau$$

$$(6.48) \qquad \sum_{j \in J^i} \gamma_{j\tau} - \sum_{j \in J^i} \delta_{j\tau} \leq 1 \quad \forall \tau$$

$$(6.49) \qquad \delta_{j\tau} \geq \gamma_{j\tau} - \gamma_{j,\tau-1} \qquad \forall j, \tau$$

Coupling conditions

Setup conditions:

$$(6.50) \qquad M^{min}\alpha_{i\tau} \leq \sum_{j \in J^i} y_{j\tau} \leq M^{max}\alpha_{i\tau} \qquad \forall i, \tau$$

Capacity conditions:

$$(6.51) \quad \sum_{i=1}^{M} s_i^T \beta_{i\tau} + \sum_{j \in J^i} (s_j^B \delta_{j\tau} + a_j^B y_{j\tau}) \leq K_\tau + \Delta K_\tau \quad \forall \tau$$

Service level constraints:

$$(6.52) \qquad Prob\{y_{j\tau}^L \geq 0\} \geq SL_j \qquad \forall j, \tau$$

Technical conditions:

$$(6.53) \qquad y_{j\tau} \geq 0, \quad \gamma_{j\tau} \in \{0,1\}, \quad \delta_{j\tau} \in \{0,1\} \quad \forall j, \tau$$

Notation

Indices

i: index of product type, $i = 1, \ldots, m$
j: index of products, $j \in J^i$
J^i: set of all products j belonging to product type i (pre-assigned)
τ: period index

Decision variables

$y_{j\tau}$:   amount of production of product j in period τ
$\alpha_{i\tau}$:   production indicator (types): product type i is produced in period τ ($\alpha_{i\tau} = 1$)
$\beta_{i\tau}$:   setup indicator (types): in period t a setup for product type i takes place ($\beta_{i\tau} = 1$)
$\gamma_{j\tau}$:   production indicator (products): product j produced in period τ ($\gamma_{j\tau} = 1$)
$\delta_{j\tau}$:   setup indicator (products): setup of product j in period τ ($\delta_{j\tau} = 1$)
$y_{j\tau}^L$:   inventory level of product j at the end of period τ
ΔK_τ: capacity adaptation in period τ [measured in working hours]
T: planning horizon [measured in units of τ]

Parameters and preset quantities

$d_{j\tau}$:   stochastic demand of product j in period τ
a_j^B: production coefficient (consumption rate [production time/item])
s_i^T: sequence independent setup time of product type i
c_i^T: sequence independent setup cost of product type i
s_j^B: sequence independent setup time of product j
c_j^B: sequence independent setup cost of product j
h_j^B: period unit holding cost of product j
K_τ: production capacity in period τ [measured in working hours]

κ: cost [per working hour] of additional capacity

M^{max}: sufficiently big number, $M^{max} := \sum y_{j\tau}^{max}$

M^{min}: positive number, $M^{min} := \sum y_{j\tau}^{min}$

SL_j: α-service level for product j (pre-assigned within the financial model)

The criterion, or more precisely, the functional equation (6.37) (see also Sec. 4.2.4) clearly reflects the two levels of the production problem. At the short term level, holding and setup costs for individual products are minimized. The medium term level then minimizes setup costs for product types. Furthermore, as in classical HPP, the production system is assumed to be capable of adapting capacity (often in form of overtime) by an amount ΔK_τ incurring costs of $\kappa \Delta K_\tau$. Also, at the medium level, the horizon T is determined which, in view of the subsequent constraints, plays the role of a cycle time within an infinite time range.

The hierarchical structure of the criterion (6.37) is not only reflected by the detailed (index j) and aggregate (index i) variables and the different decision fields A^B and A^T, it is also elucidated by the different information states $I_{t_0}^T$ and $I_{t_1}^B$. As already described in Fig. 6.3 (or Fig. 2.7), let us assume that, because of the capacity adaptation, the medium term decision is made at t_0 while the short term production decision is made only in $t_1 > t_0$, utilizing the improved information status $I_{t_1}^B$. Both information states, however, are assumed to be stochastic, i.e., they represent probabilities and, for the second stage, conditional probabilities. In order not to add any unnecessary hierarchical features to the model, we take as a universal time grid detailed periods (index τ) determined by the empirical conditions of the operational level. Furthermore, we assume the short term horizon to be the same as the medium term cycle time T.

The constraints may be separated into the two decision fields A^T and A^B. Decision field A^T mainly consists of setup and sequencing conditions (see Eqs. (6.38) through (6.42)). Eq. (6.38) represents the so-called cycle condition. It guarantees that a product type i being produced in $\tau = 0$ should, at the latest, again be produced in $\tau = T$. Eq. (6.39) says that at most two product types can be produced in one period and there is at most one setup (see Eq. (6.40)). As condition (6.41) implies, two product types in one period are only allowed in case of a change over. Finally, Eq. (6.42) describes the relation between the setup indicator $\beta_{i\tau}$ and the production indicator $\alpha_{i\tau}$. It states that a setup is necessary in case the production state is changed from 0 to 1.

Decision field A^B is similarly constructed as A^T. Again we assume stating the setup and sequencing conditions (6.45) through (6.49) that production is of the process type. It should be clear, however, that this need not be the case and that one can cope with any other type of production. The material relation (6.44) describes the lost sales case with $\tilde{d}_{j\tau}$ being the stochastic demand and $y_{j0}^{L'}$ representing the initial stock level of item j.

The most interesting conditions are the coupling constraints (6.50) through (6.52). Relation (6.50) guarantees that an item $j \in J^i$ can only be produced if at the same time the adjoint type i is produced ($\alpha_{i\tau} = 1$), and vice versa. Furthermore, for the aggregate level, Eq. (6.50) relates the production indicator $\alpha_{i\tau}$ to the aggregate production variable $\sum_{j \in J^i} y_{j\tau}$. The capacity condition (6.51) links the available capacity calculated at the medium term level to total capacity demand. Formally, it is mainly (6.51) that represents within the two-stage hierarchical system the well-known transition equation of dynamic programming. The service level constraint (6.52) may equally be considered as a coupling condition. It imposes on the operational level a service degree which, in view of the multi-component criterion (6.36), might appear to be desirable.

Primarily, the dynamic model (6.37) through (6.53) focuses on minimizing total mean costs ($\bar{C}^{TF}$) and, simultaneously, takes into account the service level criterion C^{TSL} through short term probability constraints (6.52). The robustness criterion C^{TR}, however, is only considered very indirectly. Obviously, the possible capacity adaptation ΔK_τ, the safety constraint (6.52), and the cycle condition (6.38) may contribute to the robustness objective, i.e., all three of them may contribute in stabilizing the medium term sequence of types (e.g., colors). An explicit consideration of C^{TR}, however, is not incorporated in the dynamic programming formulation. In doing so, it would be necessary to require initial aggregate inventory to be equal to final inventory

$$(6.54) \qquad \sum_{j \in J^i} y_{j0}^L = \sum_{j \in J^i} y_{jT}^L$$

and, as it was done for the model in Section 6.2, to optimize these values.

Clearly, in taking into account initial stocks $y_{j0}^{L'}$, as in the dynamic programming formulation, an optimization of inventories is no longer possible. Consequently, if the robustness criterion is of high relevance, as it is usually the case for medium term process production, the above cost minimization is unable to accomodate this additional objective.

Thus, the dynamic programming formulation implies two distinct problems: First, as is well known, a stochastic dynamic program involves unsurmountable computational difficulties; second, and this is a principle obstacle, with its focus on costs it is conceptually not capable of accommodating the complex stability objective.

It is interesting to observe that it was mainly the computational difficulties that led to a hierarchical planning formulation. Indeed, apart from the sequencing problem, classical HPP can be considered as an approximate formulation of the dynamic program (6.37) through (6.53). Clearly, like the original dynamic programming formulation, classical HPP is not able to integrate the stability objective either. Hence, HPP again turns out to be more a procedure to approximately solve a complex mathematical optimization problem rather than to provide a solution for a real-life planning task. Thus, to overcome this difficulty, a proper hierarchical planning formulation proves to be necessary.

In summary, one has the following situation: A formulation based on optimizing production costs is not able to account for stability considerations. This is due to the fact that medium term stability should not be directly affected by the short term initial stock level as it is the case for a stochastic dynamic programming formulation. Hence, from a conceptual point of view, one of the main motivations for a less tight hierarchical modeling, as compared to a dynamic program and the traditional HPP approach, is the ability to accommodate stability aspects. Indeed, to guarantee medium term stability, the two levels should be adjusted (i.e., integrated) to each other and simultaneously they should be allowed some freedom to take into account aspects that are specific for a particular level. With the integrative hierarchical production planning (IHPP) approach, such a model will now be presented.

6.3.2 Integrative Hierarchical Production Planning

In applying integrative hierarchical production planning (IHPP) to process production, we will closely follow the conceptual ideas that have already been employed for the elementary model in Section 6.2. The top-level will again be identified with the medium term level and the base-level with the short term operational decision problem. Again, the base-model is taken into account through the parameters of the top-model and the short term initial inventories are not directly affecting the top-model.

What will be new within the context of process production, however, is the way how stability is taken into account. To obtain a smooth stable behavior, it proves not to be enough to simply require equality for the initial and final stock levels and to optimize these levels. For a hierarchical approach, it will as well be necessary to closely adjust item and type production. Obviously, for an exact description, as in the previous section, such an adjustment is trivially met since no production variable for types had to be introduced. Now, for a higher decoupled system, like in the elementary model of Section 6.2.1, the short term model must build up and maintain target stocks that guarantee the medium term model not to run out of stock. A shortage of a type would not only be a problem for the particular type at hand (as discussed in Section 6.2 (Fig. 6.3 and Eq. (6.17b))), but would unduly induce through its setup a serious disturbance effecting all the other types, and hence the whole medium term production sequence. For the hierarchical model to be presented in the sequel, these considerations are formulated explicity.

(1) Formulation of the IHPP-Model

Top-level

Again the top-level describes a multi-criterion decision problem with criterion (6.36). For the financial component C^{TF} one has the following

Top-equation

(6.55)

$$a^{T^*} = \arg$$

$$\min_{(T, \Delta K_t, \beta_{it}, x_{it}, x_{i0}^L) \in A_{AF}^T} \frac{1}{T} \sum_{t=1}^{T} \left[\kappa \Delta K_t + \sum_{i=1}^{m} (c_i^T \beta_{it} + h_i^T x_{it}^L) \right]$$

Decision field A_{AF}^T

Material and production relations:

$$x_{it}^L = x_{i,t-1}^L + x_{it} - \hat{d}_{it}^T \qquad \forall i, t \qquad (6.56)$$

$$x_{i0}^L = x_{iT}^L \qquad \forall i \qquad (6.57)$$

$$\sum_{i=1}^{m} \left(s_i^T \beta_{it} + a_i^T x_{it} \right) \le K_t + \Delta K_t \quad \forall t \qquad (6.58)$$

Setup and sequencing conditions:

$$x^{min} \alpha_{it} \le x_{it} \le x^{max} \alpha_{it} \qquad \forall i \qquad (6.59)$$

$$\alpha_{i0} = \alpha_{iT} \qquad \forall i \qquad (6.60)$$

$$\sum_{i=1}^{m} \alpha_{it} \le 2 \qquad \forall t \qquad (6.61)$$

$$\sum_{i=1}^{m} \beta_{it} \le 1 \qquad \forall t \qquad (6.62)$$

$$\sum_{i=1}^{m} \alpha_{it} - \sum_{i=1}^{m} \beta_{it} \le 1 \qquad \forall t \qquad (6.63)$$

$$\beta_{it} \ge \alpha_{it} - \alpha_{i,t-1} \qquad \forall i, t \qquad (6.64)$$

Technical conditions:

$$x_{it} \ge 0, \ x_{it}^L \ge 0, \ \Delta K_t \ge 0, \ \alpha_{it} \in \{0,1\}, \ \beta_{it} \in \{0,1\} \qquad (6.65)$$
$$\forall i, t$$

Anticipation equation

$$AF(IN) = \arg \min_{(\hat{y}_{j\tau}, \hat{\delta}_{j\tau}) \in \hat{A}_{IN}^B} \sum_{\tau=1}^{T_2} \sum_{j \in J^i} \left(c_j^B \hat{\delta}_{j\tau} + h_j^B \hat{y}_{j\tau}^L \right) \ \forall i \quad (6.66)$$

Decision field $\hat{A}_{IN}^B$

Material relation:

$$(6.67) \qquad \hat{y}_{j\tau}^L = \hat{y}_{j,\tau-1}^L + \hat{y}_{j\tau} - \hat{d}_{j\tau}^B \qquad \forall j, \tau$$
$$\hat{y}_{j0}^L = \hat{y}_{j0}^{L'} \qquad \forall j$$

Coupling conditions:

$$(6.68) \qquad \sum_{j \in J^i} \left(s_j^B \hat{\delta}_{j\tau} + a_j^B \hat{y}_{j\tau} \right) \leq \left(K_t + \Delta K_t \right)_\tau \quad \forall \tau, i$$

$$(6.69) \qquad \sum_{j \in J^i} \hat{y}_{j,T_0}^L \geq x_{i,T_0}^L \qquad\qquad\qquad \forall i$$

$$(6.70a) \quad \hat{y}_{jT_1}^L \geq SS_j, \qquad\qquad\qquad\qquad j \in J^i, \forall i$$
$$(6.70b) \quad \hat{y}_{jT_2}^L \geq SS_j. \qquad\qquad\qquad\qquad j \in J^i, \forall i$$

Setup and sequencing conditions:

$$(6.71) \quad y^{min} \gamma_{j\tau} \leq \hat{y}_{j\tau} \leq y^{max} \gamma_{j\tau} \quad j \in J^i, \forall \tau, i$$
$$(6.72) \quad \gamma_{j0} = 0 \qquad\qquad\qquad\qquad j \in J^i, \forall i$$
$$(6.73) \quad \hat{y}_{j,\tau} = 0 \text{ and } \hat{\gamma}_{j,\tau} = 0, \qquad \tau \in [T_0, T_1), j \in J^i, \forall i$$

$$(6.74) \qquad \sum_{j \in J^i} \hat{\gamma}_{j\tau} \leq 2 \qquad\qquad\qquad \forall \tau, i$$

$$(6.75) \qquad \sum_{j \in J^i} \hat{\delta}_{j\tau} \leq 1 \qquad\qquad\qquad \forall \tau, i$$

$$(6.76) \qquad \sum_{j \in J^i} \hat{\gamma}_{j\tau} - \sum_{j \in J^i} \hat{\delta}_{j\tau} \leq 1 \qquad \forall \tau, i$$

$$(6.77) \qquad \hat{\delta}_{j\tau} \geq \hat{\gamma}_{j\tau} - \hat{\gamma}_{j,\tau-1} \qquad \forall \tau, j \in J^i, \forall i$$

Technical conditions:

$$\hat{y}_{j\tau} \geq 0, \hat{y}_{j\tau}^L \geq 0, \ \hat{\gamma}_{j\tau} \in \{0,1\}, \hat{\delta}_{j\tau} \in \{0,1\} \quad \forall \tau, \ j \in J^i, \forall i \tag{6.78}$$

Notations

Indices

t: macro period

τ: micro period

T_0, T_1, T_2: specific horizons (to be defined below at point (2))

For the remaining indices see Section 6.3.1.

Decision variables

x_{it}:   amount of product type i produced in macro period t

x_{it}^L: amount of stock of product type i at the end of macro period t

x_{i,T_0}^L: target stock of product type i

ΔK_t: capacity adaptation

For the remaining variables see Section 6.3.1.

Parameters and preset quantities

$\hat{d}_{it}^T$:   top-level forecast of demand of type i in period t at time t_0

$\hat{d}_{j\tau}^B$:   top-level estimate at time t_0 of the base-level forecast of demand of item j in period τ at t_1

Aggregate production: Time parameters (s_i^T, a_i^T) and cost parameters (c_i^T, h_i^T) are denoted by the suffix T. s_i^T and c_i^T are assumed to be empirically given and a_i^T and h_i^T will be determined by the aggregations (6.79) and (6.80), respectively.

x^{max}:   maximal aggregate production

x^{min}:   minimal aggregate production ($x^{min} > 0$)

Disaggregate production: Time parameters (s_j^B, a_j^B) and cost parameters (c_j^B, h_j^B) are denoted by the suffix B. They are top-level estimates in t_0. For notational convenience, we dropped the usual ' ˆ '. Only the variable $\hat{y}_j^B$ indicates the anticipative character of the base-model (6.66) through (6.78).

y^{max}:   maximal disaggregate production

y^{min}:   minimal disaggregate production $(\hat{y}^{min} > 0)$

$(K_t + \Delta K_t)_\tau$: denotes macro period capacity, broken down to a micro period.

For all other parameters see Section 6.3.1.

The **IHPP-model** has the typical structure of a decision time hierarchy. The top-equation simultaneously optimizes cycle length T, capacity adaptations ΔK_t, type setups, and inventories. Accordingly, the decision vector is given by $a^T := \left(T, \Delta K_T, \beta_{it}, x_{it}, x_{i0}^L\right)$ which, in Eq. (6.55), is an abreviation for

$$a^T := \left(T, \left(\Delta K_0, \beta_{00}, x_{00}, x_{00}^L\right), \cdots, \left(\Delta K_T, \beta_{m,T}, x_{m,T}, x_{m0}^L\right)\right).$$

Note that initial stock x_{i0}^L (of type i) is not (empirically) given but has to be determined by the top-model, and the same holds, because of the cycle condition (6.57), for the final stock x_{iT}^L. The capacity adaptation ΔK_t could also be negative. In that case two cost parameters κ^+ and κ^- would generally be necessary.

The top-decision field A_{AF}^T is defined by the material and production relations (6.56) through (6.58) and, as usual, by the setup and sequencing conditions. The inventory balance equation (6.56) is no longer assumed to be stochastic, as in the stochastic dynamic model of the previous Section 6.3.1, but is taking medium term demand forecasts $\hat{d}_{it}^T$. The capacity contraint (6.58) considers setup times s_i^T and processing times a_i^T. The expression s_i^T denotes the setup time for type i at the medium term level, while a_i^T describes a far more complicated quantity. Besides a type-specific processing time, a_i^T represents an aggregate of all processing and setup times of adjoint items (families) $j \in J^i$ (see Eq. (6.80) below).

The **anticipation equation** optimizes for the short term horizon T_2 setup and inventory costs subject to the estimated base-decision field $\hat{A}^B_{IN}$. Again, the dynamics is described by the inventory balance equation (see Eq. (6.67)) relying, however, on estimates of short term demand forecasts $\hat{d}^B_{j\tau}$. In addition, top-level forecasts of initial stock $\hat{y}^{L'}_{j0}$ incorporate further empirical knowledge. The coupling conditions are represented by three constraints. Eq. (6.68) describes the usual capacity constraint with $(K_t + \Delta K_t)_\tau$ denoting a macro period capacity broken down into a micro period. Relation (6.69) guarantees for the medium term level at time T_0 a target stock of x^L_{i,T_0} units, and (6.70) operationalizes the service degree by a safety stock SS_j. These safety stocks are to be fixed in view of the top-level service criterion C^{TSL} (see also (6.84)). Finally, setup and sequencing conditions are identical with those for the dynamic programming formulation of the previous section.

(2) The relationship between the top- and the base-level

Let us now investigate more closely the relationship of the two levels. First let us clarify the meaning of the **short term horizons T_0, T_1, T_2**, **target stock x^L_{i,T_0}**, and **safety stock SS_j**. Consider the production of type i depicted in Fig. 6.4. The **short term horizon T_2** is taken to be the interval between the setup of type i and the finishing time of the successive setup of that type. The **horizons T_1 and T_0** lie in between. T_0 denotes the finishing time of the setup at hand, and T_1 marks the setup point of the successively repeated production of type i. The horizons T_0, T_1, and T_2 are determined by the top-model, particularly by the optimal setup indicator β_{it}. Condition (6.73) assumes that, between T_0 and T_1, no production of items j belonging to type i is taking place. (Remark: Note that a fine tuning might be necessary since with (6.61) we allowed a setup within the macro period t so that the horizons need not coincide with the beginning or the end of a macro period.)

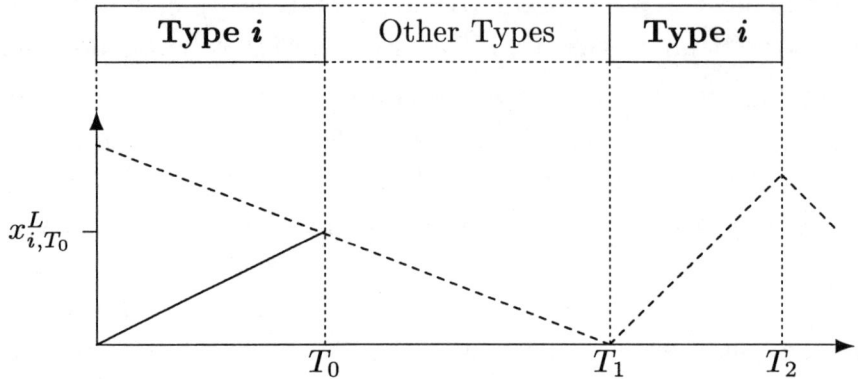

Fig. 6.4: Definition of Target Stock and Horizons T_0, T_1, and T_2

The **target stock** x^L_{i,T_0} is the stock of type i the medium level reaches by the end T_0 of its production period (note that, for notational convenience, we did not indicate the possible dependence of the horizons T_0 and T_1 on i). Since the top-model avoids stockouts (see Eq. (6.65)), the target stocks guarantee with high probability a coverage of demand for type i, and hence warrant stability for the medium term sequence of types.

Remark: Note that we are not discussing a fine tuning of the operational model, i.e., we are not discussing questions, such as, which product should be set up first in case of a capacity deficit. This type of questions will be left for the actual implementation of the model. (For a more profound discussion see [Hauth] and the subsequent 'parameter adaptation').

To buffer fluctuations in demand, product specific **safety stocks** SS_j are employed (see Eqs. (6.70a) and (6.70b)) guaranteeing the overall service criterion C^{TSL} to be observed. In determining the safety stocks $SS_j \, (j \in J^i)$, the fluctuation of cumulated demand within the period $[T_0, T_1]$ is of particular importance in which no production of type i takes place. For the immediate production period $[0, T_0]$ we assume demand to be known deterministically. The fluctuation of cumulated demand during $[T_0, T_1]$ does not only depend on the usual forecasting errors but also on the variation particularly of the horizon T_1, or, to put it differently, on the fluctuation of the demand of all other types. Consequently, in determining SS_j $(j \in J^i)$, the variance of a compound distribution needs to be estimated which gives at least a hint of how large SS_j should be. Moreover, the interval $[T_1, T_2]$ must be considered as well (see Eq. (6.70b)). In this interval, demand is not assumed to be deterministically known. Clearly, in $[T_1, T_2]$, items are again produced so that the main source of uncertainty stems from the fact that it is not clear beforehand which item is produced at which particular time.

Having clarified the role of target and safety stocks, it finally remains to explain the **aggregation of parameters**. According to the general procedure of the standard model in Section 6.2 (see Eqs. (6.23) through (6.26)), one readily has for the aggregate production coefficients

$$a_i^T = \frac{\displaystyle\sum_{j \in J^i} \sum_{\tau=1}^{T_2} \left(a_j^B \hat{y}_{j\tau}^0 + s_j^B \hat{\delta}_{j\tau}^0 \right)}{\displaystyle\sum_{j \in J^i} \sum_{\tau=1}^{T_2} \hat{y}_{j\tau}^0} \tag{6.79}$$

with the suffix "0" indicating, as usual, the optimal base-solution. Similarly, one obtains for the aggregate inventory cost parameter

$$h_i^T = \frac{\displaystyle\sum_{j \in J^i} \sum_{\tau=1}^{T_2} \hat{y}_{j\tau}^{L^0} h_\tau^B |t|}{\displaystyle\sum_{j \in J^i} \sum_{\tau=1}^{T_2} \hat{y}_{j\tau}^{L^0}}. \tag{6.80}$$

Obviously, these parameters have to be optimized in applying a hierarchical algorithm (see below). It is interesting to note that aggregation and optimization are performed simultaneously, or, to put it differently, the question how to aggregate is only answered after the overall optimal solution has been attained.

(3) Hierarchical nature of the integrative model

As for the standard model of Section 6.2, one has an exact reactive anticipation with the private criterion

$$(6.81) \qquad C^{TT} := \left\{ \sum_{t=1}^{T} \kappa \Delta K_t, C^{TSL}, C^{TR} \right\}$$

and the top-down criterion

$$(6.82) \qquad C^{TB} := \sum_{t=1}^{T} \sum_{i=1}^{m} \left(c_i^T \beta_{it} + h_i^T x_{it}^L \right).$$

The estimated base-criterion is given by

$$(6.83) \qquad \hat{C}^B := \sum_{\tau=1}^{T_2} \sum_{j \in J^i} \left(c_j^B \hat{\delta}_{j\tau} + h_j^B \hat{y}_{j\tau}^L \right).$$

Note, however, that with $\hat{d}_{it}^T$ in Eq. (6.56), a non-reactive element is present as well. This is particularly obvious if one takes aggregate values $\hat{d}_{it}^T = \sum_{j} \sum_{\tau \in t_\tau} \hat{d}_{j\tau}^B$ with t_τ being the macro period corresponding to the micro periods τ. Again, as in Section 6.2.3, $\hat{d}_{it}^T$ represents a market-oriented aggregation.

As in the simpler model of the previous section, the anticipation is re-evaluated through the top-down criterion C^{TB} and, in addition, it influences the top-level via the decision field $A^T = A_{AF}^T$.

The instruction, after having solved the multi-criterion decision problem $(C^{TT} + C^{TB}) \longrightarrow$ opt, is given by

$$(6.84) \qquad IN^* := \begin{pmatrix} K_t^* + \Delta K_t^* \\ x_{iT_0}^{L*} \\ C^{TSL*} \end{pmatrix}.$$

As discussed previously, the service-level objective C^{TSL} is at least partly operationalized by the individual safety stocks SS_j ($j \in J^i, i = 1, \ldots, m$). These stocks depend, inter alia, on the time interval between two successive setups of a production type. Hence, at least indirectly, the optimal sequence of medium term production and, in particular, T_0, T_1, and T_2 must be considered as an additional instruction for the short term level.

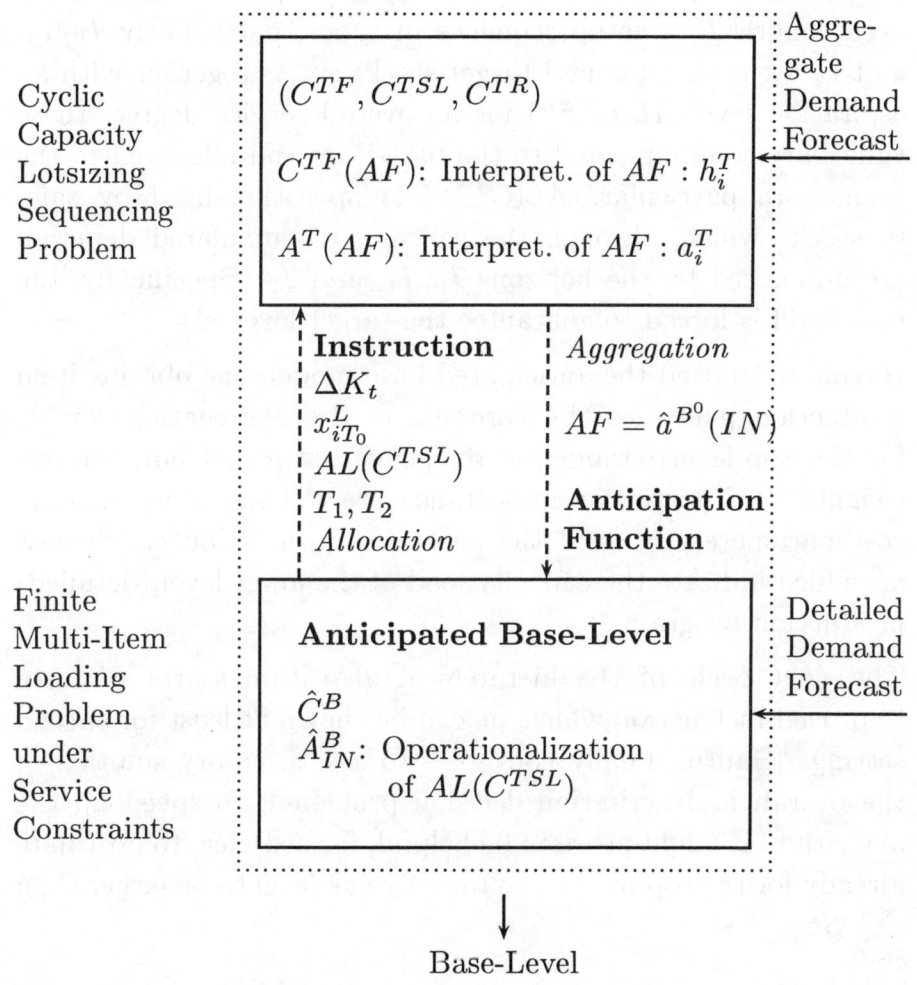

Cyclic
Capacity
Lotsizing
Sequencing
Problem

$(C^{TF}, C^{TSL}, C^{TR})$

$C^{TF}(AF)$: Interpret. of $AF : h_i^T$

$A^T(AF)$: Interpret. of $AF : a_i^T$

Aggregate Demand Forecast

Instruction
ΔK_t
$x_{iT_0}^L$
$AL(C^{TSL})$
T_1, T_2
Allocation

Aggregation

$AF = \hat{a}^{B^0}(IN)$

Anticipation Function

Finite
Multi-Item
Loading
Problem
under
Service
Constraints

Anticipated Base-Level

$\hat{C}^B$
$\hat{A}_{IN}^B$: Operationalization
  of $AL(C^{TSL})$

Detailed Demand Forecast

Base-Level

Fig. 6.5: Hierarchical Algorithm of the Top-Level

Fig. 6.5 summarizes again the relationship between the top-model and the anticipated base-model. In fact, Fig. 6.5 describes the essential interrelations of a hierarchical algorithm. The top-model represents a lotsizing sequencing problem which simultaneously optimizes the cycle length and the provision of capacity. The base-level, on the other hand, may be taken to be a finite multi-item loading problem subject to the consideration of service constraints. Starting with some non-reactive aggregate parameters, like those of Eq. (6.22), the top-level calculates a cycle length T, a setup sequence of types, particularly T_0, T_1, and T_2 for each type, and target stocks $x_{iT_0}^L$. Together with an aspiration level $AL(C^{TSL})$ for its overall service degree, these values are communicated to the base-level and allocated to the items. In particular, $AL(C^{TSL})$ is operationalized by safety stocks which, through the variance of cumulated demand, are influenced by the horizons T_0, T_1, and T_2. Specifically, the base-level is forced to guarantee the target level $x_{iT_0}^L$.

Having optimized the anticipated base-model, one obtains item production quantities which are then used as aggregation weights for the top-level parameters replacing the initial non-reactive weights. Of particular importance are the inventory holding cost parameters h_i^T and the aggregate production coefficients a_i^T which indicate the capacity load of the lower level (detailed) production program.

The next cycle of the hierarchical algorithm starts with an improved instruction which, as can be shown at least for special settings [Hauth], finally converges to a satisfactory solution of the overall multi-criterion decision problem. To speed up the algorithm, it might prove to be helpful, for instance, to postulate already for the top-model the target stock level to be larger than $\sum_{j \in J^i} SS_j$.

For a realistic parameter calibration, however, a one time calculation of the parameters is not enough. In order to capture at least some of the stochastics, the model has to be applied within a rolling horizon environment. Hence, particularly the stability aspect can only be considered to be solved in a satisfactory way if stability is maintained over a sufficiently long sequence of rolling horizon periods. Or, to put it differently, the stability of the medium term sequence of types should be insensitive with respect to substantial fluctuations of short term demand forecasts.

For a model of fairly realistic size, using extensive simulation and sensitivity studies, it can be shown that the above IHPP-model does not only lead to feasible results but is also able to successfully achieve the stability requirement (see [Hauth], Chapter 5). Particularly, in solving the capacitated lotsizing sequencing problem of the top-level, a special algorithm has been constructed [Hauth/Schneeweiss].

6.3.3 General Discussion

The presented integrative hierarchical model for medium and short term process production is not only important and interesting in itself. In fact, it may serve as an illustration for far more general problems than those of production planning. As we come back to some of these general questions, let us, for later reference, point out the general significance of IHPP.

(1) As already mentioned, the IHPP-model separates the two levels in a very cautious way. To avoid infeasibility (at least at the anticipation stage), the base-level is anticipated reactively. Its impact on the top-level, however, is only indirect through the top-parameters h_i^T and a_i^T which, on the other hand, not only affect the top-down criterion but simultaneously the top-decision field. This rather careful integration gives the levels the freedom to follow their own

particular goals, i.e., stability on the medium term level and feasibility on the operational level.

(2) It turned out that the dynamic programming formulation (see Sec. 6.3.1) which concentrated on just one aspect (C^{TF}) was not able to accommodate the rather complex stability objective. From a modeling point of view, this is an interesting observation. It shows that to take into account an objective that may not easily be operationalized, one cannot simply adapt certain parameters. In fact, the whole model must be adjusted, as has been done in applying the IHPP-approach. We will return to this important point in Section 10.1.1, but see also Section 3.2.

(3) Generally, the detailed and the aggregate level represent two different descriptions of the same organizational phenomenon. The detailed description may be considered as being empirical while the aggregate description is relying on purely intellectual constructs. These constructs only allow an incomplete description. Since there is no exact disaggregation possible, one is tied to the level of general notions (like x_{it} or x_{it}^{L}) for which no clear operationalization or interpretation is possible. Or, to put it differently, a unique explanation of the notions used on the upper level cannot be performed on the basis of the lower level. Thus, it becomes important to explain the macro notions through a network of relations that connect several 'not well defined' notions with each other, or even more adequate, with notions that do not allow a further operationalization (disaggregation) and are thus 'true' members of the macro level. For the IHPP-model, the capacity adaptation ΔK_{t} is such a quantity. Hence, the particular capability of hierarchical planning to separate two levels of description provides a deeper understanding of the subtle interrelationship of different abstraction levels in describing the real world. In particular, in organizational theory it might help to relate verbal and decision analytic

description levels more closely to each other.

(4) As a specific example for the problem just discussed, one might consider the construction of cost functions for aggregate planning. These functions are constructed relying on more detailed cost functions in following a simple aggregation device like that of the classical HPP approach. The IHPP-model clearly shows that such a simple aggregation is not only concerned with cash flows but other aspects as well. Thus, cost functions, even for the most simple case of planning a linear production program, cannot be considered as cost transformations that may empirically be verified. In fact, they can, at the most, be considered as structural relationships which may possibly be capable of accommodating empirical knowledge which, in general, is not entirely determined by empirically given cost data but by additional preference information other than costs as well.

(5) As has become clear, aggregations have to be performed in an optimal way. Hence, as is usually the case, in applying (micro economic) production theory to aggregated production processes, cost considerations cannot be avoided. Thus, the simple traditional separation of production and cost theory obviously is not possible, i.e., the quantities production theory is working with can only be defined after having introduced costs and cost functions. This clearly shows that both basic theories of management science should be replaced with the far more comprehensive and integrative theory of hierarchical planning. We will return to points (4) and (5) in Chapter 9 on cost accounting.

Chapter 7

Organizational Design and Flexibility

Design problems can be considered as typical hierarchical planning problems. Apart from formal constructional hierarchies they can belong to any of the hierarchy types defined in Chapter 2 (Fig. 2.3). That is, design problems can involve one or more decision makers, the levels can cooperate as a team, or, at the other extreme, they can behave antagonistically as in a principal agent situation.

Most of the problems we considered so far can be interpreted as design problems. Thus, the tactical-operational hierarchy, e.g., can certainly be taken to be of this character. What we have in mind with the term 'organizational design', however, is more than just providing the operational level with some capacities. Organizational design has to do with creating organizational relationships and with structuring the decision process at the operational level by decisions at the design level.

Let us focus on two prominent organizational problems. The first problem, to be treated in Section 7.1, is the design of a hierarchy at the operational level. That is, we use a hierarchical approach to design a hierarchy. As a second prominent problem, to be discussed in Section 7.2, we consider the design of flexibility. Since flexibility depends on the entire structure of a system and particularly on the dynamics of the decision processes involved, this is again an ambituous structuring problem.

7.1 Designing a Hierarchy

The problem of designing a hierarchy on the operational level will be discussed for a simple task of delegating responsibility. Consider Fig. 7.1, with the design level defining the top-level and the operational level being the base-level. The base-level itself has a hierarchical structure with an upper and a lower level. It is this hierarchical structure that has to be designed in an optimal way.

Let us consider three possible structures each of them defining a decision a_i^T, and hence, an instruction $IN(a_i^T)$ $(i = 1, 2, 3)$:

$IN_1 = IN(a_1^T)$ No delegation of decision rights: The lower level simply executes the decision of the upper level.

$IN_2 = IN(a_2^T)$ Delegation of acquiring information: The lower level provides the upper level with information which leads to a decision at the upper level (non-reactive anticipation of the lower level).

$IN_3 = IN(a_3^T)$ Total delegation: The lower level is entrusted with all operational decision activities.

Assuming that the design level and the operational upper level *represent the same DMU* (see Fig. 2.3), the formulation of the coupling equations is now straightforward.

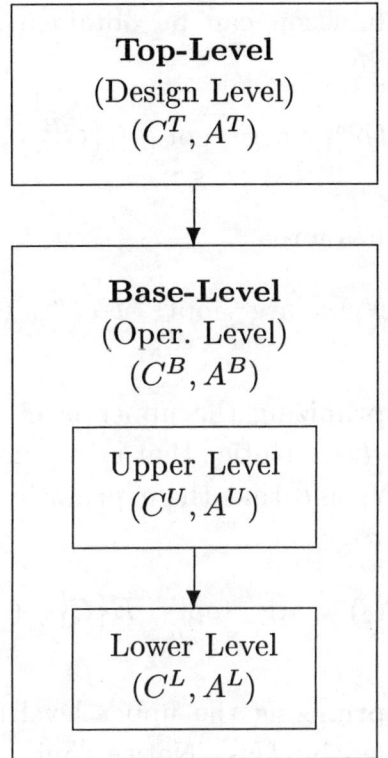

Fig. 7.1: Designing a Hierarchy

Top-level (design decision)

The top-decision is given by

$$a^{T^*} = \arg \operatorname*{opt}_{a^T \in \{a_1^T, a_2^T, a_3^T\}} \left[C^{TT}(a^T) + E\{C^{TB}(AF(IN)) \mid I_{t_0,IN}^T\} \right]$$

$$(7.1a)$$

with

$C^{TT}(a_1^T) = 0 :$ cost, if no information is acquired
$C^{TT}(a_2^T) \geq 0 :$ cost, if information is acquired
$C^{TT}(a_3^T) \geq 0 :$ cost of delegation.

The anticipation function can be obtained in optimizing the operational hierarchy

$$(7.1b) \qquad AF(IN) = \arg \operatorname*{opt}_{\hat{a}^B \in \hat{A}^B_{IN}} E\{\hat{C}^B_{IN}(\hat{a}^B) \mid \hat{I}^B_{IN}\}.$$

In particular, one has for

$$IN_1 \; : \; AF(IN_1) = \arg \operatorname*{opt}_{a^U \in A^U_{IN_1}} E\{C^U_{IN_1}(a^U) | I^T_{t_0,IN_1}\}.$$

The top-level is optimizing the upper level criterion with the information under IN_1. Notice that criterion and decision field may depend on IN_1 and that the expectation operation has to be dropped in $(7.1a)$.

$$IN_2 \; : \; AF(IN_2) = \arg \operatorname*{opt}_{a^U \in A^U_{IN_2}} E\{C^U_{IN_2}(a^U) \mid I^T_{t_0,IN_2}\}.$$

The top-level is optimizing the upper level criterion with the information provided by IN_2. Notice again that criterion and decision field may depend on IN_2 and that the expectation operation has to be dropped in $(7.1a)$.

$$IN_3 \; : \; AF(IN_3) = \arg \operatorname*{opt}_{\hat{a}^L \in \hat{A}^L_{IN_3}} E\{\hat{C}^L(\hat{a}^L) \mid \hat{I}^L\}.$$

$\hat{C}^L$ and $\hat{I}^L$ denote the top-level's estimates of the lower level criterion and information status, respectively. Note that $I^T_{t_0,IN_3}$ should not be dropped in $(7.1a)$. It contains probability distributions concerning all stochastic elements of the lower level.

Incorporating the base-level in $(7.1a)$ one has for

$$IN_1 : C^{TB} = C^U,$$
$$IN_2 : C^{TB} = C^U,$$
$$IN_3 : \begin{cases} C^{TB} \sim \hat{C}^L, & \text{for a team situation, and} \\ C^{TB} \not\sim \hat{C}^L, & \text{for a non-team situation} \end{cases}$$

with $\sim$ denoting 'C^{TB} being monotonous in $\hat{C}^L$'.

For the antagonistic non-team based situation (principal agent case) the upper and lower level have to be interpreted as principal and agent, respectively, and all agency information situations and models apply (see [Demski/Sappington] and Chapter 5).

With these explanations, the top-criterion can be evaluated for the different organizational structures. The best structure (out of the three alternatives) is then taken to be the design decision. Implementing this decision, one finally has the following optimization problem for the

Base-Level

1. If $IN^* = IN_i$ $(i = 1, 2)$, one has

$$a_i^{U^*} = \arg \underset{a^U \in A_{IN_i}^U}{\text{opt}} \; E\{C_{IN_i}^U(a^U)|I_{t_o,IN_i}^T\}. \qquad (7.1c')$$

2. If $IN^* = IN_3$, one has

$$a_3^{L^*} = \arg \underset{a^L \in A_{IN_3}^L}{\text{opt}} \; E\{C_{IN_3}^L(a^L)|I_{t_1}^T\}. \qquad (7.1c'')$$

(For a further discussion under the heading of contract theory, see [Schenk-Mathes] and more generally, e.g., [Harris/Raviv] or [Hart/Holmström].)

General remark: According to the general idea of hierarchical planning the design decision anticipates its impact on the operational consequences of the design. Usually, in practice, the operational level is only taken into account in a non-reactive way. Applying an explicit reactive anticipation presupposes a comparatively clear understanding of the consequences of a design decision which, for many organizations, is not easy to obtain.

7.2 The Design of a Flexibility Potential

As a second prominent class of design problems let us consider the design of a flexibility potential. Flexibility is one of the most important reactive properties of a system. Designing such a complex property one has first to classify which definition and measurement device one should apply. Since there exists a considerable number of rather distinct measures in the literature, a deeper discussion appears to be unavoidable. Only after this discussion the design problem can be successfully dealt with.

7.2.1 Some Preliminary Remarks

Flexibility can be characterized as the ability of a system to cope with unforeseen changes. This seemingly simple characterization is rather difficult to be put into operational terms. In fact, similar to ideas such as 'human power', 'personal freedom' or 'quality of life', flexibility has an intuitive meaning which cannot easily be cast into decision theoretic terms.

Typically, flexibility is built up at a higher managerial level then it is actually used. Furthermore, in establishing a flexibility potential one is generally less informed than at the time when the potential is actually used. Thus, flexibility can be considered as a property of a hierarchical system consisting of a top-level being responsible for the design of a flexibility potential and a base-level which makes use of it. This base-level, of course, should not only possess a flexibility potential but should also be capable of using it in an optimal way.

There have numerous attempts been made to define a quantitative measure of flexibility. All of these approaches have their own particular difficulties. In many cases they are restricted to a small class of models and problems, or they do not provide an ordinal level of scale and thus do not allow systems to be compared, which is of particular importance at the design stage. For a somewhat more elaborate discussion of this point, see [Schneeweiss/Schneider].

The measure we define is closely related to the concept of a service level as it is used in stock control. Such a measure seems to be adequate since a service level is measuring the system's ability to cope with unforeseen changes (i.e., fluctuations of demand). Furthermore, since general inventory problems are stochastic and dynamic they provide an ideal background for discussing flexibility. (For a recent example see [Jordan/Graves].)

A service degree-oriented flexibility measure has particularly three desirable properties:

1. The measure is at least of an ordinal scale and general enough to comprise a large number of different flexibility components.
2. As with stock control it accounts for the loss of goodwill, and hence, it is an additional indicator which cannot easily be replaced with a monetary criterion.
3. Management is provided with a measure which particularly in the production and operations management area has a long tradition.

7.2.2 Elementary Components of a Flexibility Measure

Flexibility can be considered as the result of various components which comprise a flexibility potential, and hence, contribute to a system's availability. Since availability can be measured by a service level, it seems to be natural to measure flexibility by an appropriate generalized service degree.

As more elementary components let us first consider the
(1a) action volume and the
(1b) reactivity.

The action volume comprises all (temporary) actions a system has available to change its state. Reactivity, on the other hand, describes the speed of this change. Both properties define a set of (dynamic) strategies which will be called a **dynamic technology** Θ. It determines all states a system can reach within a certain period of time: $Z = Z(\Theta)$.

Many flexibility concepts simply take the action volume – often only the number of its elements – as a measuring device. Think of the so-called routing flexibility of a flexible manufacturing system which is defined as the maximum number of different routes a workpiece can take through such a system. Or imagine working time flexibility which often is measured by the extension of the interval within which the weekly working time may fluctuate. Similarly, one takes just the reactivity to measure flexibility, i.e., flexibility is simply measured by, e.g., the changeover time or, as in stock control, by the lead time of replenishment orders. If the flexibility of the entire dynamic technology is measured, one often counts the number of reachable states ([Rosenhead et al.], [Benjaafar et al.]), or one takes the number of strategies that constitute the dynamic technology Θ ([Lasserre/Roubellat]).

Using this simple kind of measure, one readily encounters difficulties in comparing different kinds of flexibility potentials. Which technology is more flexible: that with a high variety of possible actions and a long reaction time or that with a small variety and a short time for reaction? Obviously, relying solely on Θ, its flexibility can only be measured at an ordinal level if for two technologies Θ_1 and Θ_2 one of the relations $Z(\Theta_1) \supset Z(\Theta_2)$, $Z(\Theta_1) \subset Z(\Theta_2)$ or $Z(\Theta_1) = Z(\Theta_2)$ holds. This, however, will only be the case for very simple systems.

Consequently, particularly in designing flexibility, one cannot simply take the volume of $Z(\Theta)$ or the dynamic technology Θ itself as a flexibility measure. In fact, in measuring the flexibility of Θ, it is necessary to evaluate its effectiveness in reacting to

a change. Such an evaluation, however, has significant consequences: Flexibility is no longer measured as a simple tech-
nological property of a system but depends on management's
attitude towards the performance of the system's technology.

In measuring the performance, let us introduce a discrepancy
D which measures the 'physical goodness of fit'. D denotes
the distance between a desired state z^d and the 'nearest' state
$z(\Theta) \in Z(\Theta)$ being reachable with $\Theta : D = D(z^d, z(\Theta))$. As an
example, take 'lost sales' or 'missing the production due date by
a certain amount of time' or, more generally, the gap between
needed and providable capacity.

A mere discrepancy will usually not be sufficient to measure the
quality of a system's adjustment. In fact, management has to
evaluate when a discrepancy actually might result particularly
in a long term loss. Let us therefore introduce as a second major
component of a flexibility measure a
(2) loss measure $L = L(D)$.
As an example, consider a missed due date. In many situations,
a small deviation might not be considered as a real problem,
whereas larger deviations might be taken more seriously. Hence,
in most situations L will depend monotonously on D. Therefore
let $L(D)$ be a function of D that measures a discrepancy which
implies a loss of goodwill, i.e., the fear of loosing in the long run
a market share.

In guaranteeing a system's availability one obviously has to take
into account, as a further component of a flexibility measure,
the
(3) uncertainty of its environment
which will be denoted as the system's information status I.

Consequently, flexibility turns out to be not only a property of
the considered system but of its environment as well (see also
[Malek/Wolf], [Rosenhead et al.], [Jordan/Graves]).

7.2.3 A General Measure of Flexibility

In deriving a flexibility measure we now combine the effect of the different components discussed before. To obtain a well-defined measure let us evaluate the conjoint effect of all components by the best adjustment they can achieve and define a (non-normalized) measure of flexibility by

$$(7.2) \qquad F = \min_{a \in \Theta} E\{L(D(a)) \mid I\}$$

with I denoting the system's information status and $a \in \Theta$ being a dynamic strategy. F aggregates a constellation $\{\Theta, I, L\}$ in just one value. Thus it becomes meaningful to compare different flexibility potentials as to their reaction with respect to their environment.

F describes a mean discrepancy that, in applying the dynamic technology Θ, cannot be avoided. That is, in view of possible disturbances, Θ is only capable of transferring the system (in a specified period of time) into a state $z(\Theta)$ which is usually not the desired state z^d at which no loss of goodwill is assumed to occur. Particularly, in the area of production and operations management, in many situations L describes the deficit between desired and (under Θ) providable resources. For inventory problems, e.g., L can be identified with non-satisfied demand. In such situations a normalization of F turns out to be straightforward. A system is defined to have lowest flexibility F^- if it is unable to react at all, thus demand for resources is entirely accumulated. Hence, one may normalize F by

$$(7.3) \qquad F^n := 1 - \frac{F}{F^-}.$$

Obviously, the (normalized) flexibility is zero for not reacting, and it takes on its highest value 1 if no mean loss remains, thus $F^n = 0$ for $F = F^-$ and $F^n = 1$ for $F = 0$.

In stock control, F^- represents mean total (non-delivered) demand for a specified period of time. Since F is non-satisfied demand, the expression $F^- - F$ can be interpreted as mean satisfied demand. Hence, the normalized flexibility measure results in

$$F^n = 1 - \frac{F}{F^-} = \frac{F^- - F}{F^-} = \frac{E\{\text{satisfied demand}\}}{E\{\text{total demand}\}}$$

which is exactly the definition of the well-known β-service degree in inventory theory (e.g., see [Schneider]).

7.2.4 Numerical Specification of Flexibility

Although the measure F (or F^n) looks straightforward, for a design purpose one is still left with the problem of assigning numerical values to it. Indeed, designing flexibility one has to consider all indicators which evaluate a system. Besides F, these indicators comprise costs K and all remaining quantitative and/or non-quantitative criteria (denoted by C in Eq. (7.4) below) which might be of relevance. In addition to the cost for establishing and maintaining a flexibility potential, K describes the expected operational cost incurred by reducing the expected loss. Hence, for design purposes, management has to solve the multi-criterion decision problem

$$\{F, K, C\} \Longrightarrow \text{opt}. \tag{7.4}$$

Strictly speaking, in the long run, an economic system has to follow some monetary goal. The reason why management tries to meet some intermediate goals, like flexibility, is caused by the complexity of the problem it has to solve. It is important to first summarize the aspects that might influence the long term goals and then to put this quantity into a 'wider' perspective. As a medium term measure, F has to evaluate the loss of goodwill which, in the long run, might have an effect on the viability of the system.

To better appreciate the complex nature of the multi-criterion decision problem (7.4), let us again consider the various evaluation steps that had to be taken:

(1) Determining a discrepancy D, which might be caused by some change. This discrepancy measures the system's deviation from some desired state z^d. Being in z^d, the system is assumed to suffer no loss of goodwill. (For a stock control problem, z^d might be taken to be zero inventory, and D describes unsatisfied demand.)

(2) Determining a loss measure $L(D)$, which evaluates those values of D that might cause a loss of goodwill. (For an inventory problem only a substantial long lasting and unsatisfied demand, e.g., might be considered to cause a loss of goodwill.)

(3) Assigning a numerical value to F (or F^n) in solving the multi-criterion evaluation (7.4). The value has to be assigned, in view of the incurred costs K and other important criteria C, resulting in an acceptable loss of goodwill. (For an inventory problem, a service level is specified in view of the expected behavior of the market and the costs necessary to maintain that level.)

In principle, one encounters two important steps of evaluation:
1. the determination of F (as a function of Θ in view of I) and
2. the assignment of a numerical value to F.
Accordingly, one has to cope with two major uncertainties:

(1) the medium (or short) term occurance of a change and
(2) the possible consequences one has to face if the system does not adjust to that change.

As to the occurrence of a change, it will often be possible to assign at least subjective probabilities. Far more difficult is the determination of probabilities for the possible consequences one has to face. These consequences are often of a long term character. Not only are the probabilities unknown, but also the events for which probabilities have to be assigned. Methods in marketing research might provide some hints.

Hence, the multi-criterion decision problem (7.4) is of a highly subjective character. This difficult situation, however, is not new for management. For instance, a debt-asset ratio or a risk measure is of the same nature. It is not that difficult to measure these quantities, but it is difficult to evaluate their significance for a system's viability. An 'intermediate measure' like flexibility, however, gives management a certain reference point. Like a debt-asset ratio or a service degree it can be objectively measured and its numerical value can be used as a bench mark. Since it combines different flexibility components, it can more easily be dealt with than $Z(\Theta)$. Indeed, for Θ_1 and Θ_2 one always has one of the three relations $F(\Theta_1) > F(\Theta_2)$, $F(\Theta_1) < F(\Theta_2)$, or $F(\Theta_1) = F(\Theta_2)$. No such statement can generally be found for Θ or $Z(\Theta)$. An ordinal relationship, however, is important, otherwise one would not even be able to derive efficient values for the multi-criterion decision problem (7.4). Consequently, one would not be able to evaluate the usefulness of flexibility.

7.2.5 Planning and Implementation Ability as Further Components of Flexibility

Up to now, in determining the flexibility of a system, we have simply relied on its dynamic technology Θ as it has been defined in Section 7.2.2. Since such a technology, however, does only describe the set of feasible strategies, it is obvious that one would only take into consideration a 'hardware-oriented' view of a system's entire flexibility. In fact, most of the measures derived in the literature (see [Sethi/Sethi] or [Gupta/Goyal]) are restricted to this more technical aspect. This is, as we have shown, too narrow a point of view. We therefore introduced a loss measure $L(D)$ and considered the information status I. Planning, communication, and implementation aspects, however, are further components that need to be taken into account.

(4) Planning and communication ability can be considered as the system's ability to fully exploit its technology. Since the technology typically is dynamic and the environment is stochastic, optimal planning can only be performed for simple settings. Approximating heuristics (i.e., efficient software) will have to be used and, obviously, the better the approximation, i.e., the better the planning ability, the lower will be F and hence (see Eqs. (7.2) and (7.3)) the higher will be the (normalized) flexibility. Clearly, the same holds for the forecasting procedures to be applied, i.e., for the system's ability to correctly perceive the probability of disturbances. Or, to put it more generally, the better the communication within a system, the more flexible it will be.

(5) Implementability represents another important component of flexibility, since a plan is only as good as its implementation. Often a decision a is not implemented as it is supposed to be. Instead, one has to accept some deviation δ. One may therefore operationalize implementability as the additional stochastics induced by a non-exact implementation. (For a deeper discussion see Chapter 8.) Clearly, leadership activities could reduce this additional uncertainty (e.g., see [Wild/Schneeweiss]). Hence, flexibility does not only depend on the system's capability to plan and to forecast but also on its leadership skill.

With these considerations, we are now ready to discuss the

design of flexibility within a hierarchical context.

7.2.6 The Design of Flexibility as a Hierarchical Planning Problem

Putting the design of flexibility into the framework of hierarchical planning is now straightforward. The coupling equations (2.5) may be stated as follows: In view of the design problem we have in mind, let us take as a top-criterion a vector of two criteria such that

$$a^{T^*} = \arg \operatorname*{opt}_{a^T \in A^T} \left\{ E\{C^{TT}(a^T) \mid I_{t_0}^T\}, E\{C^{TB}(AF(IN)) \mid I_{t_0}^T\} \right\}$$

$$(7.5a)$$

with $IN = IN(a^T)$ and

$$AF(IN) = \arg \operatorname*{\widehat{opt}_{IN}}_{\hat{a}^B \in \hat{A}_{IN}^B} E\{\hat{C}^B(\hat{a}^B) \mid \hat{I}^B\}. \qquad (7.5b)$$

The base-equation is given by

$$a^{B^*} = \arg \operatorname*{opt_{IN^*}}_{a^B \in A_{IN^*}^B} E\{C^B(a^B) \mid I_{t_1}^B\}. \qquad (7.5c)$$

Note that the optimization operator can be influenced by the top-level, that is, the design of flexibility not only endows the operational system with a dynamic technology Θ but it also provides 'handling intelligence'. Thus, all aspects described in **(4)** and **(5)** above are taken into account through opt_{IN}.

For the discussion to follow let us first consider the case that the design level and the operational level form a team. In particular, let us assume that all constituents of the operational level which are not determined by the design decision are known. Hence, one can drop all 'hats' in Eq. (7.5b) except that of $\hat{I}^B$. $\hat{I}^B$ is the information status of the base-level estimated by the design level. Note that there is uncertainty about $\hat{I}^B$ as described by the top-level's information status $I_{t_0}^T$. Taking $C^{TB} \equiv C^B$, Eqs. (7.5a) and (7.5b) may be written in the compact form

$$
a^{T*} = \arg \operatorname*{opt}_{a^T \in A^T} \left\{ E\{C^{TT}(a^T) \mid I_{t_0}^T\}, \right.
$$

(7.6a)

$$
\left. E\left\{ \min_{\substack{a^B \in A_{IN}^B}} E\{C^B(a^B)|\hat{I}^B\}|I_{t_0}^T \right\} \right\}
$$

Turning to the notations of the preceding sections, one readily recognizes the following correspondence

(a)   loss measure $L \hat{=} C^B$,

(b)   dynamic technology $\Theta \hat{=} A_{IN}^B$,

(c)   planning, forecasting, communication, and leadership ability: '$\min_{IN}$',

(d)   non-normalized flexibility measure

$$
F = \min_{\substack{a^B \in A_{IN}^B}} E\{C^B(a^B)|\hat{I}^B\},
$$

(Note that in suitably defining C^{TB} one could easily replace F with F^n.)

(e)   expected costs of designing and operating the flexibility potential: $K = E\{C^{TT}|I_{t_0}^T\}$,

(f)   range of design decisions A^T.

With these explanations except for the criteria C and the expectation $E\{F|I_{t_0}^T\}$, Eq. (7.6a) turns out to be identical with the multi-criterion decision problem (7.4). Obviously, C could have also been formulated in the hierarchical framework as a further component of C^{TT} or C^{TB} or of both. What is nicely exhibited by the hierarchical formulation, however, is the information situation. Clearly, the non-specified 'I' in Eq. (7.2) is now the information $\hat{I}^B$ the operational level is assumed to possess at the design stage. Often there will be no ambiguity about the estimate $\hat{I}^B$. In that case $E\{F|I_{t_0}^T\}$ reduces to F. What is left to be done at the operational level is to minimize expected loss employing the flexibility potential and the specific operational information status:

$$a^{B^*} = \arg \min_{\substack{IN^* \\ a^B \in A_{IN^*}^B}} E\{C^B(a^B) \mid I_{t_1}^B\}. \qquad (7.6b)$$

The flexibility potential represents the result of the design effort and is given by the properties **(1)**, **(4)**, and **(5)** above, condensed in the pair $\{A_{IN^*}^B, \min_{IN^*}\}$. The potential is measured by the pre-assigned loss measure $C^B = L$ in view of an uncertain environment of which the design level assumes that it is perceived by the operational level through $\hat{I}^B$.

Remark: In case of an antagonistic situation ideas of agency theory (see Chapter 5) could be applied using, e.g., incentives to avoid cheating. For an enforced team situation (see Fig. 2.3), C^{TB} would induce a re-evaluation showing, e.g., that the loss measure being employed by the operational level is not in accordance with the top-level. In fact, the operational level might judge a loss of goodwill in a different way than the top-level would prefer it to be done.

Chapter 8

Implementation

A decision process can be considered to be composed of two major phases: The first phase consists of planning activities, and the second one is concerned with the task of implementing the decision the planning process resulted in. Hence, planning and implementation can be looked at as forming a hierarchy which again lends itself to an investigation within the theory of hierarchical planning. This hierarchy, however, is not that distinct as it might appear. In fact, as Fig. 8.1 shows, the implementation activities often overlap the planning process. On many occasions, the implementation level is participating in the planning procedure. Furthermore, a plan is often not a clear-cut decision, it can be changed during the implementation, and short term control mechanisms often promote the implementation.

As indicated at the right hand side of Fig. 8.1, implementation

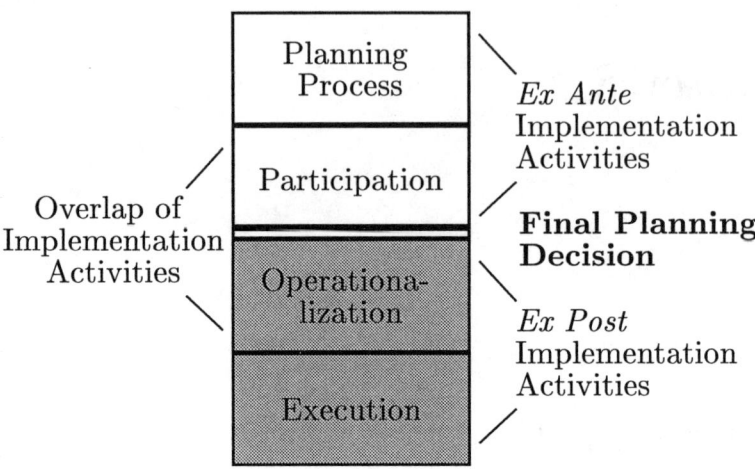

Fig. 8.1: The Overlap of the Planning and Implementation
Phases

activities can be exerted ex ante or ex post, i.e., before and
after the final plan has passed. Ex ante activities consist of
the active participation of the implementation level in the planning process. This type of feedforward involvement will not be
our main concern in the following investigation (see, however,
Chapter 12). Instead, we are focusing on the ex post part of
implementation activities. This part has to be anticipated in
the planning procedure and thus leads to an *indirect* ex ante
influence. Hence, speaking of implementation, we will always
have in mind ex post activities. For this type of implementation,
one again can find a particular structure. In fact, one can observe
two stages:

– first, the (final) planning decision is transformed into an
  operational procedure and
– second, this operational procedure is being executed.

Consequently, the planning procedure has to anticipate both, the operationalization and its final execution. This two-stage implementation process becomes particularly important in case there is more than one party involved. In that case, operationalizing often means to interpret an instruction which deliberately is somewhat vague leaving some space for final adaptations. Altogether, the implementation problem can be considered as the interrelationship between three levels, the planning level, the (operationalizing) interpretation level, and the (final) execution level.

In describing this hierarchy, let us first, in Section 8.1, briefly discuss the implementation process without explicitly taking into account the interpretation (or operationalization) stage, i.e., we are first describing the implementation process as a two-stage hierarchy consisting of a planning and an implementation level. In Section 8.2 we then investigate the three-stage implementation problem focusing particularly on activities that control the interpretation. A formal discussion of the implementation problem within the framework of hierarchical planning is then given in Section 8.3. (For a rather abstract and general discussion see also [Mesarovic et al.].) Finally, the general framework is illustrated and applied to two important problems. First, in Section 8.4, the implementation of a working time contract is considered, and secondly, in Section 8.5, the process of implementing lot sizes within a production planning and control system will be analyzed.

8.1 Planning and Implementation as a Two-Stage Hierarchy

Identifying the planning activity as the top-level and the subsequent implementation as the base-level of a hierarchy, one has the situation depicted in Fig. 8.2. The task of the implementation level is to 'reproduce' the implementation decision IM as exactly as possible. In many settings, however, this reproduction will not be exact. In fact, some **implementation disturbance**, $\tilde{\delta}_{IN}$, caused by the implementation level, might occur which has to be taken into account by the planning phase and will be represented as a random variable in the top-level. This disturbance will often be additive, implying the intuitive notation $\widetilde{IM} = IM + \tilde{\delta}_{IN}$ in Fig. 8.2. Note, however, that other types of dependencies are not excluded.

In order to keep the disturbance small, leadership activities LA are applied by the top-level (see again 'implementability' in Section 7.2.5). Hence, the influence of the top-level exerted on the base-level not only consists of the implementation decision IM, but also of the leadership activities LA which together make up the instruction $IN = (IM, LA)$ (see Fig. 8.2).

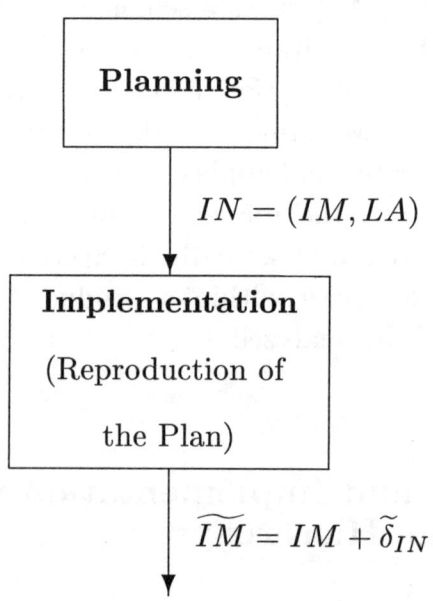

Fig. 8.2: Planning and Implementation Hierarchy

According to Fig. 8.2, Diagram 8.3 shows the general idea of how to take into account the implementation activities in the planning procedure: The top-level anticipates (all features of) the base-level and calculates an optimal instruction $IN^* = (IM^*, LA^*)$ which results in an execution $IM^{**} = IM^* + \delta_{IN^*}$, where δ_{IN^*} denotes a realization of the random variable $\tilde{\delta}_{IN^*}$. Of course, anticipating the base-level usually turns out to be an extremely tedious task.

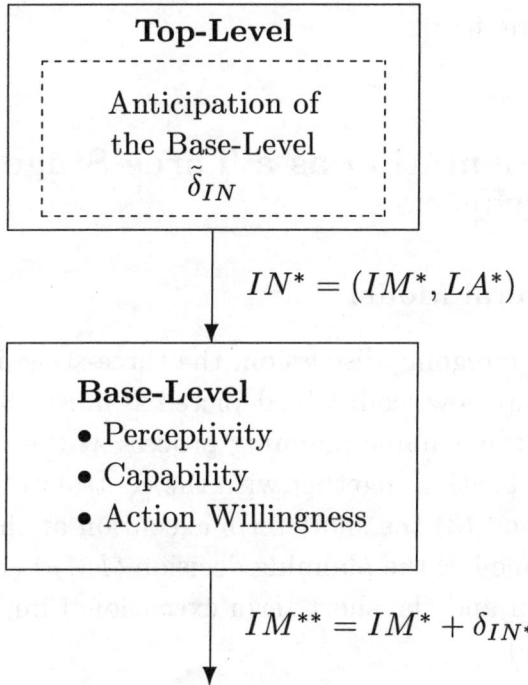

Fig. 8.3: Anticipating the Implementation in the Planning Process

As a first step, three properties can be identified to mainly determine the characteristics of an implementation level:

-   perceptivity: the ability to correctly communicate with the top-level,

- capability: the (physical) ability to execute the implementation decision, and
- action willingness: the willingness to go into action.

Obviously, operationalizing, estimating, and anticipating these properties is not easy. In what follows, we will therefore not investigate this tedious problem any further, rather we will simply combine the properties of the implementation level in some general statements about the resulting implementation disturbance. Chapter 10 will be devoted to analyze leadership aspects in more detail.

8.2 Implementation as a Three-Stage Hierarchy

8.2.1 A General Model

In view of the foregoing discussion, the three-stage implementation process may now readily be depicted as in Fig. 8.4. Diagram 8.4 shows (1) the genuine planning process at the top-level, (2) the operationalization together with the control potential at the medial-level, and (3) the short term execution at the base-level. Accordingly, one has the planning decision (IM_P) that has to be operationalized and the short term executional implementation decision (IM_E) .

The top-level's total instruction $\overline{IN}$ consists of three quantities: the planning decision IM_P^*, the leadership decision CP^* putting up the control potential, and the so-called feedforward leadership decision FF^*. This last activity describes the possibility of the planning level to directly influence the executional level. All three quantities, IM^*, CP^*, FF^*, have to be optimized simultaneously. The control potential CP^* promotes the operationalization of the planning decision IM_P^*, and the medium

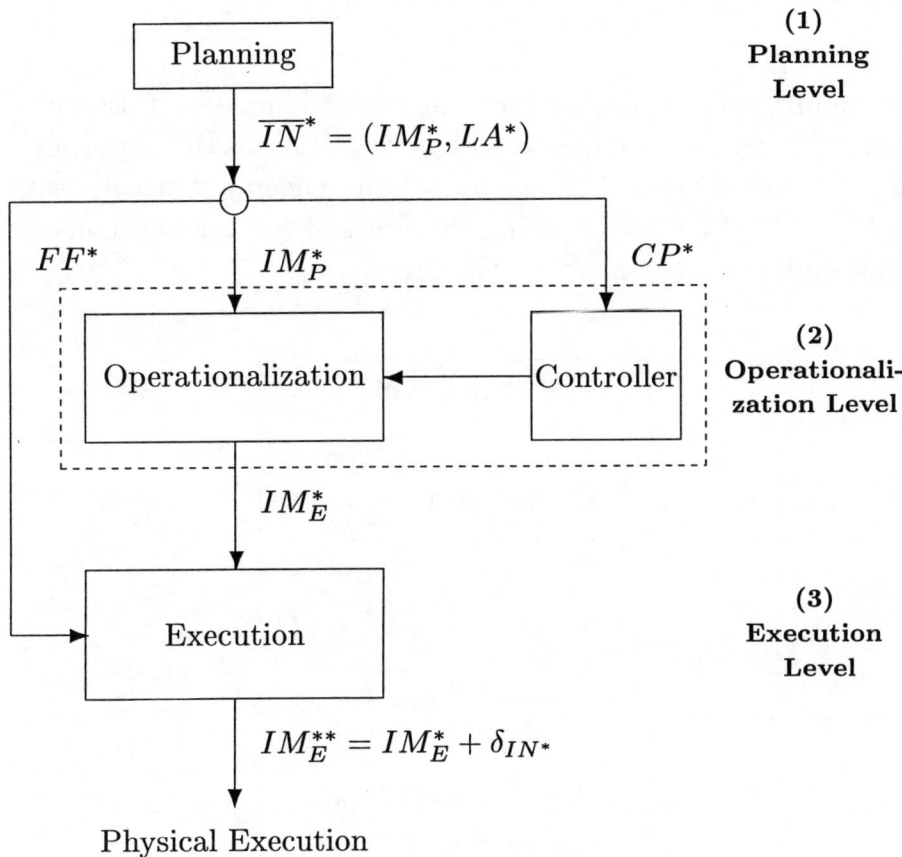

Fig. 8.4: The Three-Stage Implementation Problem

term model implements its execution decision IM_E^* through the short term execution level which is influenced by the feedforward leadership activity FF^*. Hence $LA^* := (CP^*, FF^*)$ and $\overline{IN}^* := (IM^*, LA^*)$.

8.2.2 The Solution Hierarchy

In simultaneously solving the planning and implementation problem of Fig. 8.4, one has to anticipate the respective lower level by the upper one. Fig. 8.5 shows the general structure with $IN^* := (IM_P^*, CP^*)$ defining that part of the total instruction that influences the medial-level directly.

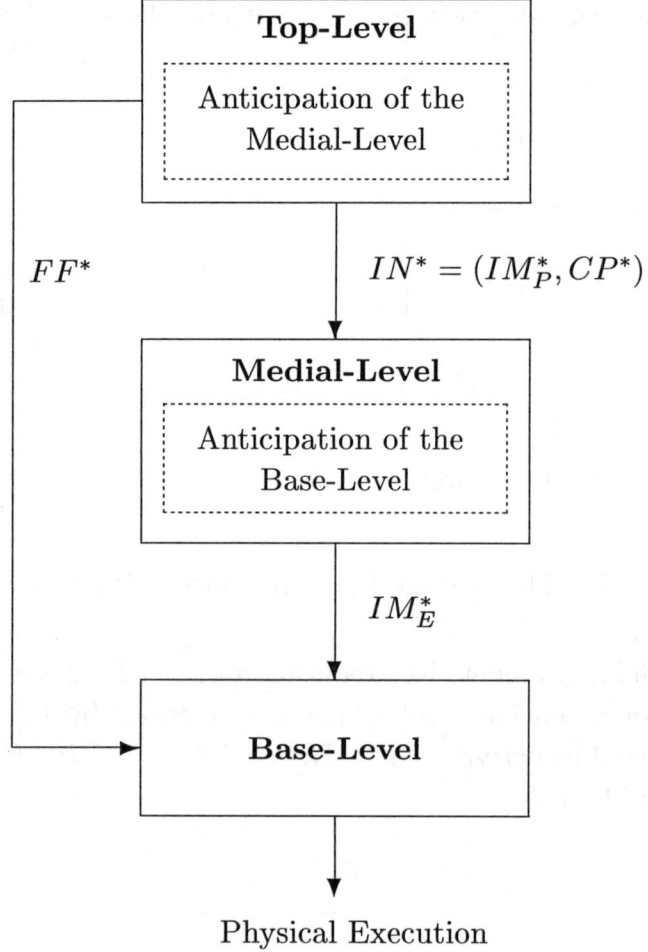

Fig. 8.5: The Three-Stage Design-Implementation Hierarchy

To be somewhat more specific, let us assume the following general relationship between the levels.

1. Between the top-and medial-level, for most planning situations in companies, it seems to be appropriate to assume a tactical-operational hierarchy (see also Section 4.2). This particularly says that both levels build a team, and hence optimize their criteria in a cooperative way.
2. Between medial- and base-level one might have an (antagonistic) principal agent relationship (see Chapter 6).
3. Between top- and base-level let us assume a non-reactive anticipation (see Sec. 2.4) and that the base-level is exclusively influenced by motivational leadership activities.

8.3 Formal Description of the Planning and Implementation Problem

8.3.1 The Coupling Equations of Hierarchical Planning

A formal description of the planning and implementation problem can again be achieved by the general equations (2.5) with the specific treatment of the 'opt-operator' as in (7.5b). For the reader's convenience, let us quote the respective coupling equations again,

$$a^{T^*} = \arg \operatorname*{opt}_{a^T \in A^T} E\left\{ C^T[C^{TT}(a^T), C^{TB}(AF(IN))] \mid I_{t_0}^T \right\} \quad (8.1a)$$

$$IN = IN(a^T)$$

$$AF(IN) = \arg \operatorname*{\widehat{opt}_{IN}}_{\hat{a}^B \in \hat{A}_{IN}^B} E\left\{ \hat{C}_{IN}^B \mid \hat{I}_{IN}^B \right\} \quad (8.1b)$$

$$a^{B^*} = \arg \operatorname*{opt_{IN^*}}_{a^B \in A_{IN^*}^B} E\left\{ C_{IN^*}^B \mid I_{IN^*,t_1}^B \right\} \quad (8.1c)$$

Using Eq. (8.1), the formal presentation of the optimization problem structured in Fig. 8.5 is now straightforward.

Let us first define the following quantities:

C^{TT} :   planning and leadership costs,

$\hat{C}_{IN}^{M}$:   operational costs and/or revenues of planning and leadership activities in view of the top-level,

IN :   instruction, $IN = (IM_P, CP)$,

IM_P :   planning decision,

$LA :=$ (C_P, FF) leadership activity,

CP :   control potential,

FF :   feedforward influence,

A^{IM_P} :   space of planning decisions,

A^{LA} :   space of leadership decisions,

$A^T :=$ $A^{IM_P} \times A^{LA}$: top-decision space,

$\hat{A}_{IN}^{M}$:   anticipated medium term operational decision, space depending on IN,

$\widehat{IM}_E$:   anticipated short term execution decision,

I^T :   information status of the top-level,

$\hat{I}_{r,\delta}^{M}$:   anticipated medium term operational information status depending on $\tilde{r}$ and $\tilde{\delta}$,

$\tilde{r}$:   exogeneous disturbance in view of the top-level, to be fully explained in Section 8.4,

$\tilde{\delta}$:   endogeneous disturbance caused by the implementation activities of the top- and medial-level in view of the top-level.

With these definitions, the hierarchy depicted in Fig. 8.5 results in the following specification of the general Eq. (8.1a):

$$IN^* = \arg \operatorname*{opt}_{IN \in A^T} E\left\{ C^{TT}(IN) \right.$$

$$\left. + \operatorname*{opt}_{\widehat{IM}_E \in \hat{A}_{IN}^M} E\{\hat{C}_{IN}^M(\widehat{IM}_E)|\hat{I}_{r,\delta}^M\} \Big| I^T \right\}.$$

$$(8.2)$$

In fact, Eq. (8.2) describes the top-equation of a three-stage hierarchy. According to Section 8.2.2 , we reasonably assume a cooperative regime between the design and medium term operational level. Hence, aggregating the private and the medium term criterion additively seems to be natural. Furthermore, there is no re-evaluation, i.e., Eq. (8.1b) is incorporated without any change in the top-equation. The third level, i.e., the execution level, is only described through the executional disturbance $\tilde{\delta}$. In fact, $\tilde{\delta}$ can be considered as a base-anticipation function which is estimated by the top-level: $\tilde{\delta} = \widehat{AF}^B(IM_E, FF)$. This estimation is simply performed in establishing a subjective probability, i.e., no attempt is made to derive $\tilde{\delta}$ from a fully anticipated base-level as it is done with the medial level.

Eq. (8.2) nicely exhibits the structure of a dynamic program. Solving this program, one readily obtains, as a component of the optimal instruction IN^*, the optimal plan IM_P^*. Two examples may illustrate the general considerations.

8.4 Working Time Contract

The general procedure depicted in Fig. 8.4 may readily be illustrated by the implementation of a working time contract. The tactical level consists of the choice of a particular contract W^* (see Fig. 8.6). The medium term operationalization level transforms the regulations of the contract into the optimal sequence of monthly working hours $h^* := (h_1^*, \ldots, H_T^*)$. The control potential can be identified with the allowance of a certain maximum amount of overtime $OT := (OT_1, \ldots, OT_T)$ during a particular period $t, t = 1, \ldots, T$. This potential helps to smooth medium term capacity fluctuations and hence supports the (medium term operational) implementation of the contract. The instruction for the short term (executional) implementation level is the optimal number $h_t^* = h_t^{r*} + o_t^*$ of regular hours h_t^{r*} and of overtime hours (o_t^*) an employee must work.

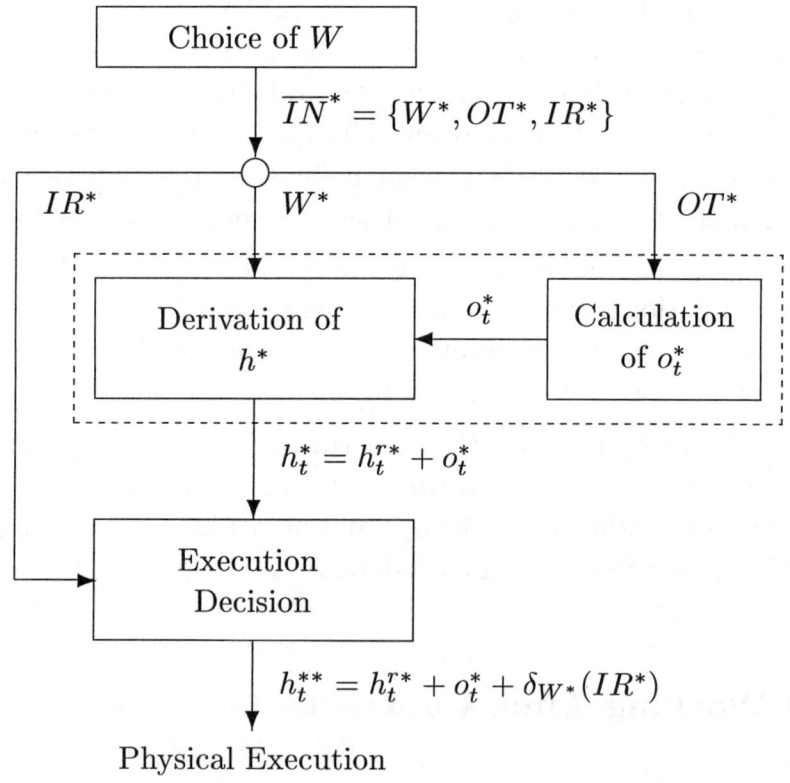

Fig. 8.6: Design and Implementation of a Working Time Contract (W)

Particularly, for overtime, however, a working time contract can foresee a certain freedom for the employee not to accept the demanded amount of overtime. Hence, one has an implementation uncertainty $\tilde{\delta}_W(IR)$ which not only depends on the contract but also on the industrial relations IR. This latter quantity, however, is influenced by the (tactical) planning level and provides a nice example how the tactical level can communicate directly with the short term executional level.

Let us illustrate Eq. (8.2) with a simplified version of this example for which overtime is not allowed. That is, in this first example, we are not examining the effect of a control potential. This aspect will be left for the example given in the next section.

The aim now consists in finding an optimal working time contract W^* from a finite set of feasible contracts $A^T := \{W_i, i = 1, \ldots, n\}$. The planning criterion mainly has two components: the costs $C^{TT} = C^{TT}(W_i)$ attributed to a particular contract W_i and the penalty (e.g., stockout) cost for a deficit in capacity. Hence, in view of Eq. (8.2), one readily has

$$W^* = \arg \operatorname*{opt}_{W_i \in A^T} E\left\{ C^{TT}(W_i) + \operatorname*{opt}_{h \in \hat{A}^M_{W_i}} E\{\hat{V}(h)|\hat{I}^M_{r,\delta^B_{W_i}}\}|I^T\right\}.$$

$$(8.3)$$

$\hat{V}(h)$ is a top-level estimate of a penalty function

$$V(h) = \sum_{t=1}^{T} c_t v_t(h_t) \qquad (8.4)$$

with c_t being penalty unit cost of period t, and $h = (h_1, ..., h_T)$ is the vector of weekly working time for weeks 1 to T. The function

$$v_t(h_t) := \begin{cases} r_t - g(h_t) - INV_t & \text{if } r_t - g(h_t) - INV_t \geq 0 \\ \\ & \text{else} \end{cases} \qquad (8.5)$$

represents a capacity deficit with r_t and INV_t being demand and inventory in week t, respectively, and $g(h_t)$ denotes implemented working hours. All quantities are being measured in man-hours.

The vector $(h_1, ..., h_T)$ gives the distribution of the working time over a horizon of T weeks. Its medium term optimization can be interpreted as the result of an operationalization of a working time contract, i.e., of a planning decision. The particular contract W_i is partly determining the medial-level decision space $A_{W_i}^M := \{(a), (b), (c)\}$. Particularly, the properties (a) and (b) represent the working time contract i:

(a) Flexibility corridor:

$$h_{ti}^l \leq h_t \leq h_{ti}^u \qquad\qquad \forall \quad i, t$$

h_{ti}^l and h_{ti}^u being lower and upper bounds respectively, depending on the working time contract.

(b) Balance of total working time $H_i := H(W_i)$ after $T_i := T(W_i)$ periods:

$$\sum_{t=1}^{T_i} h_t = H_i \qquad\qquad \forall \quad i$$

(c) Inventory Balance Equation:

$$INV_{t+1} = \max\{INV_t + g(h_t) - r_t; 0\}$$

This last property represents the operational production part of the medium term decision space. Its most interesting quantity certainly is the implemented working time

$$g(h_t) = h_t + \tilde{\delta}_{W_i}^B(IR),$$

which is affected by the disturbance of the short term execution.

Working time orders have not always to be strictly obeyed. Many working time contracts allow for a certain degree of freedom not to accept an order (instruction) h_t. Hence, in deciding upon a working time contract, management has to obtain subjective probabilities whether an order might be accepted or not. Let us assume that this probability does only depend on the particular working agreement W_i and on the industrial relations. And let us further assume, for contracts having the same weekly working time h_t, the better the industrial relations , the smaller the variance of $\tilde{\delta}_{W_i}^B(IR)$ will be. The industrial relations can be improved by motivational leadership activities. Eq. (8.3) shows (as a side effect) how these activities might in principle be measured.

Specifying $C^{TT}(W_i)$, I^T, and all other quantities numerically and solving Eq. (8.3) finally results in an optimal contract, i.e., in an optimal planning decision. Of course, this example is extremely simple, still it proves to be sophisticated enough to illustrate the main features of the hierarchical planning approach to solve a planning-implementation problem. (For a more realistic and comprehensive example, see [Wild/Schneeweiss] and [Wild]).

8.5 Implementation of Lotsizes

The implementation of lotsizes within a stochastic production planning and control system may serve as a further example to show the effect of an implementation uncertainty. Again, one has a three-level system involving medium and short term production planning, and job shop control. To hold the discussion simple, however, let us focus on only the two upper levels, i.e., on medium and short term planning. Thus, at the medium term level, lotsizes are calculated which are then, at the short term level, actually implemented.

Using the terminology of a production planning and control system, the medium term level represents aggregate production planning (APP) (or the master production schedule), and the implementation level can be identified with the MRP level. In contrast to traditional PPC systems (see Fig. 1.8), however, lotsizing is already performed at the medium term level. In fact, for many production systems, capacity adaptations must be achieved well in advance, and since capacities often mainly depend on the frequency of setups and since this frequency, on its part, depends on the size of the lots, it is necessary to determine lotsizes not at the MRP level - as it is done in traditional PPC-systems - but on the higher APP level. This redesign of a traditional PPC-system has for many production systems the crucial consequence that the medium term level must be described stochastically.

Hence, we are adopting the following procedure summarized in Fig. 8.7. First we calculate at the 'planning level' for each product i so-called target lotsizes q_i^{opt} which are later, at the 'implementation level', adapted to the improved state of information, resulting in adapted lotsizes q_i^0.

What has to be done, however, and this is the advantage an integrative hierarchical planning is actually bringing about, one has to anticipate the adaptation activity. Clearly, adapting a plan, that is to say, being flexible, simultaneously implies nervousness which we previously identified as implementation uncertainty. Again, as in Eq. (8.2), this uncertainty has to be taken into account by the medium term level as an additional stochastic influence.

Let us proceed as follows. The next two sections will separately present the calculation of target lotsizes and the respective adaptation procedure. Section 8.5.3 will then show how the anticipation can be performed. Finally, Section 8.5.4 will again embed the entire approach into the general framework of hierarchical

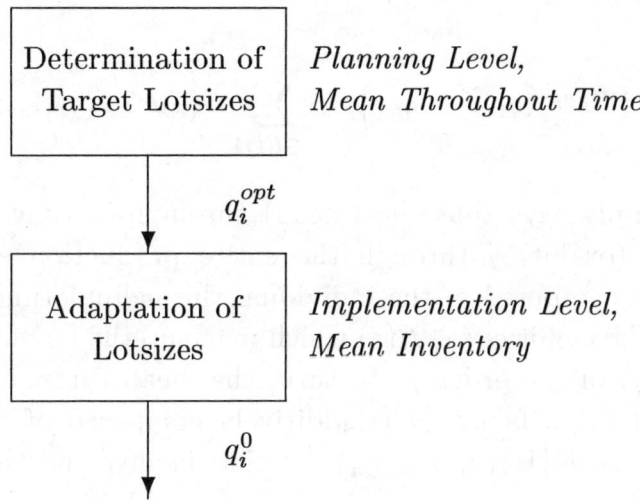

Fig. 8.7: Implementing Lotsizes as a Two-Stage Hierarchy

planning.

8.5.1 The Planning Level: Determination of Target Lotsizes

At the APP level, one obviously has not only to determine lotsizes but capacities as well. Since we are here mainly interested in the lotsize adaptation problem let us leave the determination of capacities aside. (For a more comprehensive presentation see [Söhner/Schneeweiss], [Söhner].)

As mentioned above, from a medium term point of view, the arrival of orders i, and hence of lots to be manufactured, must be described as a stochastic process. Consequently, let us modelize the entire production system as a queueing network and let us take the throughput time as the main optimization criterion. For lot $j\,(j = 1, \ldots, n)$ the expected throughput time TPT_j is given by

(8.6) $E\{TPT_j(q_1,\ldots,q_n)\} = \sum_{i \in R(j)} E\{TPT_{ij}(q_1,\ldots,q_n)\}$

which simply says that the (mean) throughput time TPT_j of an order (or lot) j through the entire production system is additively composed of the individual throughput times TPT_{ij} through the facilities $i \in R(j)$ which make up the manufacturing route $R(j)$ of the order j. In turn, the mean throughput time of a production facility i is additively composed of the mean waiting time $E\{W_i(q_1,\ldots,q_n)\}$ at that facility and the service time ST_{ij}

(8.7) $E\{TPT_{ij}(q_1,\ldots,q_n)\} = E\{W_i(q_1,\ldots,q_n)\} + ST_{ij}$

Obviously, the waiting time depends on all lotsizes $q_1, \ldots, q_n$ being involved. The service time, finally, can be obtained from

(8.8) $$ST_{ij} = p_{ij}q_j + s_{ij}$$

with p_{ij} being unit processing time and s_{ij} denoting the setup time of order j at machine i. (Note that according to the Just-in-Time principle all lotsizes q_j along route $R(j)$ are assumed to be identical, hence we dropped the index i at q_j.)

In view of Eq. (8.7), calculating the throughput time clearly amounts to determine the waiting time at the nodes of a queueing network. Taking into account all relevant data of the network, particularly those of the stochastic demand processes, one can use standard software (Queueing Network Analyzer [Whitt]) in establishing $E\{W_i(q_1,\ldots,q_n)\}$.

With the individual throughput times, the formulation of the optimization problem is now straightforward, following the consideration that lotsizes should be optimized with respect to the weighted mean of all possible orders. With MTPT being mean total throughput time, one finally has the following optimization problem for the (non-adapted) target lotsizes

$$E\{MTPT(q_1^{opt},\dots,q_n^{opt})\} =$$

$$= \min_{q_1,\dots,q_n} \sum_{j=1}^{N} \frac{n(j)}{\bar{n}} \sum_{i\in R(j)} E\{TPT_{ij}(q_1,\dots,q_n)\} \qquad (8.9)$$

with $\bar{n}$ being the total number of lots and $n(j)$ representing the amount of lots of type j $(j = 1,\dots,n)$.

8.5.2 The Implementation Level: Adaptation of Target Lots

Having calculated q_j^{opt} $(j = 1,\dots,n)$, let us now describe the adaptation procedure at the implementation level (see Fig. 8.7). Let us assume that the demand processes have been revealed so that we now have deterministic demands d_{jk} for an order of type j in period, k. (Note that period k is not necessarily identical with the period at the APP level.)

In adapting the (optimal) target lotsizes, our main concern will be the minimization of inventory costs. Setup costs need no longer be considered since they have mainly been taken into account by the capacities (see the above remark) and the throughput time. As an important consequence, the following optimization problem may be separated with respect to the order type j. Hence, the adaptation may optimally be achieved by the following dynamic program. With y_{jk} being the amount of inventory of type j in period k and T_{IM} being a short term implementation horizon, for each j, one minimizes total stock

$$\sum_{k=1}^{T_{IM}} y_{jk} \longrightarrow \min \qquad (8.10)$$

s.t. the static decision space to be defined below and the dynamics given by the inventory balance equation

(8.11) $$y_{jk} = y_{j,k-1} + u_{jk} - d_{jk} \qquad \forall k$$

(8.12) $$y_{jk} \geq 0 \quad \forall k.$$

The production quantity u_{jk} should result in the adapted lotsizes q_{jk}^0. Let us assume that these lotsizes are only allowed to deviate from the (optimal) target lotsizes q_j^{opt} by a percentage of a maximum of Δ_j, i.e.,

(8.13) $$q_{jk}^0 \in \{q_j^{opt}(1 - \Delta_j); q_j^{opt}(1 + \Delta_j)\} \forall k.$$

Obviously, the relationship between the optimal production quantity u_{jk}^0 and q_{jk}^0 is given by

(8.14) $$u_{jk}^0 = q_{jk}^0 f_{jk}$$

with f_{jk} being the setup frequency in period (week) k, i.e., f_{ik} denotes the number of lots of kind j to be produced in period k. Hence, the feasibility region for u_{jk}^0 can be expressed as

(8.15) $$u_{jk}^0 \in \cup_{f_j=0}^{f_j^{max}} \{f_j q_j^{opt}(1 - \Delta_j); f_j q_j^{opt}(1 + \Delta_j)\}$$

with f_j^{max} being defined as

(8.16) $$f_j^{max} = \left\lceil \frac{\sum\limits_{k=1}^{T_{IM}} d_{jk}}{q_j^{opt}(1 - \Delta_j)} \right\rceil$$

(and $\lceil x \rceil$ denoting, as usual, the smallest integer $\geq x$).

Optimizing (8.10), one obtains u_{jk}^0 which is an element of one of the intervals comprising the set (8.15) and which corresponds to a particular frequency. Let us call this frequency f_{jk}^0. Hence, one obtains for the optimally adapted lotsize

(8.17) $$q_{jk}^0 = \frac{u_{jk}^0}{f_{jk}^0}.$$

8.5.3 Anticipation

The approach described in the two preceding sections is of a pure top-down nature. As we know, however, it is one of the main concerns of an implementation theory to explicitly anticipate the implementation task in the planning activity. Following our general idea of implementation uncertainty, let us consider the adaptation as an additional source of randomness. In that case the medium term criterion (8.9) will be influenced by changed values of the mean processing time, and Eq. (8.8) has to be replaced with

$$E\{ST_{ij}\} = p_{ij}E(Q_j) + s_{ij} \tag{8.18}$$

where q_j is now replaced with the random variable Q_j. Moreover, the waiting time in Eq. (8.7) is influenced by the additional stochastics which requires not only the mean value of Q_j but also its variance.

To determine the probability distribution of the optimally adapted lotsizes Q_j^0, a risk analysis is necessary. This is performed in solving the short term optimization problem (8.10) through (8.16) for numerous values of demand d_{jk} being chosen from a probability distribution that is estimated at the medium term level.

Having recalculated all quantities for the medium term optimization problem (8.9), the optimally adapted (optimal) lotsize q_j^* can now readily be obtained in solving again (8.9). Note that q_j^* is depending on the adaptation range $\Delta_j : q_j^* = q_j^*(\Delta_j)$. Fig. 8.8 summarizes the described procedure.

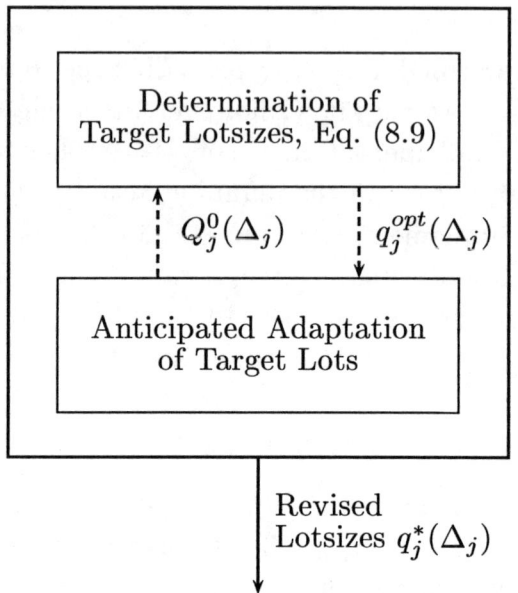

Fig. 8.8: Determination of Reviewed Targets

8.5.4 Description within the Framework of Hierarchical Planning

In describing the lotsize adaptation problem within the general framework of the implementation problem, one has the lotsize as the actual implementation. Besides the lotsize, however, the implementation level is endowed with a flexibility potential being expressed by the maximal percentage Δ_j of adaptation.

Hence, the top-level consists of two criteria:

- the throughput time criterion (8.9) denoted by

$$C_{TPT} := E\{MTPT(q_1,\ldots,q_n)|I^T\} \qquad \text{and}$$

- the adaptation criterion

$$C_\Delta = (C_{\Delta_1},\ldots,C_{\Delta_n}), \qquad \text{with} \quad C_{\Delta_j} := E\{Y_j(\Delta_j)|I^T\}$$

and $Y_j(\Delta_j)$ being the stochastic inventory level in view of the top-information I^T.

Hence, the top-criterion is given by

$$C^T := (C_{TPT}, C_\Delta).$$ (8.19)

Clearly, C^T only possesses top-down components. The top-decision is given by

$$a^T := (a_q^T, a_\Delta^T) \qquad \text{with}$$
$$a_q^T := (q_1, \ldots, q_n) \qquad \text{and} \qquad a_\Delta^T := (\Delta_1, \ldots, \Delta_n).$$

For the respective decision spaces, one has

$$A_q^T := \{q_j \in I\!N : 1 \le q_j \le Cumd_j, j = 1, \ldots, n\}$$
$$A_\Delta^T := \{\Delta_j \in I\!R : 0 \le \Delta_j \le 1, j = 1, \ldots, n\}$$

with $Cumd_j$ being the maximal possible cumulated demand for product j.

The anticipation function is the vector random variable

$$AF(a^T) := (Q_1^0, \ldots, Q_n^0).$$ (8.20)

Hence, the top-equation represents a two-criterion decision problem

$$a^{T*} = \arg \min_{a^T \in (A_q^T, A_\Delta^T)} \{C_{TPT}, C_\Delta\}$$ (8.21)

resulting in the (final) instruction

$$IN^* = (q_1^*(\Delta_1^*), \ldots, q_n^*(\Delta_n^*); \Delta_1^*, \ldots, \Delta_n^*)$$ (8.22)

with $q_j^*(\Delta_j^*)$ and Δ_j^* $(j = 1, \ldots, n)$ being the (two-criterion) optimal lotsizes and adaptation ranges, respectively.

The result (8.22) clearly shows that not only the target lotsizes have to anticipate the adaptation activity at the implementation level but, in addition, the flexibility range must be determined within which an adaptation is believed to be profitable. In fact, the larger Δ, the longer the throughput time will be, reducing the (market) flexibility of the system. (Considering a service degree flexibility measure, as proposed in Section 7.2, this nicely shows that for more complicated systems the size of the action volume cannot be related to flexibility in a straightforward way.) On the other hand, for large Δ, it will be easier to adapt target lotsizes to the actual demand situation and thus to reduce inventories.

Finally, the base-equation is given by

$$(8.23) \qquad a_j^{B^*} = \arg \min_{a_j^B \in A_{j,IN^*}^B} \sum_{k=1}^{T_{IM}} y_{jk}, \qquad j = 1, \ldots, n$$

with the base-criterion

$$C_j^B := \sum_{k=1}^{T_{IM}} y_{jk}, \qquad j = 1, \ldots, n$$

and deterministic demand as base-information status I^B. The general base-decision is defined as

$$a_j^B := \left(q_{j1}, \ldots, q_{j,T_{IM}}\right), \qquad j = 1, \ldots, n$$

and for the base-decision field one has

$$A_{j,IN^*}^B := \left\{(8.11) \wedge (8.12) \wedge (8.15)\right\}, \qquad j = 1, \ldots, n$$

with q_j^0 being replaced with $q_j^*(\Delta_j^*)$. As an overall final result one ends up with in the ultimate lotsize $q_{jk}^{**} = \frac{u_{jk}^{**}}{f_{jk}^{**}}$ with u_{jk}^{**} and f_{jk}^* being optimal values for the information situation at the time when the operational decision is actually made.

Chapter 9

Cost Accounting

As pointed out earlier, there exists a close relationship between cost accounting and hierarchical planning. In fact, many modern developments in cost accounting, like behavioral accounting or investment-oriented cost evaluations, can be extracted from the basic concepts of hierarchical planning. Up to now production and cost theory is still taken as a theoretical basis for cost accounting. This proved to be more or less sufficient as long as one considered traditional cost systems like full cost or direct cost systems. For modern production systems involving stochastics, dynamics, and even non-continuous variables, traditional cost theory, however, is a too narrow concept. This becomes even more obvious if one abandons the traditional one-person decision making paradigm and considers real management decision processes with more than one decision maker.

As modern cost accounting concepts which have a particular relationship to hierarchical planning, let us consider
– steering costs,

- investment-oriented costs,
- strategic costs,
- transactional incentive costs, and
- behavioral costs.

Steering Costs are specific opportunity costs that result from an insufficient representation of a system. They are used to adapt the optimal decisions derived in the insufficient representation to the criteria of the more comprehensive description.

Investment-oriented costs are closely related to steering costs. These are costs, like the rate of depreciation, that occur in a production model. Their value is determined such that the net present value (NPV) is optimized. To put it differently, investment-oriented cost values are derived from the well-established net present value criterion, thus relating medium term investment calculus to short term cost accounting (e.g., see [Küpper], [Hotelling]).

Strategic costs are used to evaluate, at least partially, strategic or tactical decisions. Target Costing (e.g., see [Sakurai]) and Activity Based Cost accounting (e.g., see [Cooper/Kaplan], [Kaplan/Atkinson]) may serve as prominent examples. The hierarchical aspect here is to combine strategic cost evaluations with short term cost concepts.

Incentive costs arise in principal agent settings that have already been discussed in Chapter 5 (e.g., see [Rajan]).

Behavioral costs are studied in behavioral accounting (e.g., see [Siegel/Ramanauskas-Markoni]) where costs are not primarily used for planning purposes but for leadership reasons. Costs are employed to motivate management permanently and thus are often leading to transformational changes of management's preference structure (see Fig. 2.5). Only these characteristics of a *transformational* change will be taken here as 'behavioral cost accounting'.

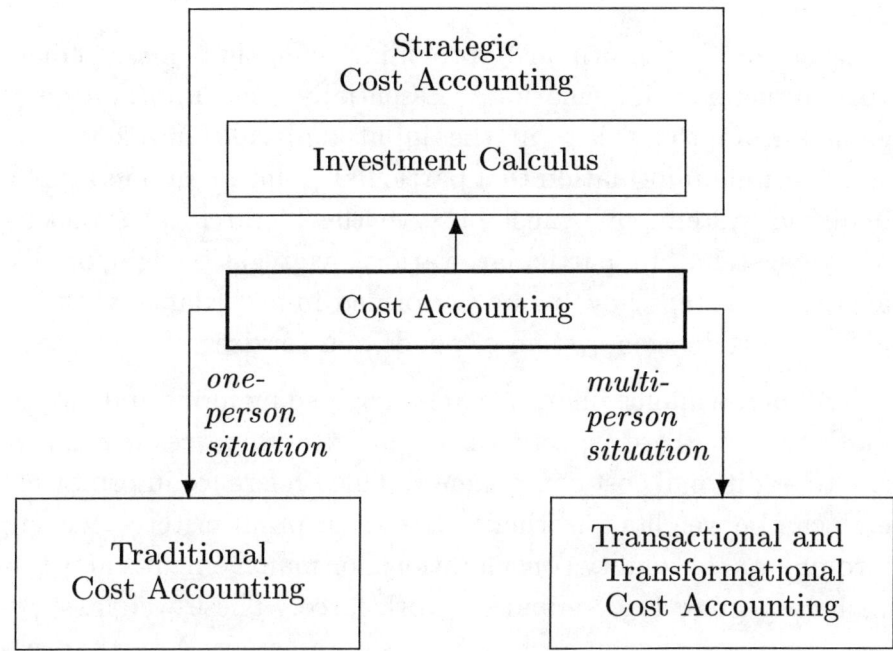

Fig. 9.1: Modern Trends in Cost Accounting

Fig. 9.1 summarizes some of the main directions in modern cost accounting. It shows the extension in the strategic direction and to multi-person situations. In particular, it points out that, for reasons of coordination, transactional or transformational costs must be taken into account. In addition, costs in relation to communication processes might occur which, however, will not be considered in this chapter. In fact, communication problems, particularly in the case of opportunistically behaving agents, break the framework of cost accounting and has to be treated in a broader context of managerial accounting.

9.1 General Considerations

Cost accounting is primarily providing operations management with preference information. Essentially, this information is gained from the prices in the input and sales markets. In transforming information to a particular point in an operational planning system, one must observe the hierarchical structure of the system. In particular, various aggregation and/or disaggregation steps have to be performed in accordance with the physical production system of goods and services.

Not all performance information is provided by input and output markets. There are aspects other than external prices which give rise to additional cost components. This preference information, e.g., can be weights for other than cost or profit criteria, like environmental or quality considerations, or management's attitude with respect to the company's work force. These weights play the role of so-called opportunity cost parameters. A further reason for such costs can be seen in replacing parts of a decision field with cost values: Transfer prices for the output of a company's subdivision give a prominent example. In all these cases an evaluation is necessary giving rise to a hierarchy in which the top-level determines the (optimal) value of the opportunity costs to be used at the base-level.

A further reason for hierarchical planning to be of relevance can be seen in the multi-person situation resulting in antagonistic or non-antagonistic interdependencies. Since, as we have seen in Chapter 5, agency problems can readily be described within the framework of hierarchical planning, its suitability to evaluate incentive costs is obvious, and the same holds true for costs that are used to inherently influence the other party's preference behavior.

In summarizing, the following hierarchies, depicted in Fig. 9.2, will be of importance in dicussing modern cost accounting.

We first consider the one-person or team situation (see Fig. 2.3) taking into account two types of hierarchies which are particularly related to steering costs, investment-oriented costs, and strategic costs, respectively ((1), (2), and (3) in Fig. 9.2). The last two types of costs, incentive and behavioral costs, will then be discussed within the framework of a non-team situation.

(1) First we investigate the case of symmetric information within a relaxation hierarchy. As in Section 3.2, the realistic (master) model describes the complete problem, whereas the decision generator is used to actually determine a decision. One applies steering parameters that can be adapted to the master model. If these parameters are cost parameters, their optimal value will be called **steering costs**.

(2) The second type of opportunity costs are those arising in a tactical-operational hierarchy, or, to be more specific, we are determining costs within an investment-production hierarchy. This hierarchy will usually be of the decision time type, and hence the information status is asymmetric. Section 9.3 will discuss these **investment-oriented cost** parameters in some detail.

(3) The hierarchy induced by the **strategic cost** concept will briefly be discussed for the case of Activity Based Costs in Section 9.4. The hierarchy one has to consider in this case is identical with the general strategic-operational hierarchy with the cost driver volumes being the instructions for the operational model.

(4) **Incentive costs** for an antagonistic agent are considered in utilizing the principal agent hierarchy of Fig. 9.2.

(5) Finally, **transformational costs** are determined within a leadership hierarchy giving rise to an intrinsic change of a non-antagonistic agent's preference structure. These costs will briefly be considered in Section 9.5.

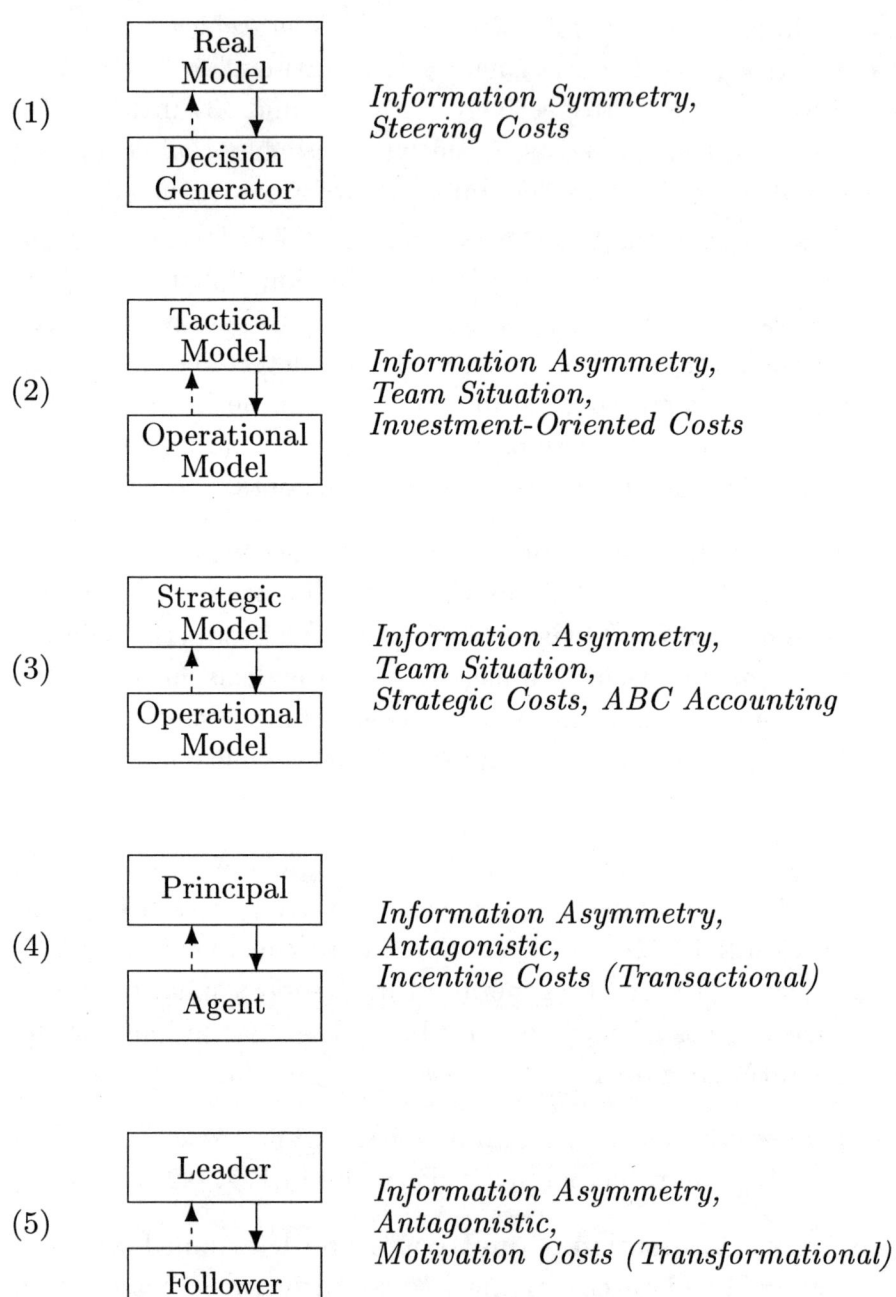

Fig. 9.2: Hierarchies and Costs

9.2 Steering Costs

Steering costs can be described within the general relaxation hierarchy of Section 3.2. Considering decision generators that only differ in the values of their cost parameters, one is looking for that set of cost parameters, or simply for that cost parameter $p = p^*$, which optimizes the criterion of the adjoint comprehensive master model (see Eq. (3.22a))

$$p^* = \arg \operatorname*{opt}_{p \in P} E\{C^{TB}(AF(p))|I^T\}. \tag{9.1a}$$

The top-criterion explicitly depends on the optimal solution $(AF(p))$ of the decision generator characterized by the cost parameter p

$$AF(p) = \arg \operatorname*{opt}_{a^B \in A^B} E\{C^B_p | I^B\}. \tag{9.1b}$$

To put it differently: The cost parameter is taken as an additional decision variable which is used (via parametric optimization) to adapt the decision generator to the original (master) model.

As can readily be seen, steering costs depend on both the formulation of the master model and the construction of the decision generator. Obviously, the master model describes the empirical situation, whereas the decision generator has only to generate promising solutions. Hence, it is highly important to carefully determine the master model. The better this model is determined, the less important is the empirical significance of the decision generator. This observation is often not enough taken into account. All too often one does not derive an empirically validated master model, instead one directly takes the decision generator and derives decisions to be implemented in practice without any pre-check by a more realistic description of the problem.

As a prominent example to illustrate this situation, consider the EOQ-model of inventory theory. This model in most cases is a rough approximation to reality, and although this fact is well-known the cost parameters are still determined from empirical data. This does not make much sense. The correct procedure to be adopted provides Eq. (9.1): First, derive a master model by truly describing the real-life inventory problem at hand. In particular, describe all empirically measurable financial quantities (like out of pocket costs) of the problem carefully. Second, derive the adjoint EOQ-model and calculate solutions. As a third step, evaluate these solutions with respect to the criterion of the empirical (master) model. Finally, use setup and holding costs (within the EOQ-model) as free parameters and optimize them, i.e., take those cost parameters that result in the best adapted EOQ-solution with respect to the empirically described inventory problem. These costs are then the steering costs of the EOQ-model.

This simple example is highly significant. It shows that the empirical parameters used in most of the formal models of Operations Research are not of empirical relevance and should not be extracted from empirical data. Rather it is necessary to construct an adjoint empirically realistic model providing a description such that the data have empirical significance.

For cost accounting this means that at the empirical (top-)level one has empirically measurable cash flows (out of pocket costs) while on the decision generator level the cost parameters usually are of no empirical relevance. They depend on the cash flow, not through a simple tracing procedure, but through the parameter adaptation process guided by Eq. (9.1).

Remark: A particular case occurs when the top-criterion is not only made up of cash flows but has multiple criteria that have to be taken into account by the decision generator. In that case, the decision generator generates solutions being used to solve the multi-criterion decision problem. The parameter $p = p^*$ for which a compromise is reached defines the steering costs. For cardinal criteria, multi-attribute utility theory (MAUT, [Keeney/Raiffa], [French]) may be used to derive a linear value aggregation. If one has, however, only ordinal criteria, the aggregation procedure can, in principle, no longer be solved in a rational way. This has as a consequence that for ordinal criteria there is no rational way of determining cost parameters (e.g., see [Arrow/Raynaud], [Zeleny]).

9.3 Tactical-Operational Cost Evaluation

The idea of 'tactical-operational' costs is similar to that of steering costs. In analogy to the hierarchy between the master model and the decision generator, the cost parameters for tactical-operational costs are selected through the tactical level relying on the optimal solution of the operational level. The coupling equations which describe this relationship are those of the tactical-operational model (see Eq. (4.7)) and can be stated as

$$a^{T^*} = \arg \operatorname*{opt}_{a^T \in A^T} E\{(C^{TT}(a^T) + C^{TB}(AF(p))) \mid I_{t_0}^T\} \quad (9.2a)$$

$$AF(p) = \arg \operatorname*{opt}_{\hat{a}^B \in \hat{A}_K^B} E\{\hat{C}_p^B(\hat{a}^B) \mid \hat{I}^B\} \quad (9.2b)$$

As a specification of the general case, the instruction depends on the investment K and a cost parameter p, $IN = (K, p)$. The cost parameter influences the base-criterion C_p^B, whereas the investment affects the base-decision field A_K^B. At the base-level, one has

$$a^{B^*} = a^{B^*}(p^*) = \arg \operatorname*{opt}_{a^B \in A_{K^*}^B} E\{C_{p^*}^B \mid I_{t_1}^B\}. \quad (9.2c)$$

As a particular case, one may take for the top-criterion the net present value (NPV) of an investment problem and for the base-model a production problem with the marginal contribution as base-criterion. The optimal production calculated from the production model provides the investment model with a positive cash flow resulting in a NPV which is then used to determine cost parameters of the production model. To illustrate this procedure let us consider the specific case of determining the rate of depreciation as a particular case of an investment-oriented cost evaluation.

9.3.1 Investment-Oriented Cost Evaluation

(1) Preliminary description

In illustrating the evaluation of the depreciation parameter, let us first give a rough outline. Consider an investment being evaluated by a NPV-criterion which, as is well-known, consists of negative and positive discounted cashflows. The effect of the investment on the production level is twofold. First, it provides the operational level with capacities and hence influences A^B. Second, it determines the rate of depreciation. Considering a depreciation within the short term model seems reasonable since production has to 'earn' the reinvestment depending on the use of the capacity. The utilization-oriented depreciation describes the loss in value of the investment depending on the use of the capacity.

This loss has to be taken into account in the production model. As is common practice, the rate of depreciation increases variable unit cost c by an additive constant c^a resulting in a rate of contribution margin $q - (c + c^a)$ with q being the unit price for sold goods at the operational level. (To avoid incompatabilities with the NPV, let us assume c to be out of pocket costs of the period in question.) With this base-criterion, an optimal production program is calculated resulting in a positive cashflow for the NPV.

Hence, in principle, we have the following hierarchical situation (see Fig. 9.3). The top-level determines, within an infinite investment chain, a rate of depreciation and transmits this value to the production model as an instruction. The production model, on its turn, is anticipated through its (estimated) positive cashflow influenced by the depreciation. Solving this problem allows to determine the rate of depreciation in an optimal way.

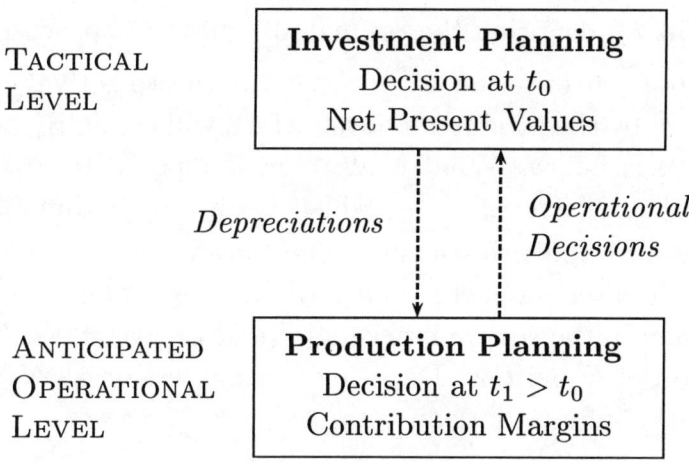

Fig. 9.3: Investment and Production Planning as a Tactical-Operational Hierarchy

(2) More detailed description

Let us now give a slightly more detailed description (see also [Eichin/Schneeweiss]). Let us consider a production facility which, after every D periods, is replaced by an identical facility resulting in an infinite investment chain. (Taking such an infinite chain simply avoids the problem of arbitrarily choosing an end condition.) Hence, the **top-equation** may readily be formulated as

(9.3a)

$$a^{T*} = \arg\operatorname*{opt}_{a^T \in A^T} \left[C^{TT}(a^T) + \sum_{t=1}^{D} C_t^{TB}(AF_t(a^T))\rho^t \right] \frac{1}{1-\rho^D}.$$

As usual (see (4.9a)), the private criterion C^{TT} stands for investment costs. In addition, it contains the (discounted) liquidation proceeds of the desinvested used fixed assets. Hence, one has

$$C^{TT}(a^T) := \hat{L}(K, D)\rho^D - A(K)$$

with $A(K)$ being the investment expenditure for investment K and $\hat{L}(K, D)$ denoting the estimated liquidation proceeds.

The top-down criterion C^{TB} evaluates the (positive) cashflow generated by the production level, which will explicitly be stated in Eq. (9.4) below. What is also new compared to Eq. (4.9) is the 'projection factor' $\frac{1}{1-\rho^D}$ which is due to the infinite cyclic repetition of the investment. The parameter $\rho = \frac{1}{1+i}$ is, as usual, the discount factor and i the interest rate. Clearly, the expression in the square brackets in (9.3a) represents a NPV for a horizon of D periods. Denoting this expression as NPV_1, one has for the infinite horizon

$$NPV_\infty = \sum_{t=0}^{\infty} NPV_1 \rho^{tD} = NPV_1 \frac{1}{1-\rho^D},$$

and hence the expression in Eq. (9.3a).

Together with the investment K, the duration D is a decision variable of the investment level, hence

$$a^T := (D, K),$$

and the **top-decision space** is

$$A^T := \{(D, K) : 0 \le D \le D^{max}, 0 \le K \le K^{max}\}$$

with D^{max} and K^{max} as given maximal values.

The investment model is defined on macro periods t, say years, being composed of $\bar{\tau}$ micro periods, say months, of the production model. Hence, the first micro period is $(1,1)$ and the last one is denoted as $(D, \bar{\tau})$. The linkage from one production model to the other is achieved, as usual, through

$$x_{t1}^L = x_{t-1,\bar{\tau}}^L + x_{t-1,\bar{\tau}} - \hat{d}_{t-1,\bar{\tau}},$$

where $x_{t\tau}^L$ stands for stock, $x_{t\tau}$ for production, and $\hat{d}_{t\tau}$ for forecast demand (see also Sec. 4.2.2).

The anticipated production criterion is simply the contribution margin (over the year t) adapted by the depreciation rate $c_{t\tau}^a$

$$\hat{C}_{t,c_t^a}^B = \sum_{\tau=1}^{\bar{\tau}} (\hat{q} - (\hat{c} + c_{t\tau}^a))\hat{x}_{t\tau}$$

with $\hat{q}$ being the estimated selling price, $\hat{c}$ the variable out of pocket cost per unit, and $c_{t\tau}^a$ as being defined below. Note that as inventory cost we only consider costs of bounded capital which are taken into account on the top-level by the NPV.

Thus as **anticipation function**, one readily obtains

$$AF_t = \hat{a}_t^{B^o}(c_t^a) = \arg \max_{\hat{a}_t^B \in \hat{A}_K^B} \hat{C}_{t,c_t^a}^B \qquad (9.3b)$$

with $\hat{a}_t^B := (\hat{x}_{t1}, \cdots, \hat{x}_{t\bar{\tau}})$, $c_t^a := (c_{t1}^a; \cdots, c_{t\bar{\tau}}^a)$, and $\hat{A}_K^B$ being a suitably defined base-decision field depending, of course, on the investment decision K.

Having determined the anticipation function $AF_t = \hat{a}_t^{B^o}$, we can now formulate the top-down criterion as

$$C_t^{TB} = \sum_{\tau=1}^{\bar{\tau}} (\hat{q} - \hat{c})\hat{x}_{t\tau}^0(c_t^a) - RM(\hat{\hat{x}}_t^0) \quad (t = 1, \ldots, D). \qquad (9.4)$$

Obviously, since C_t^{TB} needs to be a cashflow, the cost term does not contain the non-cashflow quantity c_t^a. In fact, $\hat{c}$ stands exclusively for out of pocket costs. The term $RM(\hat{\bar{x}}_t^0)$ defines the repair and maintenance payments. They are assumed to depend on the 'production history' $\bar{x}_t := (x_1, \dots, x_t)$ up to period t, with $x_{t'} := (x_{t'1}, \dots, x_{t'\bar{\tau}})$ for $t' \le t$. Clearly, repair and maintenance costs need to be considered in the investment equation, since they are reducing the contribution margin of the production level. In considering repair and maintenance costs we (simultaneously) assume that the capacity of the invested production facility is maintained irrespective of the actual use. Since these costs will usually increase with the (cumulated) utilization of the facility, a reinvestment turns out to be economically reasonable resulting in an optimal 'economic' life D^*.

Having explained almost all quantities of the two coupling equations (9.3a) and (9.3b), there still remains to define the quantity the whole effort is aiming at, namely the rate of depreciation. Let us adopt the following definition:

$$(9.5) \qquad c_{t\tau}^a := \frac{NPV'(\text{prod. in}(t, \tau)) - NPV'(\text{no prod. in}(t, \tau))}{\hat{x}_{t\tau}}$$

with NPV' being the discounted estimated outgoing cashflow of future payments induced by the production decision in t.

The difference in the numerator of Eq. (9.5) measures the (discounted) loss caused by a production $\hat{x}_{t\tau}$ in period (t, τ) as compared to the case of no production in that period. This definition connects the two hierarchical levels and ultimately allows a rational evaluation of the (utilization-oriented) depreciation rate as a cost parameter that guarantees an optimal reinvestment. In fact, $c_{t\tau}^a$ is part of the instruction for the operational level and must be optimized within a hierarchical algorithm determined by (9.3a), (9.3b), and (9.5). (For a more extensive discussion, see [Eichin/Schneeweiss].)

The second part of the **instruction** is made up by the duration D which determines the number of short term models that must be linked and simultaneously optimized to provide the investment model with the necessary positive cash flow. Thus D has only an indirect influence. The third part, of course, is the investment K. Hence,

$$IN = IN(a^T) = \Big((c_1^a, \ldots, c_D^a), K\Big).$$

Finally, for the (operational) base-model one may readily take (9.3b) with $IN = IN^*$ and all estimates replaced with their revealed values. In view of Section 4.2.2, let us take, as the **base-decision field** A_K^B, the following set of conditions

$$ax_{t\tau} \leq K \qquad \forall t, \tau \tag{9.6}$$

$$x_{t\tau}^L = x_{t,\tau-1}^L + x_{t,\tau-1} - d_{t,\tau-1} \quad \forall t, \tau = 2, \ldots, \bar{\tau} \tag{9.7}$$

$$x_{t1}^L = x_{t-1,\bar{\tau}}^L + x_{t-1,\bar{\tau}} - d_{t-1,\bar{\tau}} \quad \forall t \tag{9.8}$$

$$x_{t1}^L = x_{D\bar{\tau}}^L + x_{D\bar{\tau}} - d_{D\bar{\tau}} \tag{9.9}$$

$$x_{t\tau}^L, x_{t\tau} \geq 0 \qquad \forall t, \tau \tag{9.10}$$

with (9.6) being the capacity relation defining, as usual, the coupling inequality of the top-model and the base-decision field. Eqs. (9.7), (9.8), and (9.9) are material balance equations with (9.7) describing the material flow within a year, (9.8) between the years, and Eq. (9.9) closes the investment cycles. In particular, Eq. (9.10) does not allow for stock outs ($x_{t\tau}^L \geq 0$) which, for a medium term production model, is a reasonable postulate. As in Section 4.2.2, of course, one could have not just one but several products and instead of known demand, forecasts could have been used.

Remark: Defining the depreciation rate $c_{t\tau}^a$ by the expression (9.5) is not compelling. Other definitions could be used. In particular, disregarding its economic meaning, one could consider

$c_{t\tau}^a$ as a steering cost parameter (see Sec. 9.2) and could apply a 'free search'. From this point of view, one could regard (9.5) as an iteration device defining a special search. Having this in mind, optimal depreciations might not be the best steering costs one could determine.

Occasionally it is argued that determining optimal depreciation rates is only of limited significance. It only shows that cost accounting is, in principle, capable of yielding the (overall) optimal NPV. To obtain the depreciation rate, the adjoint investment problem would have to be solved. Hence, rather than determining $c_{t\tau}^a$, one could have employed the investment calculus straight away. This type of argument is definitely wrong, and it is one the main contributions of hierarchical planning to be able to show that both levels are necessary. As has been pointed out, the depreciation rate was determined on the top-level using information and approximations at that level. No operational decision had actually been made. These cost-dependent decisions are made at a later point in time using possibly more recent information and are thus decoupled from the investment level. In addition, note again that the formalism of hierarchical planning with its re-evaluation device C^{TB} is perfectly suited to separate the cost level from the cashflow-dependent investment level.

9.4 Strategic Costs

Let us contribute only a brief remark on the hierarchical character of ABC accounting which is one of the most prominent strategic cost systems. ABC accounting as a strategic instrument separates the short term volume related cost evaluations from more general strategic evaluations (see [Cooper/Kaplan]). In doing so, one determines cost drivers which determine the overhead capacity usage of a (strategic) decision. The amount of a cost driver can then be taken as a measure for the overhead costs the particular driver is incurring. Thus overhead capacities are not traced down to the operational level of single items but only to more aggregate quantities (like cost drivers). On the other hand, strategic decisions often have an impact on operational decisions. Hence, in a second step, it is necessary to allocate cost driver costs to operational cost objects (like items or lots) [Schneeweiss (1998)].

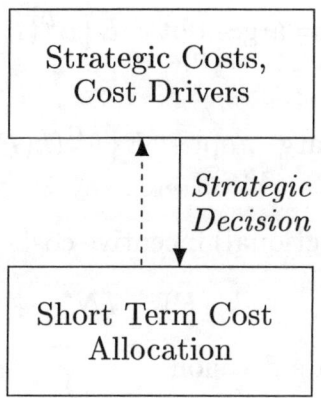

Fig. 9.4: Two-Step Cost Allocation

Fig. 9.4 clearly shows the explained two-step character of the cost allocation. Rather than tracing overhead costs directly to single items, as it is done within the traditional full cost systems, ABC supports strategic decisions which, on the operational level, induce a short term cost allocation. Obviously, for an important operational level, this pure top-down approach would not be adequate, and it would indeed be necessary to anticipate the operational cost consequences within the strategic decision.

9.5 Incentive and Transformational Costs

(1) Incentive Costs

In Chapter 5, we optimized incentives within the framework of a hidden action situation. What remains here is to repeat the coupling equations (5.6), with the general incentive $\phi(P)$ being replaced with incentive costs

$$k(P) \equiv \phi(P).$$

Hence, in view of the definitions given in Section 5.2, one has

$$(9.11a) \qquad k^*(P) = \arg \operatorname*{opt}_{k(P) \in A^T} E\{u^T(P - k(P)) \mid I^T\},$$

$$(9.11b) \quad AF(k) = \arg \operatorname*{opt}_{\hat{a}^B \in \hat{A}^B_{k(P)}} E\{\hat{u}^B(k(P) - \hat{V}(a^B)) \mid \hat{I}^B\}.$$

The optimal (transactional) incentive costs define the instruction

$$k^*(P) = IN^*$$

and imply the agent's decision

$$(9.11c) \qquad a^{B^*}(k^*) = \arg \operatorname*{opt}_{a^B \in A^B_{k^*}} E\{u^B(k^* - V(a^B)) \mid I^B\}.$$

Eq. (9.11c) again exhibits the different character of costs within a multi-person setting. They are not used for mere planning purposes but for coordinating the actions of different decision makers.

(2) Transformational costs

Transformational costs are intrinsically motivating a decision maker. They are actually changing his or her preference structure (or utility function). The general coupling equations (2.5) may therefore be written (see also (3.22) or (9.1)) as

$$(9.12a) \quad a^{T^*} = \arg \operatorname*{opt}_{a^T \in A^T} E\{C^T(C^{TT}(a^T), C^{TB}(AF(p))) \mid I^T\}$$

$$AF(p) = \arg \operatorname*{opt}_{\hat{a}^B \in \hat{A}^B} E\{\widehat{\widetilde{C}}_p^B (\hat{a}^B) \mid \hat{I}^B\} \qquad (9.12b)$$

with $\widehat{\widetilde{C}}_p^B$ denoting an estimate of the base-criterion changed by the transformational effect of the cost value p. Again, $p^* = IN^*$ is a motivational steering cost parameter.

PART III

Leadership

Part III will be devoted to a discussion of general leadership questions that can be treated within the framework of hierarchical planning and distributed decision making. Of course, only a few aspects can be touched, particularly those that lend themselves to a comparatively simple description within the formal concept of hierarchical interactions.

At several occasions we already encountered leadership issues, particularly in Chapter 5 on agency problems and in Chapter 8 on implementation questions. In principal agent hierarchies, the principal is offering incentives, and within the framework of implementation strategies, we explicitly formulated leadership activities as an additional component of the instruction (e.g., see LA in Fig. 8.3). In fact, both strategies are coping with leadership problems from a different angle. While in agency theory communication aspects play a predominant role, one has for implementation activities more the problem of how an instruction is actually processed by the (implementing) base-level. In both cases, however, the base-level still plays a more or less passive role. It is only described through the top-level's anticipative planning activities.

For a general discussion of leadership questions the base-level should be allowed some reaction, possibly initiating a negotiation between the levels. Hence, leadership questions need an extension of general planning hierarchies (see Fig. 2.3) in at least three directions:

– One should achieve a more explicit description of the base-level, particularly of the way how the base-level is processing the top-level's instructions,
– the leadership instructions of the top-level should be described in more detail, and finally
– the communication process between the levels should be analyzed more carefully.

In what follows, these three requirements will lead, in Chapter 10, to a reformulation of the coupling equations (2.5), extending general hierarchical planning settings to hierarchical configurations (see Fig. 2.3). This extension will provide an adequate framework within which typical leadership activities, such as coordinations and negotiations, can conveniently be described, as will be shown in detail in Chapters 11 and 12, respectively.

Particular emphasis will be put on the discussion of the different kinds of instruction and the way how the base-level is handling them. In doing so, it proves to be adequate to raise the theory, we have developed so far, to a higher level of conceptualization. This enhancement will be achieved in representing the involved decision makers (i.e., the levels) by their individual decision processes, so that the coupling equations will not describe the intervention of just a single top- and a base-model but will involve complete segments of the interfering decision processes.

Chapter 10

Hierarchical Configurations

Up to now we have confined our presentation to general planning hierarchies as they were introduced in Chapter 2 (see Fig. 2.3). They were characterized as hierarchies that do not allow the base-level to react. The *possibility* of such reactions, however, was anticipated and taken into account by the top-level decision maker. Thus, in general, it turned out to be necessary to carefully estimate and forecast the base-level's behavior.

We are now in a position to surpass this comparatively narrow setting and to include actual reactions of the base-level. From a practical point of view, this means an extension of hierarchical planning to the situations before and after the actual planning activity. Prior to the concrete planning task, there will often be some negotiations allowing the top-level to attain some knowledge about the base-level's position and opinions. From a leadership perspective, such 'negotiations' are typical of an involvement of all parties in the mutual decision process. On the other hand, if a hierarchical planning decision has been made, ex post reactions might be of interest, particularly in cases when decisions are made within a rolling horizon scheme. Thus, an extension to negotiations will considerably enrich the pure planning perspective.

From a more formal point of view, taking into account actual reactions of the base-level, means an enhancement of the simple top-down instruction to at least one full cycle, incorporating the base-reaction and a real bottom-up influence (see Fig. 10.1). Of course, to describe actual negotiations, usually several cycles would have to be considered.

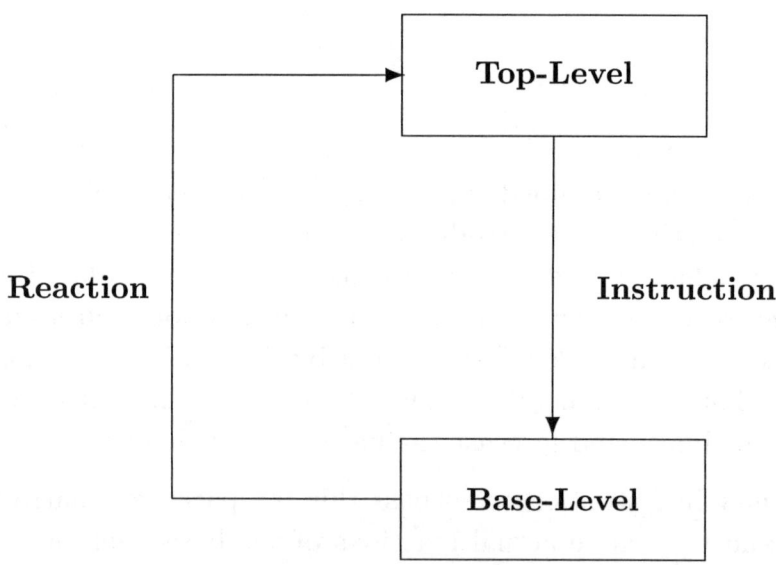

Fig. 10.1: Negotiation Cycle

Fig. 10.1 is just a simplified version of Fig. 2.1 which straightly had been reduced to the hierarchical planning situation of Fig. 2.4. Now, for the more comprehensive setting of hierarchical configurations (comprising general hierarchies and negotiations),

Fig. 10.1 or Fig. 2.1 will not be reduced, so that a reformulation of the coupling equations is necessary. The hierarchical character of these equations will no longer be that obvious, and it will be necessary to describe the base-level more carefully than it has been done so far. In fact, the whole theory has to be raised to a higher level of conceptualization containing hierarchical planning as a special case. Or, to put it differently and less formally, hierarchical planning has to be extended to a structural theory which allows to comprise at least some of the issues leadership has to deal with.

Up to now we have restricted our discussion to cognitive relations. For leadership questions, however, this is a too narrow perspective. In fact, in addition to negotiation processes, we need to extend the analysis to non-cognitive notions, like power, charisma or enthusiasm. Following the general procedure in leadership theory, however, we try to describe non-cognitive relations through the cognitive results they are provoking. In doing so, the general framework will be maintained having as an important consequence that hierarchical planning and leadership problems can be discussed within the same hierarchical setting.

To arrive at such a more comprehensive view, let us consider hierarchical configurations as interactions of individual decision processes. Hence, in Section 10.1, let us first briefly explain the main features of an individual decision process and let us then, in Section 10.2, derive the general coupling equations of such an interaction. Since these coupling equations do not only describe negotiations but simultaneously present a more elaborate way of interaction, they will enable us to model leadership relations more profoundly than we could do in Chapter 8 within the context of the implementation problem.

10.1 The Individual Decision Process

10.1.1 General Two-Step Structure

An individual decision process may be described as a sequence of decision models. Running through some kind of learning process, these models are continuously reformulated, finally reaching a stage which provides an acceptable solution to the problem at hand. At least for quantitative decisions, this process usually has a two-stage structure (see Fig. 10.2).

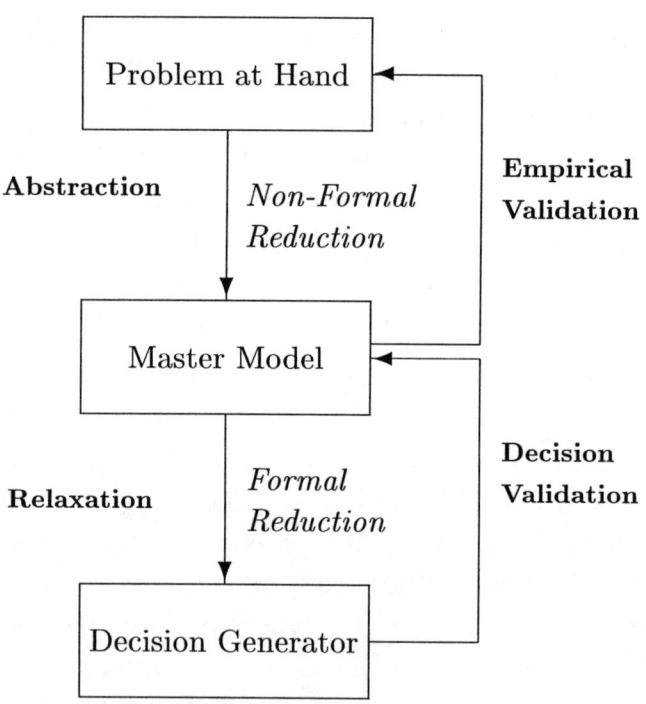

Fig. 10.2: Two-Stage Structure of the Decision Process

Starting with an often not well-defined problem at hand, one tries to substantialize those aspects of the problem one believes to be of major relevance.   As a result of this **abstraction process** one arrives at a **master model** that gives a first, fairly comprehensive description of the problem. For a quantitative analysis, however, the master model will usually be far too complicated to be manipulated in a formal way.   Hence, a second (formal) reduction step is added resulting in a **decision generator** whose single task it is to generate decisions. This reduction is known as **relaxation** and has already been described in Section 3.2.

The abstraction process is related to **real constructional hierarchies**, while the relaxation process is evolving within a (formal) **relaxation hierarchy** (see Fig. 10.2).   As mentioned in Section 3.2, for quantitative planning tasks in Operations Research, the relaxation process with its two hierarchical levels described by the master model and the decision generator, is of essential significance. Particularly, the parameter adaptation, giving rise to the important notion of steering costs, plays an essential role in cost accounting and quantitative decision making (see Sec. 9.2).

The two stages of the general decision process differ in their way of processing the information. The abstraction process concentrates only on relevant information and discards or not even registrates information that does not seem to be of importance. The relaxation process, on the other hand, does only temporarily disregard some information. In fact, in adapting the solution of the decision generator to the master model, one again relies on the full information available in that model.

Accordingly, the validation task of a decision process is split up into two main steps.   The master model, as a result of the abstraction process, is validated *empirically*, that is, single empirical hypotheses of that model are tested with respect to their empirical validity.   In contrast, for the decision generator only a so-called **decision validation** can be achieved (see Fig. 10.2). I.e., only that decision generator is accepted which provides the best solution with respect to the master model. Thus, the decision generator is merely used to *generate* decisions whereas the master model has the (passive) task of *selection*. Consequently, the master model need not be described completely, in fact, it should only be able to select a given decision. Often its decision space will not totally be known and one will have only a limited knowledge of the criterion, which is particularly true for the weights of the objectives. Within a multi-criterion decision problem, such weights can reasonably be fixed by the decision maker only together with the decisions generated by the decision generator.

In general, let us refer to the master model as representing the **empirical level**, while the decision generator makes up the adjoint **formal level**.

10.1.2 A More Refined Description

(1) The cycle process

Obviously, the individual decision process is not that simple as depicted in Fig. 10.2. The learning process has to undergo many loops in which not only the decision field is improved but also the preferences by which decisions are selected. In abstract terms, such a loop may be represented as in Fig. 10.3.

One of the crucial points of a decision process is the formulation of **aspiration levels** AL_κ. As explained earlier, these are critical values of a criterion the decision maker wants to reach, in any case. Considering the decision process, the criterion C_κ does not only consist of components which evaluate the performance with respect to the problem at hand but it also consists of components that characterize the decision process itself, like information costs or planning time. Hence, aspiration levels are of essential significance for the process. They are the reason for a possible **discrepancy** (or deviation) $DIS(C_\kappa^*, AL_\kappa)$ between the optimal value C_κ^* of the criterion and the aspiration level AL_κ. Only if this discrepancy can be removed, i.e.,

$$DIS_\kappa = DIS_\kappa(C_\kappa^*, AL_\kappa) \leq 0,$$

the whole process can terminate, and a final decision will be made and implemented.

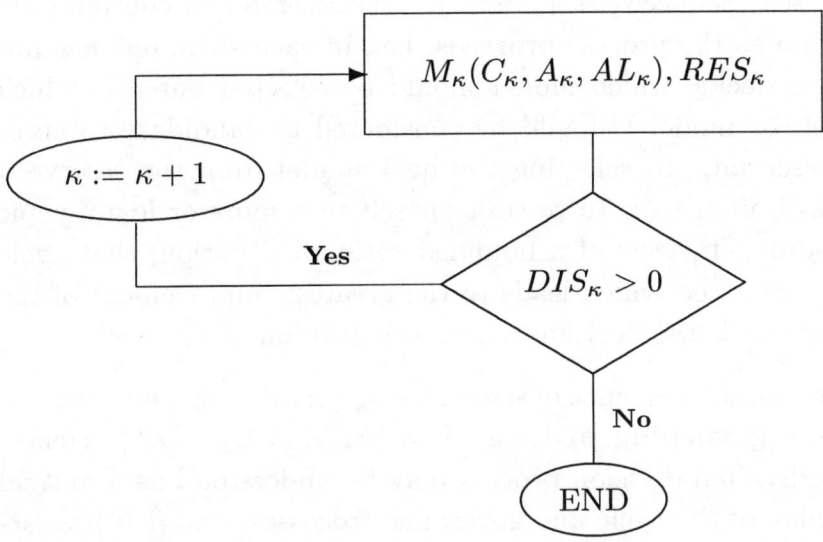

Fig. 10.3: Cycle Process

Fig. 10.3 describes the situation of stage κ of the entire process. Let us call M_κ and its transition to a new model $M_{\kappa+1}$ a **cycle** Z_κ, and consequently let us denote the sequence of all those cycles the **cycle process** $Z := \{Z_\kappa : \kappa = 1, \dots, \kappa^*\}$ with κ^* indicating the model that is actually used to determine the final decision.

One of the most crucial problems is the 'meta-decision problem' of selecting the next cycle ($\kappa + 1$ in Fig. 10.3). Of course, for an unbounded rational decision maker, there would not be a problem. All possible future cycles would be known, and one could select the best sequence of cycles. In fact, the whole process could be viewed as a (dynamic) optimal stopping process (e.g., see [Schneeweiss (1992)]). For bounded rationality, the situation is far more restrictive. One can assume, however, that in stage κ the decision maker is able to look ahead into the near future such that she/he knows at least some small segment of the set of all possible future cycles. This segment will be called reservoir RES_κ. (To a certain extent it is comparable with the changing set of rules of a rule based *learning* Expert System (e.g., see [Schneeweiss (1992)].) The reservoir is continuously built up as the process proceeds, i.e., in each stage one has not only to decide which model should be selected but also which model (or models) should be considered as candidate to enter the reservoir. In selecting the next model from the reservoir, one will often have to restrict oneself to a more or less myopic procedure. In view of a bounded rational situation, that cycle will be selected which leads to the greatest improvement of the general goals the decision maker has in mind at stage κ.

Let us call the sequence of selections S_κ (of cycle Z_κ and reservoir R_κ) the **governing process** $G := \{S_\kappa, \kappa = 1, \ldots, \kappa^*\}$. Hence, the individual decision process may be understood as a mutual interplay of the cycle and governing processes, *and it is precisely through the governing process that a second (hierarchically related) decision maker may interfere.*

(2) Types of hypotheses

The cycles can be very different in nature. During the abstraction phase, and particularly for the first steps, the cycles may be less precisely defined than in the relaxation stage. In fact, the whole process represents a learning process in which one learns from the experiences with earlier cycles. In this process, especially in the abstraction phase, it is essential to operationalize not well-defined properties and to clarify the goals (preferences) the

decision maker would like to follow. To gain some insight into this crucial problem, let us differentiate between three types of statement:
- hard facts,
- solid facts, and
- vague hypotheses.

Hard facts can be measured without any difficulties. One may think, for instance, of certain quantities defining the physical structure of the problem (like numbers of items or facilities), institutional and legal requirements, certain well defined (exogeneous) economic parameters or unalterable (ex ante) prescriptions by the decision maker or instructions of a (hierarchically related) external decision maker.

Solid facts are similarly easy to specify. Those facts shall be called solid, for which, in principle, an empirical specification is possible, i.e., for which the empirical data-basis is sufficiently large.
As simple examples consider the specification of a particular stochastic process or of a linear production function.

Vague hypotheses will be called all statements that are not hard or solid. Especially for situations characterized by rapidly and non-stationary changing information, it will, in general, be extremely difficult to obtain projections for the time at which the so-called **final decision** has to be implemented and is in operation. The same is true for the description of an antagonist's behavior which, in general, will only be known in 'vague terms'.

A vague hypothesis may be taken as a statement which ultimately has to be operationalized, i.e., all vague expressions have to be made measurable at least to the degree necessary for the purpose one has in mind. In particular, all uncertainties have to be measured by (subjective) probabilities or, in case of fuzziness, by membership functions. Usually, in real-life situations, vague hypotheses cannot be avoided. They are typical at least of the first (often not well-defined) cycles of a decision process. Indeed, it is one of the main tasks of the decision process gradually to transform a vague messy situation into a well-defined decision model.

There are different degrees of operationalization which may easily be explained with an example. Consider the following statement: "In the near future the situation of the company will improve considerably." Operationalizing this vague expression, one has at least to clarify the meaning of "near future", "situation", and "improve considerably". In many situations, people simply 'know' what is meant by these expressions at least with respect to the purpose the statement is pursuing. This is due to the fact that often a specific vague statement was used in the past or, for the present problem, in a different context, so that a whole network of statements is delimiting its meaning. This characterization will then be used within a decision process. Let us call this type of indirect operationalization *'horizontal semantics'*.

A completely different situation occurs if one tries to operationalize each single expression in regressively posing questions like: "What is the meaning of ...?", that is, if one tries to rely on quantities being measurable more easily. This way of clarifying the meaning of a vague hypothesis may be denoted as 'vertical semantics'.

Obviously, in the case of horizontal semantics, the meaning of an expression depends on the entire context. For vertical semantics, at least at a first glance, this seems not to be necessary. In general, however, this is only true to a certain extent. Operationalizing vertically opens an additional dimension of knowledge, but it is clear that in general various operationalizations are possible and, furthermore, that the detailed knowledge must again be recombined, and here, at the latest, some kind of horizontal semantics is again involved. Thus, it turns out that operationalizing vague knowledge may be interpreted as a hierarchical process in which the upper level with its often only verbal and holistic description has to be combined with a lower level at which a more analytic approach is applied. Which of the levels will prove to be the more predominant depends, of course, on the purpose one is pursuing (see also remark (3) of Section 6.3.3).

Vague hypotheses and their operationalization or interpretation play an important role in leadership. This is due to the fact that instructions (or reactions), particularly those of a non-cognitive (emotional) nature, are often only vague devices that need to be interpreted by the other level. Again it should be stressed that an interpretation usually cannot be performed in considering merely a small part of the problem, in fact, all features that might be of some relevance must be taken into account.

10.1.3 The Entire Decision Process

Having clarified the meaning of a typical cycle, let us now return to the entire decision process. The flow diagram of Fig. 10.4 gives a general impression. It shows a general cycle which simultaneously covers the abstraction and the relaxation phase and, as a specific case, cycles that are solely restricted to one of the phases. Each cycle is closed in checking whether the aspiration levels are reached or not. If they are reached, the final decision can be made, that is, an 'instruction' is leaving the process for implementation.

If, on the other hand, a discrepancy still remains, the governing process selects a new cycle from the reservoir. Within the abstraction phase, the governing process is primarily concerned with two problems: first, creating a new operationalization and, second, adapting the aspiration levels. Both tasks are closely related to each other. Considering new operationalizations, in most cases results in a reformulation of aspiration levels. On the other hand, if aspiration levels are changed, other aspects not taken into account before might be of importance, possibly implying a new operationalization.

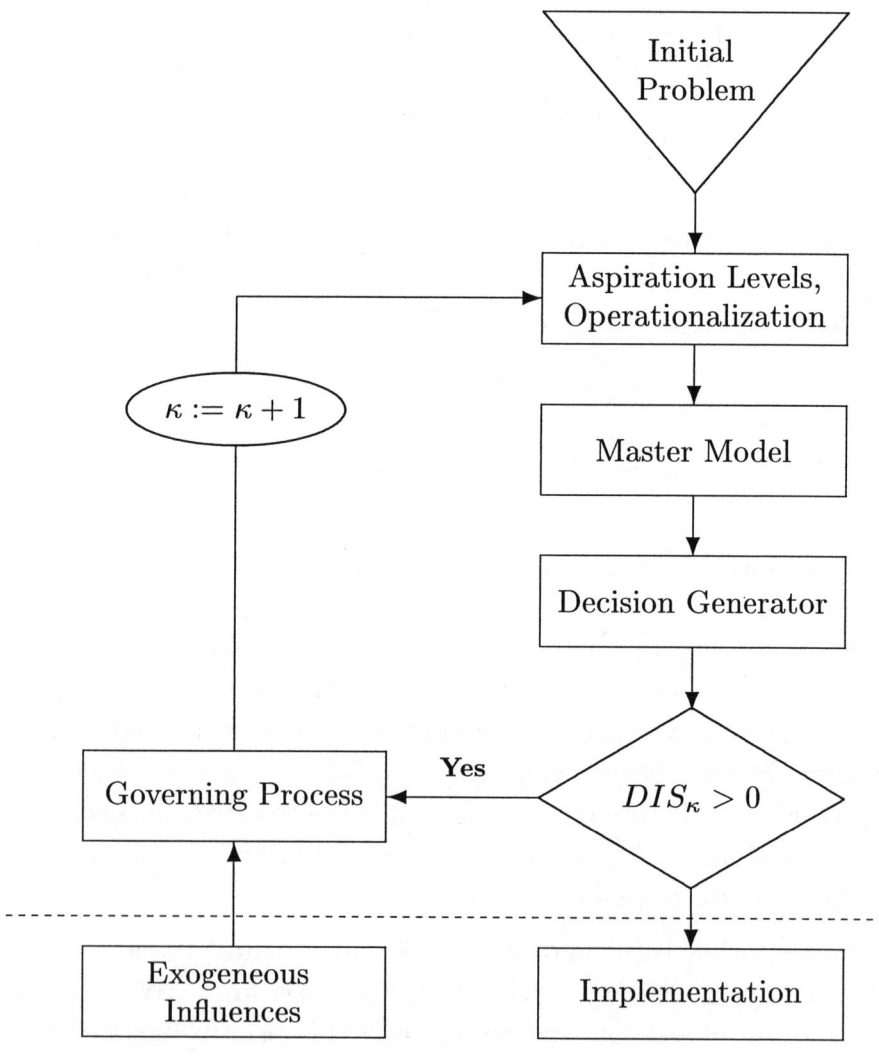

Fig. 10.4: The Entire Individual Decision Process

As mentioned before, the choice of an aspiration level is one of the most crucial tasks during a decision process. Starting with very general vague cycles, the process progressively gets to know its own proficiency and is experiencing external constraints. Setting aspiration levels particularly means for the decision maker to consider the entire development of the process and the insight she/he has gained thus far. Asking to state some aspiration levels implicitly assumes the decision maker to possess some knowledge of a possible outcome of the whole procedure. Like in the early stages of a cost-benefit analysis, often some crude decision alternatives may be known, possibly employing some kind of incremental analysis. It is precisely the purpose of the decision process to generate an increasing number of possible solutions for an 'evolving' problem which consequently will lead simultaneously to more refined aspiration levels.

In summary, the entire decision process generally starts with cycles that are not well defined and which are predominantly located in the abstraction phase. In proceeding, the cycles are becoming more and more precise and are shifting to the relaxation phase. Holistic arguing is progressively replaced with a more analytic style of investigation. The whole process can be viewed as a hierarchical system in that the decisions made at a particular cycle (i.e., level) depend on earlier cycles and on the anticipation of future cycles. For strategic decisions, in most cases, a too precise operationalization is not appropriate. Therefore the decision process stops at an earlier cycle.

The hierarchical nature of the decision process is of significant importance. Analytic models evolve from more holistic descriptions through the distinct interface of only two quantities, the instruction and the anticipation. No 'naive' operationalization is performed destroying the cycles autonomy (see also the discussion of Section 6.3.3).

The exchange with the environment is made by the implementation and the governing process. Hence, another decision maker might influence all parts of the process, in particular the aspiration levels and the way how the multi-criterion decision problem is solved in reducing the aspiration levels. The following section will discuss these questions in more detail. (For an earlier and to some extent more comprehensive version of the individual decision process the reader is referred to [Schneeweiss (1987)].)

10.2 A Formal Description of Hierarchical Configurations

10.2.1 The Interaction of Individual Decision Processes

Having explained the main features of an individual decision process, it is now straightforward to describe the relationship between two decision makers formally. Let us first assume the two parties to be equally ranked. Hierarchical elements will later be introduced according to further elaborations of the theory.

As depicted in Fig. 10.4, the interface between the two levels is achieved through the implementation activity defining the output, and the governing process representing the input unit. An interference of the individual decision processes may occur in any stage of the processes. To attain a formal description, let us consider the top- and the base-processes

$$P^T := \left\{ M_\kappa^T : \kappa = 1, 2, \ldots \right\} \quad \text{and} \quad P^B := \left\{ M_\kappa^B : \kappa = 1, 2, \ldots \right\},$$

respectively. If the top-process is in some stage $\kappa = k$ in state M_k^T, its decision $a_k^T \in A_k^T$ implies an instruction IN_k^* for the base-process, being in some state M_k^B. The base-level takes this instruction into consideration and, possibly after some cycles ΔP^B, communicates a reaction RE_k^* to the top-level (see Fig. 10.5). This reaction is perceived by the top-level, and, again possibly after some top-cycles ΔP^T, a new instruction is developed and passed down to the base-level.

As indicated in Fig. 10.4, both cycles interfere through their governing processes, i.e., they influence the other party's selection of the next cycle, and hence of the next decision model and the reservoir. In doing so, each level may interpret (and operationalize) the other's instruction. Instructions of a specific far-reaching nature are those concerning the other level's process-related aspiration levels. They, in particular, may give the other process a significant (strategic) direction.

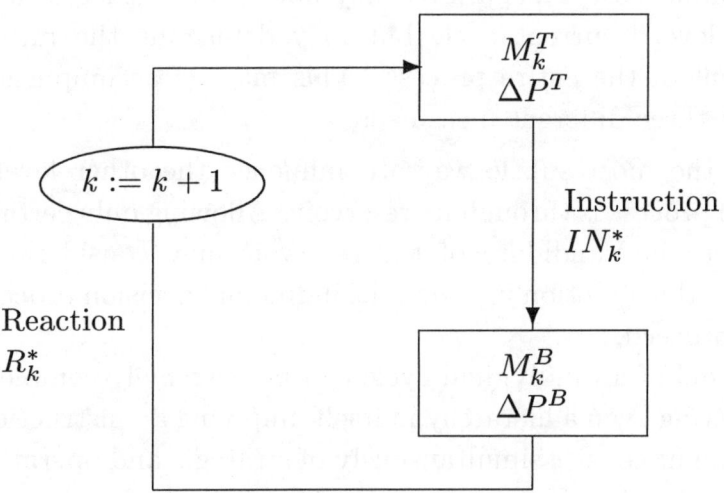

Fig. 10.5: The Coupling Process

Let us call the complete communication cycle a **coupling cycle** and the process of all these cycles the **coupling process**. This process which in fact describes a negotiation, generally consists of the interacting communications IN_k^* and RE_k^*, and of some individual cycles ΔP^T and ΔP^B the decision processes proceed on their own. These individual cycles are needed to determine optimal instructions IN_k^* and reactions RE_k^*. In particular, they have to perform the necessary anticipations giving rise to hierarchical algorithms, i.e., to individual cycles to be passed in the relaxation phase (see Chapter 3 on constructional hierarchies). It seems to be obvious that in many situations there will be a trade off between the number of coupling cycles and the individual cycles. The tighter the information exchange during a negotiation is, the less effort is needed to anticipate the other party's possible behavior. In fact, in many cases a hierarchical algorithm being applied to calculate $a_k^{T^*}$ or $a_k^{B^*}$ may be interpreted as a hypothetical negotiation, thus internalizing an external process.

The interactions IN_k^* or RE_k^* of a coupling cycle can exert far reaching influences. Thus a level may not just influence locally the other level's current cycle but may determine the future development of the entire process. This may be accomplished by at least three different measures:

1. One of the most subtle ways to influence the other level's decision process is through its reservoir. Allowing only certain models to be candidate of the reservoir may considerably influence the direction in which the individual decision process has to proceed.

2. The model of an individual cycle can be extremely complex, representing even a hierarchy in itself, implying an instruction which might consist simultaneously of strategic and operational components. Hence, in particular, it might be through the strategic components that the long term development of the other level is influenced.

3. In Section 10.1 it was argued that not only problem-related attributes may influence an individual decision process but process-related attributes as well. These attributes, like planning time, information costs, implementation friendliness, etc., may have far-reaching consequences. They will often imply multiple instructions such that each component represents a conditional instruction for a future cycle of the others' process. These components may be determined as decisions

that have been applied during an anticipative hierarchical algorithm and may thus be understood as a projection of the inner world (of a level) onto the external real-life situation (represented by the other level).

In general, the communications IN_k^* and RE_k^* will not always be clearly defined guidelines but must be interpreted and operationalized. In doing so, some freedom will be left to the subordinate level which, of course, will be limited such that possible interpretations are still compatible with the leading level's own ideas. It is exactly these limitations one has to communicate either in one step, possibly influencing all future cycles of the subordinate process at once, or during a negotiation process. In fact, the negotiation procedure described in Chapter 12 may serve as an example.

10.2.2 The General Coupling Equations

A conceptual formalization of the preceding considerations is now straightforward. Let us proceed according to the more elementary formalizations of the general planning situation depicted in Fig. 2.4. The general coupling process of Fig. 10.5 may serve as a starting point. Replacing the individual process segments ΔP^T and ΔP^B by some interior anticipative cycles, one readily obtains, as an 'operationalization' of Fig. 10.5, the more detailed description of Fig. 10.6.

For a symmetric description, we now use anticipations at each level denoted by $ANT^T(M^B)$ and $ANT^B(M^T)$, and accordingly one has the anticipation functions $AF^T(IN)$ and $AF^B(RE)$. Hence, $AF_k^T(IN_k)$ represents an (optimal) anticipation of the reaction RE_k, and $AF_k^B(RE_k)$ anticipates the instruction IN_{k+1}.

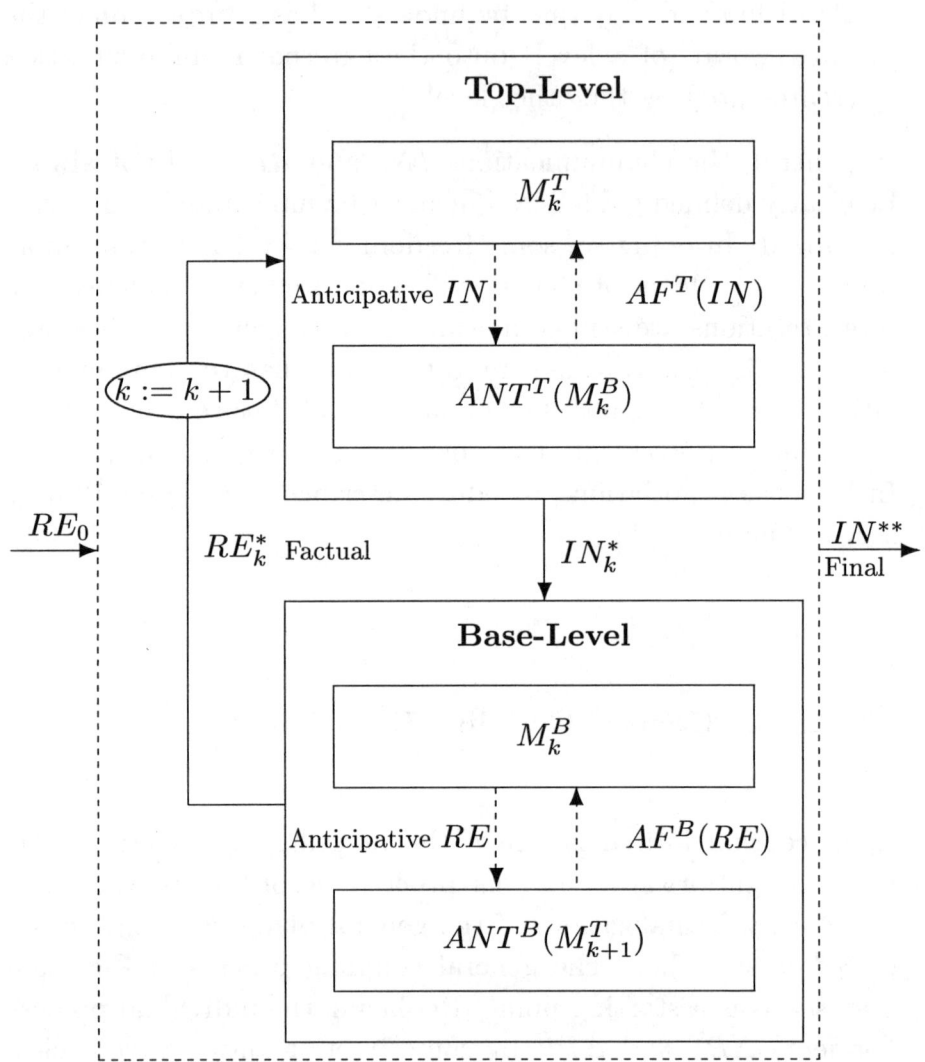

Fig. 10.6: Detailed Description of the Coupling Process

The coupling process starts with an initial information RE_0 which, in principle, could be an organizational design of the hierarchy (see Sec. 7.1), and ends up with the final decision IN^{**} (see also Fig. 2.1), representing the compromise reached in the negotiation. Note that RE_0 may not only initially define the levels of a hierarchy but may, in addition, determine the (initial) rules under which the whole coupling process is to evolve. By the exchange of factual signals IN_k^* and RE_k^*, the organization (i.e., the hierarchy) may be adapted through the actual problem it has to solve. Thus the organizational structure could be changed while solving real-life non-organizational problems.

With the description in Fig. 10.6, the formulation of the general coupling equations is now straightforward. Again, in accordance with the simpler equations (2.5), one has

$$a_k^{T^*} = \arg \operatorname*{opt}_{a_k^T \in A_k^T(RE_{k-1}^*)} E\left\{ C_k^T[a_k^T | RE_{k-1}^*, AF_k^T(IN_k)] | I_{k,t_0}^T \right\}$$

$$(10.1a)$$

$$a_k^{B^*} = \arg \operatorname*{opt}_{a_k^B \in A_k^B(IN_k^*)} E\left\{ C_k^B[a_k^B | IN_k^*, AF_k^B(RE_k)] | I_{k,t_1}^B \right\}$$

$$(10.1c)$$

The meaning of Eqs. (10.1a) and (10.1c) can be explained as follows: At time t_0 the top-level calculates the optimal instruction $IN_k^* = IN(a_k^{T^*})$. In doing so, the base-level is taken into account by the reaction RE_{k-1}^* of the last coupling cycle and the anticipation function AF_k^T. The (optimal) instruction $IN(a_k^{T^*})$ is passed on to the base-level, possibly influencing all its components, particularly its aspiration levels and possible operationalizations and interpretations. Finally, the base-level calculates an (optimal) reaction $RE_k^* = RE_k(a_k^{B^*})$ under its information I_{k,t_1}^B, possibly making use of an anticipation function AF_k^B.

Notice that, in order to hold the notation simple, not all possible dependencies on IN_k or RE_k are explicitly stated. Particularly, the opt-operators will frequently depend on rather subtle instructions and reactions. The same is due for the anticipations which might not only influence the criteria but the decision fields as well.

Furthermore, through RE_{k-1}^* the reaction of only the last coupling cycle is explicitly taken into account by the top-level. All former reactions have already been 'absorbed' by an appropriate adaptation. Formally, however, it would of course not be a problem to take the whole history RE^{k-1^*} instead of RE^*_{k-1}. Obviously, for the base-level an analog argument holds.

One of the most crucial points is the way how the optimizations are performed. As in the pure planning case, this will heavily depend on the specific criteria one takes into account and on the particular operationalizations being described by the decision fields. The next subsection will investigate this problem somewhat further.

Closely related to the optimization problem is the determination of the instruction (or reaction), i.e., $IN^*_k = IN_k(a_k^{T^*})$. Particularly, for process-related criteria, the instruction will have to be split up into a sequence of components influencing not only the present base-cycle but future cycles as well. As explained above, such instructions might be extracted from a hierarchical algorithm, specifically constructed to solve the anticipation problem. Thus, an instruction does not only optimize the local (solely k-dependent) criterion C_k^T but one has to take into account general organizational goals which the decison makers would finally like to achieve through their negotiation. As already discussed in the preceding section, these goals are continously changing for the individual decision process. The coupling equations (10.1a) and (10.1c) could accommodate these non-local (process-oriented) aspects, for instance, in prescribing appropriate aspiration levels through their interactions. Hence, the coupling equations provide only a general framework and need further specifications in describing the individual decision processes. This situation is not entirely new, since already in the general planning case the optimization procedure of the top-level often possesses several cycles. What is different now, is the possible guidance of the interior processes by the other level.

The general equations (10.1) allow several important specifications to be discussed in the remaining chapters of Part III. Two
specifications, however, are fundamental and, to a certain extent,
represent extreme situations,
- *general hierarchical planning* and
- *pure negotiations.*

(1) For general hierarchical planning situations the Eqs. (10.1)
    reduce to just half a cycle. Hence, in dropping the index k
    and not allowing for any reaction RE and consequently not
    considering a base-anticipation function AF^B, one ends up
    with the general hierarchical planning equations (2.5).
(2) Pure negotiations are defined as negotiations not regarding
    any reactive anticipation. That is, the anticipation func-
    tions AF^T and AF^B will be removed from the Eqs. (10.1).
    Moreover, the negotiation takes place at a particular point in
    (physical) time: $t_0 = t_1 = t$, i.e., no external information is
    entering the system during the negotiation. Hence, the time
    index may be dropped, too, resulting in the pair of equations

$$a_k^{T^*} = \arg \operatorname*{opt}_{a_k^T \in A_k^T(RE_{k-1}^*)} E\left\{ C_k^T[a_k^T | RE_{k-1}^*] | I_k^T \right\} \qquad (10.2a)$$

$$a_k^{B^*} = \arg \operatorname*{opt}_{a_k^B \in A_k^B(IN_k^*)} E\left\{ C_k^B[a_k^B | IN_k^*] | I_k^B \right\}. \qquad (10.2c)$$

Obviously, an instruction or reaction will only be determined if
the decision makers are not yet satisfied, that is, if a discrepancy
(see Fig. 10.3) still exists, i.e.,

$$DIS_k = DIS_k(\bar{C}_k^*, AL_k) > 0.$$

The flow chart of Fig. 10.7 plainly shows the different stages
in passing through a negotiation cycle. Taking explicity into
account discrepancies seems to provide a somewhat more comprehensive description than the coupling equations (10.2).

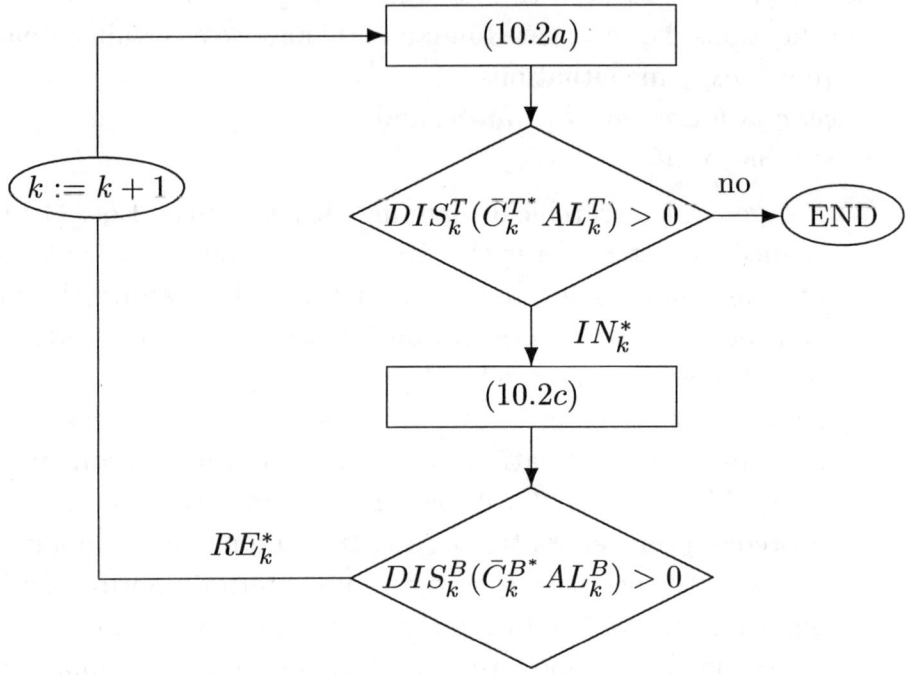

Fig. 10.7: Pure Negotiation

This is, however, not really the case. Formulating explicitly the function $IN_k(a_k^T)$ in Eq. (10.2c) usually calls for the formulation of a discrepancy. (For an example, see the definition of a depreciation rate in Eq. (9.5).)

Chapter 12 will further investigate negotiation processes. In particular, it will be shown how hierarchical aspects can be incorporated in the coupling equations (10.2) which, up to now, are still symmetric.

10.2.3 Leadership Properties of the Coupling Equations

The theoretical extension we achieved in deriving the general coupling equations (10.1) may mainly be seen in the more explicit description of the base-level. The increased importance we are attributing to the base-level is two-fold. First, the equations allow for a reaction of the base-level which results in negotiations to be described in the next chapters. Second, and this is less obvious, because of the more exposed position of the base-level, particularly the base-criterion has to be described in more explicit terms. Furthermore, it is necessary to describe more carefully how the base-level is handling the instruction and is arriving at a reaction. It is this second aspect which we are now going to investigate more closely.

(1) Specification of the coupling equations by their criteria

According to its increased significance, let us now describe the base-level not simply by one monolithic criterion C^B but, in analogy to the top-criterion, by two components

$$C^B = C^B(C^{BB}, C^{BT})$$

with C^{BB} being the private criterion of the base-level and C^{BT} defining a bottom-up criterion.

Within a leadership context, one may interpret C^{BT} as the role perception of the base-level and C^{TB} as the role expectation of the top-level with respect to the base-level.

With these interpretations, one may – in accordance with Sections 2.3 and 2.4 – employ the criteria C^{TT}, C^{TB}, C^{BT} and C^{BB} to characterize several leadership situations:
(a) $C^T = C^{TT}$:   egocentric top-level,
(b) $C^T = C^{BB}$:   altruistic, employee-oriented top-level,
(c) $C^B = C^{BT}$:   task-oriented base-level,

(d) $C^B = C^{TT}$:   'obsequious' base-level,

(e) $C^B = C^{BB}$:   heteronomous base-level,

(f) $C^T = C^{TB} \wedge C^B = C^{BB}$: Top- and base-level pursue only their own interests. One has the typical constellation of a principal agent hierarchy (see Sec. 5.2, Eq. (5.1)).

(g) $C^B = C^{BT} \wedge C^{TB} = C^{TB}(C^{BT})$ strictly monotonous increasing: team situation (see Sec. 2.3). In case there is no role ambiguity, i.e., $C^{TB} \equiv C^{BT}$, a re-evaluation is not needed.

(h) $C^T = C^{TT} \wedge C^B = (C^{BB}, C^{BT})$: patriarchal leadership style. In this case the base-level does not participate explicitly in the top-level's evaluation of decisions.

(i) $C^T = (C^{TT}, C^{BB}) \wedge C^B = (C^{BB}, C^{BT})$: participative leadership style: The top-level is employee-oriented, whereas the base-level is both, heteronomous and task-oriented.

To understand the relationship between the two levels more closely, some general model as to how the two decision processes might interfere proves to be necessary. In doing so, it seems to be sufficient to restrict the discussion to the (top-down) instructions. Similar considerations would apply for the (bottom-up) reaction.

(2) The instruction as a leadership problem

An appropriate starting point to investigate the way how the instruction might actually be applied to the base-level may be seen in the discussion of implementation activities, as illustrated with Fig. 8.3. The main idea is to build up the instruction of two components, of a problem- (or task-) related part (IN_P) and a leadership part (IN_L). These partial instructions can be of a cognitive or a non-cognitive character as indicated in Fig. 10.8.

Usually the leadership part will have a higher proportion of non-cognitive instructions than the problem-related part. Hence the problem of vague statements and their interpretation, as discussed in Section 10.1.2, will be of crucial significance.

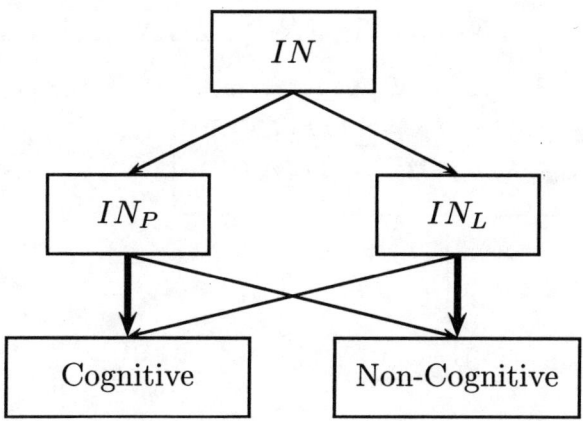

Fig. 10.8: Composition of Instructions

To be more specific, consider Fig. 10.9. The partial instructions IN_P and IN_L may consist of hard, solid, and/or vague communications which have to be interpreted (or operationalized) by the base-level. If the top-level wants the interpretation to guarantee a certain minimum level of achievement, it has to state, as a leadership instruction, an appropriate aspiration level $AL(IN_P)$, i.e., $IN_P \geq AL(IN_P)$. Let us assume that this latter instruction is not vague. Similarly, leadership aspiration levels might be applied to guarantee some minimum achievement of the base-level's decision process ΔP^B, i.e., '$\Delta P^B \geq AL(\Delta P^B)$'. In addition, there might be some further leadership instructions IN'_L for which, in many cases, an interpretation through the base-level will be necessary. One of the reasons of the top-level to be not too precise as to its instructions IN_P may be seen in the freedom it is intending to grant the base-level.

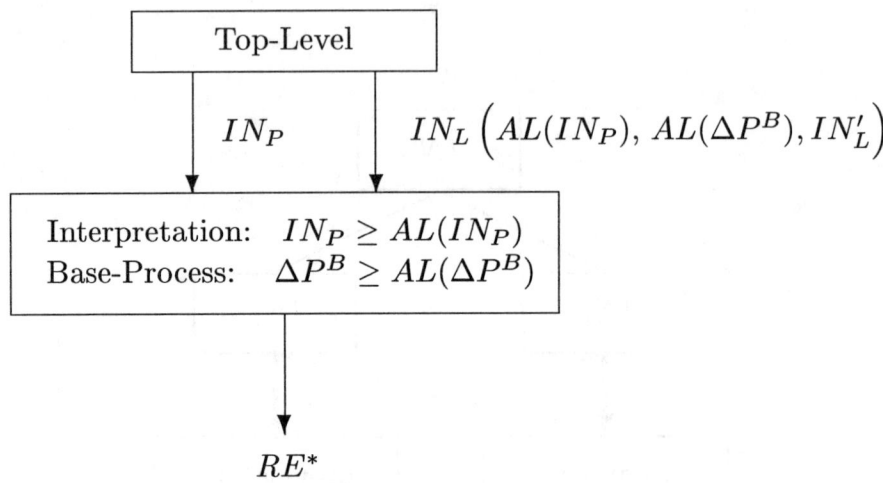

Fig. 10.9: Composition of Instructions

How can these very general ideas be made explicit? Considering the coupling equations (10.1), the instruction materializes in certain directives for the base-criterion and in aspiration levels defining constraints for the base-decision field. Of particular importance is the optimizing operator of the base-level. This operator can be used to impose certain procedures on the base-level, that is, it can be used to prescribe parts of the individual base-decision process (ΔP^B). This is particularly important in the case of process-related aspiration levels. These prescriptions can frequently only be accommodated by certain cut-off criteria for a decision process. As an example, think of an instruction defining the maximal number of base-cycles to be used in calculating the reaction RE^*. This might be the number of parameter adaptation steps in a relaxation analysis (see Sec. 3.2).

Clearly, for an explicit anticipation, the reaction with respect to all components of an instruction must be anticipated. In principle, Chapter 8 is showing how for specific situations such an anticipation can be performed.

Chapter 11

Coordination

Coordination activities can be considered as one of the most important issues in planning and leadership. As long as they are not of a self-organizing nature, they typically exhibit a hierarchy. Taking the top-level as the coordinator and the base-level as the units to be coordinated one may readily apply the general coupling equations (10.1) to analyze and design coordination processes.

There exist a large number of different coordination schemes depending on how the top-level is influencing the base-level. Generally, one might influence the base-criterion or the base-decision field, or both. Influencing the criterion, one has the prominent case of management by objectives (MBO). The Dantzig/Wolfe coordination scheme, for instance, which, in a different context, has already been presented in Section 3.1.2, provides an example for a coordination by transfer prices, whereas other procedures describe a coordination in allocating resources (e.g., see [Ten Kate], [Benders]). In fact, there are an extensive number of papers investigating various aspects of formal organizational coordination schemes (e.g., see [Bogetoft et al.], [Burton et al.], [Burton/Obel], [Holmberg], [v.d. Panne], and for a very general treatment see [Mesarovic et al.]).

Typical coordination procedures can be met in modern management accounting making use of steering costs and the payment of incentives (e.g., see [Demski], [Zimmerman]). Of particular importance is the case of information asymmetry for a non-team situation. For this situation principal agent theory may give a hint (see Chapter 5 and in particular [Holmström/Tirole]). Further problem areas, investigating particularly the role communications play for a coordination process, may be seen in the Groves mechanism [Groves/Loeb] and the Weizman scheme [Weizman].

In what follows, let us focus on a particular coordination setting describing a subtle hierarchical influence of a company's top management on its divisions. The divisions are assumed to possess private information, but no cheating will be allowed. The coordinating top management exerts its influence in changing the criteria and the decision fields of the divisions. Particularly, for the criteria, this is not simply achieved in totally prescribing all parts of the criteria but, in fact, in allowing the base-level some freedom of choice. This kind of coordination may be regarded as a particular participative leadership style.

Let us proceed as follows. To provide a framework, let us first state in very general terms the interactions of the control unit and the divisions (Sec. 11.1). We then, in Section 11.2, reduce the problem to a coordination of linear decision models, allowing, however, for multiple objectives. In a final step (Sec. 11.3) we then refine the interaction of the control unit in enabling it to interfere in the divisions' decision processes.

11.1 General Features of a Coordination Process

Returning to the general coupling process depicted in Fig. 10.5, we may readily specify the general diagram to describe the coordination of S divisions as shown in Fig. 11.1. The top-criterion is simply assumed to be additively composed of the contributions C^{Ts} of the divisions: $C^T := \sum_{s=1}^{S} C^{Ts}$.

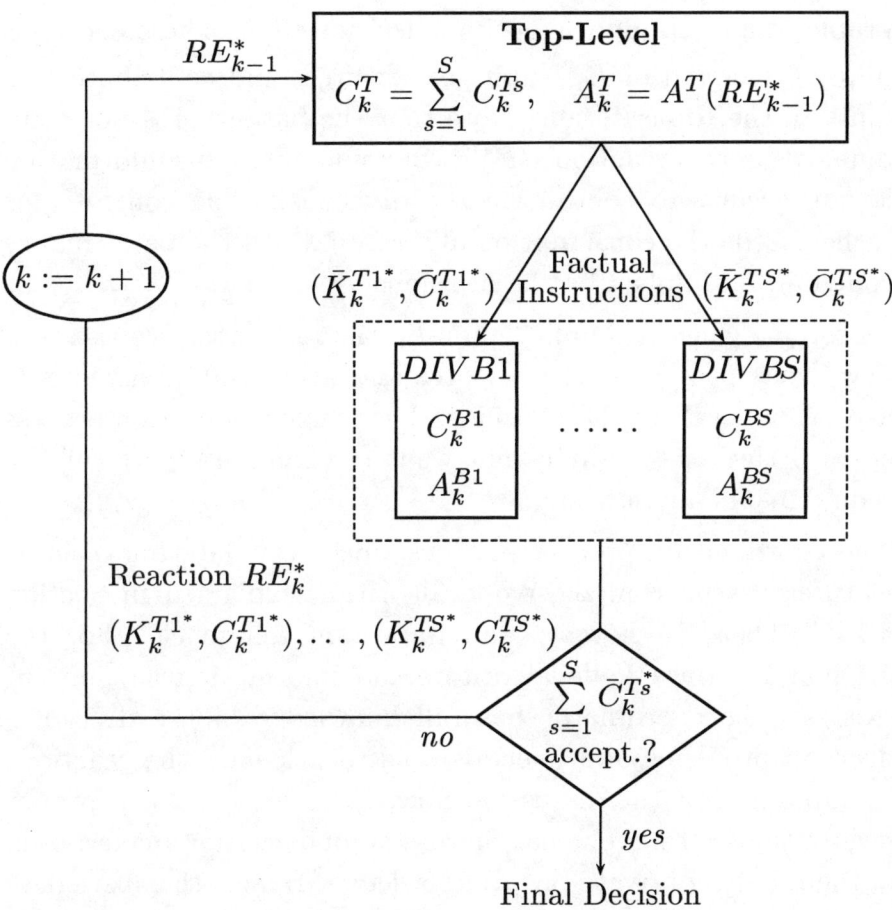

Fig. 11.1: Coordination as a Negotiation Process

In cycle k, the (coordinating) top-level is promising the divisions to allocate the amount $\bar{K}_k^{T\overset{*}{s}}$ of resources. Simultaneously, it is requiring a certain performance level, i.e., an amount $\bar{C}_k^{T\overset{*}{s}}$ of the top-level's goal. These factual instructions enter the base-level's decision field A_k^{Bs} ($s = 1, \ldots, S$). In particular, one has, (at cycle k) for the performance contributions C_k^{Ts}, the constraints

$$C_k^{Ts} \geq \bar{C}_k^{T\overset{*}{s}} \quad (s = 1, \ldots, S).$$

Subject to the constraints communicated as instructions ($\bar{K}_k^{T\overset{*}{s}}$, $\bar{C}_k^{T\overset{*}{s}}$) to the base-level, the divisions optimize their decision problems and obtain the optimal decisions $a_k^{B\overset{*}{s}}$. These decisions imply a demand of $K_k^{T\overset{*}{s}}$ units of resources and contribute $C_k^{T\overset{*}{s}}$ units to the top-criterion. Note that the base-level is not communicating as a reaction RE_k^* its decision $a_k^{B\overset{*}{s}}$. This information is not needed to coordinate the divisions. The control unit rather needs the consumption of resources and the performance contribution implied by the decisions $a_k^{B\overset{*}{s}}$ ($s = 1, \ldots, S$).

As for the general coupling process, the reactions give rise to a new cycle, passing a new resource allocation and adjusted goal aspiration levels to the divisions. The whole negotiation process stops if the top-level does not want to change its performance requirements any longer.

The coordination process just described has the same *general* features as the Dantzig/Wolfe algorithm explained in Section 3.1.2. There is, however, an important difference. For the original Dantzig/Wolfe algorithm, no information asymmetry exists. The coordinator has full knowledge of the divisions' decision problems and hence is able to calculate the reactions by himself. For the discussion now, however, i.e., for a proper negotiation setting, one has more than one decision maker, each of them having private (local) knowledge. Hence, the answers of the divisions are important, providing the coordinator with the knowledge he actually needs.

In what follows, we specialize the general framework for the case that all decision makers decide on the basis of linear systems. These are exactly the assumptions of the Dantzig/Wolfe algorithm. We are extending this standard situation, however, by two steps. First, in the next section, we realistically assume that all criteria may have multiple objectives. The next step, to be discussed in Section 11.3, will then allow the top-level to interfere in the multi-criterion decision processes of the divisions. This will be achieved in prescribing weights for the single objectives. Thus, an additional hierarchical element drives the coordination process. In discussing this particular and very instructive hierarchical coordination scheme, we are following [Homburg (1998b)] and [Homburg/Schneeweiss]. (For a more comprehensive treatment see Chapter 3 of [Homburg (1996)]. The reader is also referred to the paper of [Goedhart/Spronk].)

11.2 A Linear Coordination Process

Focusing on a *linear* multi-criterion coordination process, let us first assume that all characteristics be known. Hence, one has the following simultaneous decision model for the control unit and the divisions in which all decision makers are guided by multiple objectives expressed by vectors C^T and C^B

$$C^T = \sum_{s=1}^{S} D^{Ts} x^s \longrightarrow \max \tag{11.1}$$

$$C^{Bs} = D^{Bs} x^s \longrightarrow \max \quad s = 1, \ldots, S \tag{11.2}$$

s.t.

$$\sum_{s=1}^{S} A^{BTs} x^s \leq K^T \tag{11.3}$$

$$A^{Bs} x^s \leq K^{Bs} \quad s = 1, \ldots, S \tag{11.4}$$

$$x^1; \ldots, x^s \geq 0 \tag{11.5}$$

Indices

$s = 1, \ldots, S$: division

Decision variables and derivatives

x^s: decision vector of division s
C^T: vector of top-criteria
C^{Bs}: vector of base-criteria

Parameters

D^{Ts}:   matrix of top-criteria coefficients evaluating x^s
D^{Bs}:   matrix of base-criteria coefficients evaluating x^s
K^T: vector of resources controlled by the top-level
K^{Bs}:   vector of resources controlled by the base-level
A^{BTs}: matrix of production coefficients with respect to K^T
A^{Bs}:   matrix of production coefficients with respect to K^{Bs}

The simultaneous model (11.1) through (11.5) describes with (11.1) and (11.2) a vector maximum problem subject to the common constraints (11.3) and the local constraints (11.4). Assuming $D^{Bs} \equiv D^{Ts}$ $\forall s$ and D^{Ts} representing a vector and not a matrix, the above model reduces to the ordinary one-criterion Dantzig/Wolfe model (see (3.11) through (3.14)) of Section 3.1.2.

As mentioned before, for different decision makers having private information, the simultaneous model has to be restructured to allow for a proper negotiation process. According to the general coupling equations (10.1) and in view of Fig. 11.1, the divisional models for iteration k may readily be formulated. Hence, one has the following **base-model**

(11.6) $$C_k^{Ts} := D^{Ts} x_k^s \longrightarrow \max$$

(11.7) $$C_k^{Bs} := D^{Bs} x_k^s \longrightarrow \max$$

s.t.

(11.8) $$C_k^{Ts} \geq \bar{C}_k^{Ts^*}$$

(11.9) $$A^{TBs} x_k^s \leq \bar{K}_k^{Ts^*}$$

(11.10) $$x_k^s \geq 0$$

with $\bar{\boldsymbol{C}}_k^{T_{\tilde{s}}^*}$ and $\bar{\boldsymbol{K}}_k^{T_{\tilde{s}}^*}$ being temporary (factual) top-level instructions (see Fig. 11.1).

The divisions solve for their part their multi-criterion decision problems resulting in compromise solutions $\boldsymbol{x}_k^{s*}$ $(s = 1,\ldots,S)$ and, as reaction RE_k^*, report their performance contributions

$$\boldsymbol{C}_k^{T_s^*} = \boldsymbol{D}^{T_s}\boldsymbol{x}_k^{s*} \tag{11.11}$$

and their utilization of scarce (common) resources

$$\boldsymbol{K}_k^{T_s^*} = \boldsymbol{A}^{TB_s}\boldsymbol{x}_k^{s*} \tag{11.12}$$

to the coordinator.

As for the original Dantzig/Wolfe algorithm, these reactions are then combined with earlier reactions giving rise to new (feasible) instructions for each division $s = 1,\ldots,S$

$$\left(\sum_{l=0}^{k-1}\lambda_l^s\,\boldsymbol{K}_l^{T_s^*},\ \sum_{l=0}^{k-1}\lambda_l^s\boldsymbol{C}_l^{T_s^*}\right) \tag{11.13}$$

with $\lambda_l^s \geq 0$ and $\sum\limits_{l=0}^{k-1}\lambda_l^s = 1$. Before communicating these instructions to the base-level, the top-level optimizes the performance requirement of expression (11.13) with respect to λ_l^s, taking into account the common constraints. Hence, one has the following
top-model

$$C^T = \sum_{s=1}^{S}\sum_{l=0}^{k-1}\lambda_l^s\,\boldsymbol{C}_l^{T_s^*} \longrightarrow \max \tag{11.14}$$

s.t.

$$\sum_{s=1}^{S}\sum_{l=0}^{k-1}\lambda_l^s\,\boldsymbol{K}_l^{T_s^*} \leq \boldsymbol{K}^T \tag{11.15}$$

$$\sum_{l=0}^{k-1}\lambda_l^s = 1 \qquad \forall s \tag{11.16}$$

$$\lambda_l^s \geq 0 \qquad \forall s, l \tag{11.17}$$

As a result, the coordinating control unit attains new resource allocations

(11.18)
$$\bar{K}_k^{T_s^*} = \sum_{l=0}^{k-1} \lambda_l^{s*}(l) K_l^{T_s^*}$$

and performance requirements

(11.19)
$$\bar{C}_k^{T_s^*} = \sum_{l=0}^{k-1} \lambda_l^{s*} C_l^{T_s^*}$$

to be communicated to the divisions. The negotiation process terminates as soon as the top-level is content with its performance requirements. Since the top-level's instruction implies feasible solutions for the base-level, the optimal decisions $x_{k^*}^{s^*}$ for the terminating iteration k^* become final (see Fig. 2.1), i.e.,

(11.20)
$$x_{k^*}^{s^*} = x^{s^{**}}, \quad s = 1, \ldots, S.$$

Remark: In contrast to the divisions, we solved the *top-model* as a vector maximum problem. In looking for a multi-criterion compromise solution, the top-level would have to incorporate criteria preferences generally resulting in a proper re-evaluation of the base-level decisions. Formally, this re-evaluation would then be denoted, as usual, by C^{TB}.

11.3 Hierarchical Interference in the Base-Level Decision Processes

After having illustrated the general structure of a coordination process, let us now demonstrate how the coordinator might exert a further (hierarchical) influence on the divisions. Up to now the instruction exclusively consisted of a resource allocation $\bar{K}^{T_s^*}$ and a performance requirement $\bar{C}^{T\overset{*}{s}}$. No influence was exerted on the individual multi-criterion decision process of a division.

Let us now assume that the top-level causes the divisions to solve their multi-criterion decision problems in assigning appropriate weights to their criteria. In doing so, the Zions-Wallenius (ZW) interactive MCDM-algorithm [Zionts/Wallenius] seems to be particularly appropriate. The ZW procedure accommodates preference information in implicitly adjusting the weights of a linear preference functional. Hence, the top-level may easily interfere in the division's multi-objective decision problem. The main idea of the particular hierarchical interference to be described in the sequel consists in not to prescribe crisp values for the weights, but to specify regions W^{Ts} ($s = 1, \ldots, S$) in which the weights should lie.

The principle idea of the ZW-algorithm can easily be explained. The algorithm starts with calculating efficient solutions in assigning appropriate weights to the criteria. In doing so, it makes use of the efficiency theorem of linear vector optimization [Keeney/Raiffa]. This theorem says that each efficient extreme point can be calculated in optimizing a suitably chosen linear combination of the criteria. Having an efficient solution, the algorithm then calculates adjacent solutions and asks the decision maker to articulate preferences with respect to these points on the efficient border, which results in certain constraints for the weights. That is, the given preference information implies in case of an indifference between adjacent points an additional equality constraint and in case of a preference an inequality constraint. With this interactively gained information, being modeled through linear constraints, the algorithm finally ends up with an accepted compromise solution, which is expressed by a specified set of weights.

Influencing the ZW-procedure in the above mentioned cautious way, the division has to make sure that all weights generated during the ZW-algorithm lie in the set W^{Ts} of prescribed weights. If W^{Ts} is represented by linear constraints, it can easily be incorporated in the linear models to be solved within the ZW algorithm.

In calculating the weight restrictions W^{Ts}, the top-level has to be informed about the ideal and the pessimistic values of the various criteria. This is done by confronting each division with a minimal and a maximal resource allocation resulting in a report of a corresponding ideal and pessimistic performance contribution. These values are then the starting point for a MAUT-like procedure to calculate weight ranges W^{Ts} (see [Homburg (1998a)]).

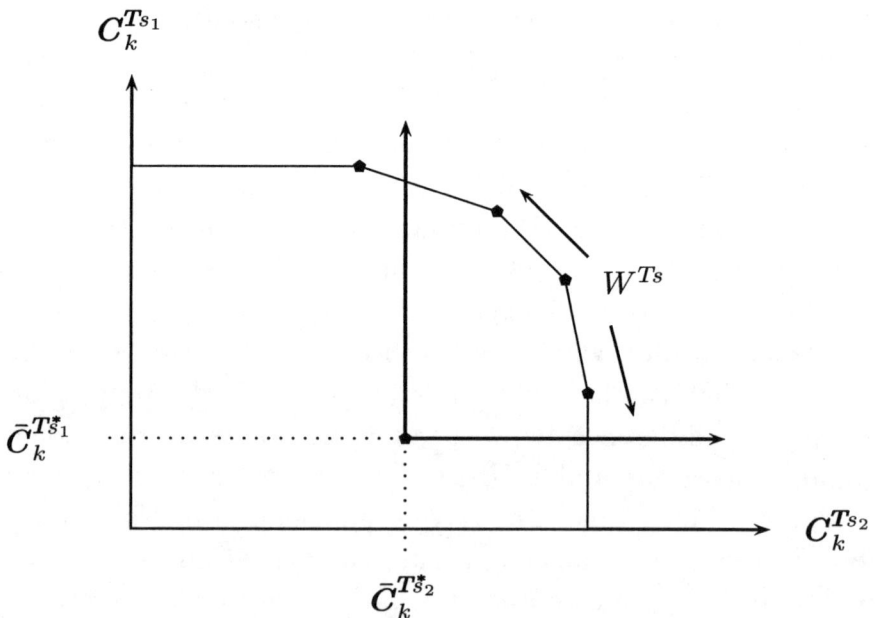

Fig. 11.2: Constraints on the Division's Decision Problem

Returning to the general procedure explained in the previous section, the top-level's influence is, of course, not restricted merely to control the base-level's compromise process. This is only the second step. The first step concerns the instructions $\bar{K}_k^{Ts^*}$ and $\bar{C}_k^{Ts^*}$ which influence the division's decision space, while W^{Ts} has an impact on the criteria. Fig. 11.2 indicates the situation. The top-level needs not to be perfectly informed about the base-level's decision space to calculate W^{Ts}; the reports on the pessimistic and ideal performance contributions are sufficient. Thus, weight restrictions are particularly appropriate in early cycles of the coordination process when the knowledge about the divisions is still rather poor. Later, when the decision space is further reduced, weight restrictions are no longer that important.

11.4 The Entire Coordination Process

Summarizing the considerations of the previous two sections, the entire coordination process consists of two phases, the initial phase and the subsequent negotiation process.

The process starts with minimal and maximal resource allocations and calculates in this *initial phase*, using a first response of the divisions, via a MAUT-like procedure, weight restrictions W^{Ts}, and, in addition, determines first performance requirements. These values are then communicated as an instruction to the base-level.

During the subsequent *negotiation process*, depicted in Fig. 11.3, the top-level constructs a linear combination of past reactions, solves the top-model (11.14) through (11.17) and determines new instructions via (11.18) and (11.19). Possibly the weight restrictions are adjusted as well. Taking into account those instructions, the base-level solves its divisional models (11.6) through (11.10) and reports as a reaction performance contributions (11.11) and resource utilizations (11.12) to the top-level. With these reactions, a new negotiation cycle starts. The negotiation process terminates when the top-level considers its performance requirements to be sufficient. In this case, the factual instructions become final and are actually to be executed.

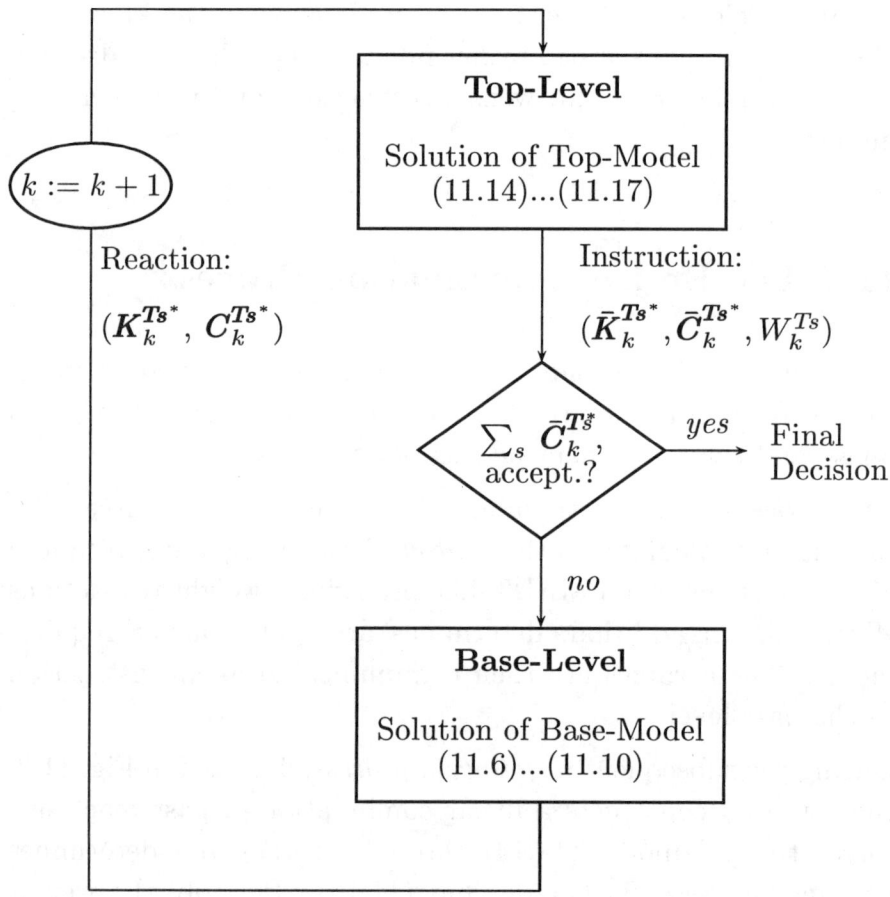

Fig. 11.3: The Entire Hierarchical Negotiation Process

The whole negotiation process shows several hierarchical features. With the initial resource allocations and the weight restrictions the first cycles are driven into a direction being favorable for the coordinator. Moreover, in repeatedly applying resource allocations and demanding performance contributions, the top-level continuously exercises its power. Finally, it is the top-level that is authorized to stop the negotiation.

On the other hand, the central unit cannot behave authoritarian-like. In fact, it practices some kind of a participative leadership style. It leaves the divisions some freedom to allocate resources to criteria they are particularly interested in. This might even be the case for the local criteria. Thus the top-level might, indeed, allow and actually urge the divisions to put a particular high weight on their local (private) objectives. Finally the control unit seriously takes into account the reports of the divisions.

Chapter 12

Negotiations

The previous chapter considered negotiations as part of a coordination process. They were simply employed as a leadership instrument to integrate the divisions of a company. We are now investigating negotiations from a more fundamental point of view. Thus, in contrast to the Dantzig/Wolfe coordination scheme, negotiations will not be reduced to a formalized information exchange between the members of a team. In fact, we now investigate negotiations in describing the levels to be more autonomous than in the pure team situation. Furthermore, the negotiations will not only lead to *transactional* (and hence temporal) modifications of the base-level's preferences but will imply true *transformational* changes in attitude (see Fig. 2.5d).

The situation we are going to analyze is neither antagonistic nor of a pure team character. We are rather investigating a limited team situation which, besides a role perception C^{BT}, allows the base-level to follow a private goal C^{BB}. For this private goal, top management is assumed to guarantee the base-level a certain aspiration level $AL^B \leq C^{BB}$; and it is exactly this aspiration level the two parties are suggested to negotiate.

Generally, a pure planning activity describes only a limited segment of the entire planning process. Prior to the planning phase, information must be collected and, especially when more than one party is involved, the individual preferences have to be balanced. Therefore, very often, negotiation processes precede the planning activity. On the other hand, in implementing a final plan, negotiations might be necessary just as well. Thus, for realistic applications planning is, indeed, embedded in leadership activities.

The negotiation process we are going to investigate will cope with all the above raised questions. It will discuss negotiations in relation to planning activities and will contribute additional features to the implementation problem treated in Chapter 8. Furthermore, it will shed new light on the design problem of Section 7.1 with its information collection strategy, and it will show how preferences may be transformed within a limited team setting.

In doing so, let us proceed as follows. In the next section, we first characterize the general situation we are going to analyze. Sections 12.2 and 12.3 will then progressively describe the negotiation process in greater detail. Section 12.4 incorporates pure planning activities, and Section 12.5 will finally describe the entire planning and negotiation process. The presentation follows [Homburg (1995)]. (For a more comprehensive treatment see Chapter 4 of [Homburg (1996)].)

12.1 A Hierarchical Negotiation Situation

Let us consider a situation as depicted in Fig. 12.1. The inner part of the diagram describes a negotiation between a top- and a base-level as it has already been shown in more detail in Fig. 10.7. Following the design problem of Section 7.1, however, let us assume that there exists an additional (strategic) level having an impact on the negotiation.

The setting described in Fig. 12.1 can be found in many practical circumstances. Imagine a price negotiation between a seller (top-level) and a buyer (base-level). This negotiation might well be influenced by the production facilities, i.e., the resources with which the strategic level is providing the company (seller). Similarly, the resource decision might depend on the outcome of the price negotiation [Pesenti].

As a further example, think of the working time contract we already encountered in Section 8.4 (see also [Wild/Schneeweiss]). As a strategic decision, one has a specific working time contract, and at the operational level the foremen negotiate with the workers about the amount of overtime being necessary to remove a bottleneck. Clearly, the arrangements of the contract will depend on the short term negotiations, and vice versa. In fact, let us take this latter case as an illustrative example for the following analysis. To be specific, let us assume that the strategic decision refers to the amount of manpower to be provided. Thus, the better the manpower provision the less tight the operational negotiations will be.

The interplay between the strategic (planning) decision and the negotiation may now be described as follows (Fig. 12.1). The strategic decision (contract) about the resources is made in t_0. Prior to t_0, a negotiation takes place which has to be performed for each possible provision of resources. Later, in t_1, the operational decision is made. Thus, the negotiation we are considering

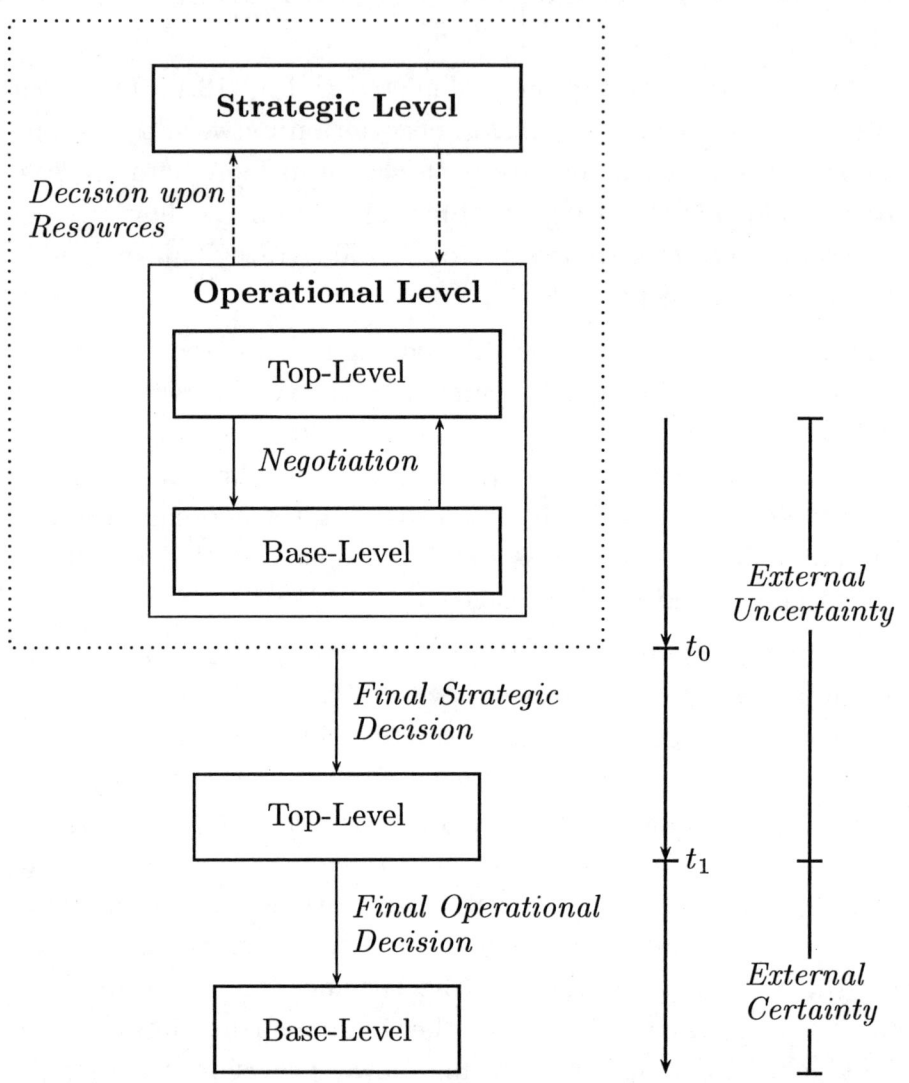

Fig. 12.1: The Negotiation as Part of the Entire Planning
Process

here may be understood as being precautionary. It is used to
determine the strategic decision. Its precautionary character is
becoming even more obvious if we realistically assume that at

time t_0 there exists uncertainty about the future situation at the operational level. Only in t_1, the external uncertainty is assumed to be removed. Hence, the negotiation must be performed with respect to expected scenarios.

In a way, the outcome of the negotiation can be considered at the strategic level as an anticipation. There is, however, an important difference. It is not just an anticipated (forecast) value as in the pure planning context. In fact, the achieved compromise is considered to be an obligatory commitment for the two levels. In contrast to influencing the base-criterion in the pure planning case, a negotiation often implies not only a transactional but also a transformational change of the levels' preferences.

For the **overtime example** one could have the following situation. The company has to decide on its manpower provision for the next year, which usually depends on the willingness of the employees to accept overtime. For different scenarios, i.e., demand situations, management has to discuss with the employees how much overtime they might be willing to accept. Since the amount of necessary overtime depends on the provided manpower, the mutual interdependance of the manpower decision and the negotiation is obvious. Moreover, it can generally be taken for granted that the outcome of the discussion can be considered as a commitment for the employees to actually accept the agreed overtime whenever a particular scenario occurs in t_1 on which the negotiation in t_0 was based .

12.2 A Formal Description of the Negotiation

To formalize the problem explained in the previous section, let us first assume that a specific strategic provision $a^s \in A^s$ and a certain scenario $S_i \in \{S_1, \dots, S_n\}$ are given. For this situation, the negotiation process may readily be described by the general Eqs. (10.2a) and (10.2c). Within a company, it seems to be realistic to assume that the top- and the base-levels neither behave antagonistically nor that they form a pure team (case (g) in Sec. 10.2.3). Rather we expect the levels to follow a limited team behavior as indicated in the previous section, i.e., primarily one has case (g) (Sec. 10.2.3) of a team situation with $C^T = C^{TB}$ and $C^B = C^{BT}$, and, in addition, for the private criterion C^{BB} of the base-level one requires a certain aspiration level $AL^B \leq C^{BB}$. The aspiration level restricts the decision fields A^B and A^T and may therefore be an obstacle for the top-level. As a consequence, the two parties will negotiate about the base aspiration level AL^B exhibiting an important feature of a participative leadership style.

Assuming that there is no role ambiguity (see Sec. 10.3.2), i.e., $C^{TB} = C^{BT}$ and that the private criterion C^{BB} is known to the top-level, the negotiation equations (10.2) may readily be written as

$$(12.1a) \quad a_k^{T^*} = \arg \opt_{a_k^T \in A_k^T(RE_{k-1}^*)} \left\{ (C^{TB}(a_k^T), C^{BB}(a_k^T)) | RE_{k-1}^* \right\}$$

$$(12.1c) \quad a_k^{B^*} = \arg \opt_{a_k^B \in A_k^B(IN_k^*)} \left\{ (C^{TB}(a_k^B), C^{BB}(a_k^B)) | IN_k^* \right\}.$$

Both equations represent multi-criterion decision problems with the same criteria C^{BB} and C^{TB}, i.e., the top-level has an employee-oriented part represented by C^{BB} and the employee complies with the role expectation of the top-level. Though both levels have the same criteria, the solutions $a_k^{T^*}$ and $a_k^{B^*}$ of their multi-criterion decison problems need not be the same. In fact, solving (12.1a), the top-level arrives at a solution C^{BB^*} and C^{TB^*}, and it is the value C^{BB^*} which is passed down to the base-level as a proposal AL^{BT} for the base-aspiration level AL^B. Hence, one has the instruction $IN^* = C^{BB^*} = AL^{BT}$. The base-level, on the other hand, takes this value into consideration, solves its own multi-criterion decision problem, and communicates a new aspiration level AL^{BB} as a reaction to the top-level, hence $RE^* = AL^{BB}$.

Let us describe this negotiation cycle in some more detail. Fig. 12.2 may illustrate the crucial concession step. To be specific, let us assume C^{TB} to represent costs and the concession line in Fig. 12.2 to be strict convex.

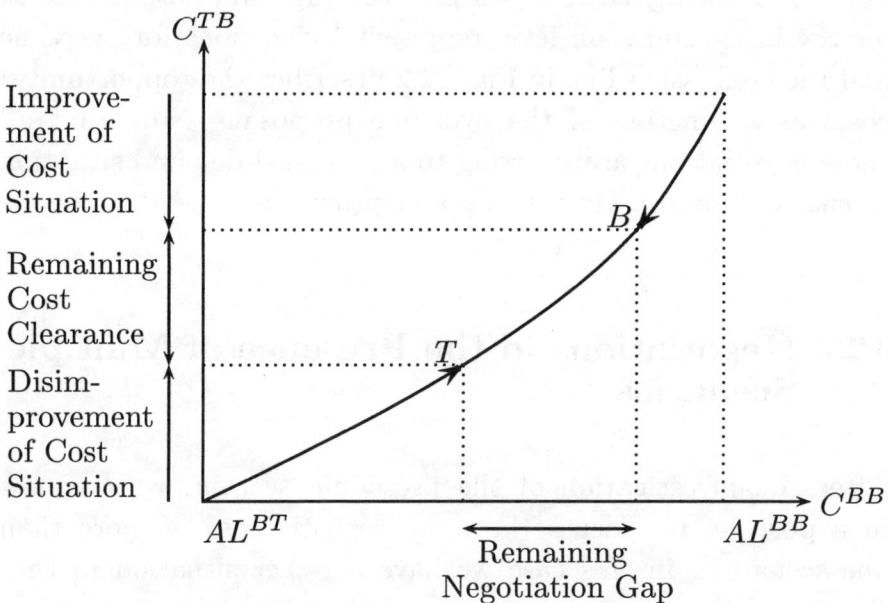

Fig. 12.2: Concession Step for One Scenario

Let us start with the concession step of the top-level, i.e., the top-level solves its multi-criterion decision problem (12.1a) and arrives at point T on the concession line in Fig. 12.2. This means that, compared to the starting position at the origin, the top-level has to incur a certain increase in costs, i.e., a disimprovement of its cost position. As a compensating concession, the base-level is expected to solve its multi-criterion decision problem (12.1c) to arrive at point B on the concession line. This means that it lowers its aspiration level which, for the top-level, implies an improvement of the cost situation, or, to put it differently, the position of the base-level is improved with respect to the top-level (see Fig. 12.2). Clearly, in the eyes of the top-level, the concession of the base-level will be assessed in view of the balance between the loss and the gain in C^{TB}. After this concession step, the next cycle starts negotiating now about a reduced negotiation gap and a corresponding cost clearance.

For the **working time example**, the top- and base-proposals for the base-aspiration level represent suggestions for overtime and the concession line in Fig. 12.2 describes the (opportunity) costs as a function of the overtime proposal. Note that all these negotiations are referring to a proposed demand situation (scenario S) and a given manpower provision.

12.3 Negotiations in the Presence of Multiple Scenarios

After the investigation of the preceding section, we are now in a position to discuss the more realistic case of more than one scenario. In this case we have a richer situation in that the contracting parties may now negotiate simultaneously about different scenarios.

The aspiration level AL^B for each scenario $S_i \in \{S_1, \ldots, S_n\}$ may be considered as a separate objective, and each scenario occurs with an estimated probability p_i $(i = 1, \ldots, n)$. Of course, usually it will not be possible to negotiate about all n

scenarios. One therefore restricts the negotiation to $m < n$ **representative scenarios**. (How these scenarios are to be selected is shown in detail in [Homburg (1996)].)

Considering the negotiation cycle k, the one-scenario case of the preceding section may readily be extended to the m-scenario situation giving rise to the following multi-dimensional instructions

$$\boldsymbol{IN}_k^* := \left(AL_1^{BT}, \dots, AL_m^{BT}\right)_k \qquad (12.2a)$$

and reactions

$$\boldsymbol{RE}_k^* := \left(AL_1^{BB}, \dots, AL_m^{BB}\right)_k. \qquad (12.2c)$$

Correspondingly, the negotiation equations now describe multi-dimensional negotiations with decisions $\boldsymbol{a}_k^{T^*} := (a_{1k}^{T^*}, \dots, a_{mk}^{T^*})$ and $\boldsymbol{a}_k^{B^*} := (a_{1k}^{B^*}, \dots, a_{mk}^{B^*})$ being vectors. Restricting the discussion to a negotiation in the presence of only two scenarios, one has the criteria $C_1^{TB}, C_2^{TB}, C_1^{BB}, C_2^{BB}$. For the role expectation it seems to be reasonable to assume that C_1^{TB} and C_2^{TB} describe the same attribute C^{TB}, for example, costs in the working time contract. The significance of these quantities is mainly determined by the probability p_i with which scenario S_i occurs. Hence, one has as relevant top-down criteria $C_1^{TB} := p_1 C^{TB}$ and $C_2^{TB} := p_2 C^{TB}$. The private criteria C_1^{BB} and C_2^{BB}, on the other hand, will usually not describe the same attribute.

The antagonists may now negotiate 'across two scenarios'. This means that a concession of the top-level for scenario 1 is compensated by a concession of the base-level for scenario 2. Hence, one has the following negotiation equations

$$a_{1k}^{T^*} = \arg \opt_{a_{1k}^T \in A_{1k}^T(AL_{2,k-1}^{BB})} \left\{p_1 C^{TB}, C_1^{BB}\right\}, \qquad (12.3a)$$

$$a_{2k}^{B^*} = \arg \opt_{a_{2k}^B \in A_{2k}^B(AL_{1k}^{BT})} \left\{p_2 C^{TB}, C_2^{BB}\right\}, \qquad (12.3c)$$

with 1 and 2 in A_{1k}^T and A_{2k}^T denoting sceario dependent decision fields. As in multi-criterion decision theory, C^{TB} serves as a pricing out quantity [Keeney/Raiffa] which allows for a comparison of C_1^{BB} and C_2^{BB}, and hence for a negotiation across different scenarios.

Fig. 12.3 illustrates the concession step across the scenarios $i = 1, 2$. Obviously, choosing scenario 1 for its concession, the top-level could go a big step into the direction of the base-level without incurring too much cost. On the other hand, in compensating this step, the base-level could, for the scenario 2 being presented by the top-level, considerably improve the top-level's cost situation without too much lowering the proposal for its aspiration level.

The example clearly shows how a negotiation should proceed in the presence of more than two scenarios. Providing the top-level with the additional hierarchical feature of having the right to choose the pair of scenarios across which it is willing to negotiate, it will try to choose pairs as those illustrated in Fig. 12.3. To put it more formally, the top-level will present the base-level those scenarios for which the concession lines have the shapes as indicated in Fig. 12.3. Selecting pairs for all scenarios finally brings the aspiration levels for each of the scenarios more closely together.

As briefly mentioned earlier, negotiating across scenarios is not only necessary because of the prevailing uncertainty, it has also the advantage that the number of different concession opportunities is increased. Moreover, in adding new representative scenarios, the negotiation can be restructured. Both instruments could be employed by the top-level to control, to a certain extent, the outcome of the negotiation and to avoid deadlocks.

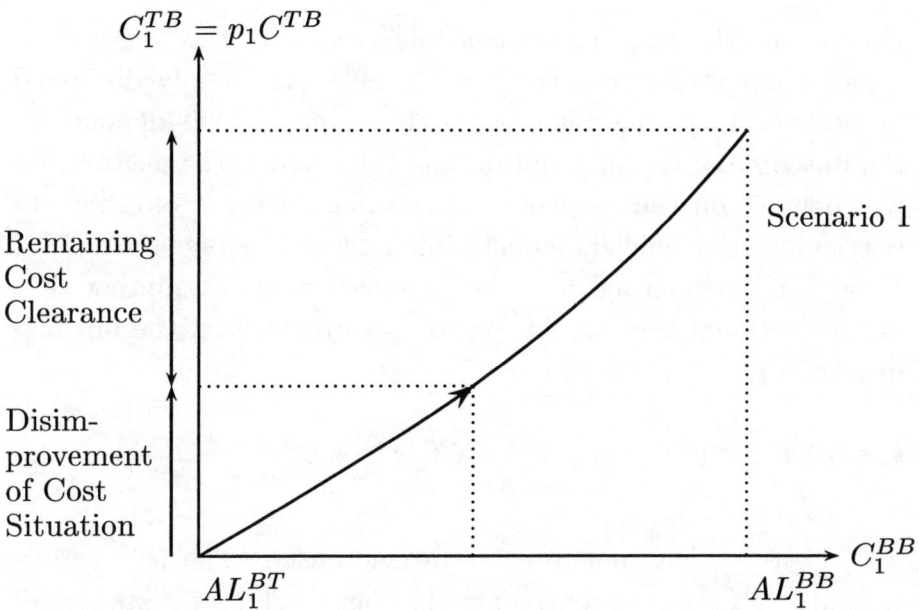

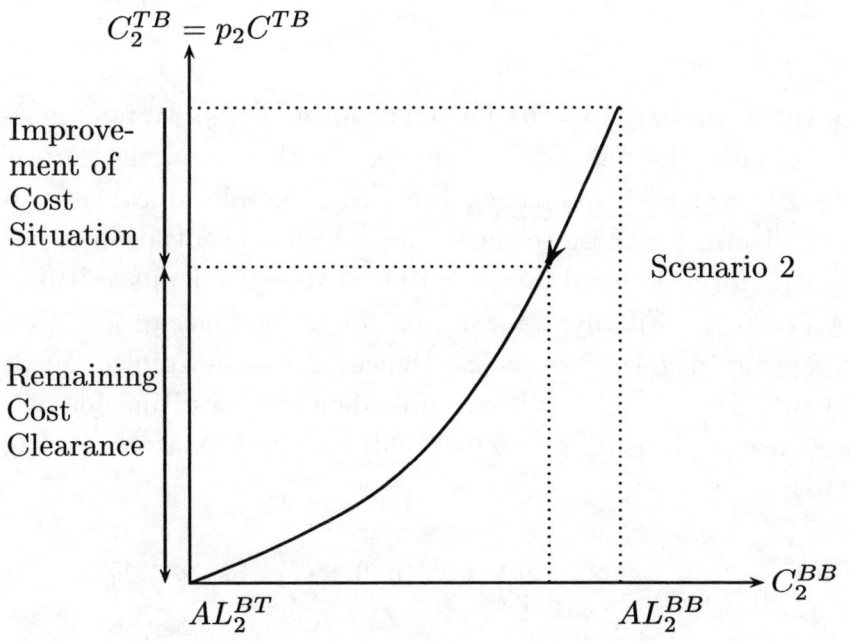

Fig. 12.3: Concessions Across Two Scenarios

12.4 The Strategic Decision

Up to now the negotiation has taken place in the presence of a particular strategic decision $a^S \in A^S$. As already discussed in Section 12.1 (see Fig. 12.1), this decision will depend on the outcome of the negotiation and, vice versa, the negotiation will depend on the provision the strategic level is offering. In particular, the efficient concession lines will change with a^S. Hence, in considering only the cost aspect and assuming that the operational decision a^{T^*} is going to be chosen, the optimal provision a^{S^*} is given by

$$(12.4a) \qquad a^{S^*} = \arg \operatorname*{opt}_{a^S \in A^S} \left\{ C^S(a^S) + \bar{C}^{TB}(a^S, a^{T^*}) \right\}$$

with $C^S(a^S)$ denoting direct strategic costs. The role expectation $\bar{C}^{TB}(a^S, a^{T^*})$ represents the mean value of costs for all scenarios

$$\bar{C}^{TB}(a^S, a^{T^*}) = \sum_{i=1}^{n} p_i C_i^{TB}(a^S, a^{T^*}).$$

Note that, compared to the formulation in (12.1), we now marked explicitly the dependence on a^S. Furthermore, the sum is over all n-scenarios indicating that, in principle, one needs to find C_i^{TB} also for those scenarios for which a negotiation is not intended (for a detailed investigation of this problem see [Homburg (1996)]). Finally, a^{T^*} stands for a top-level proposition of a specific negotiation cycle. Hence, if a compromise is not (yet) reached, a^{T^*} and a^{B^*} are not identical, resulting for a^{B^*} in a strategic decision a^{S^0} which will usually deviate from Eq. (12.4a),

$$(12.4b) \qquad a^{S^0} = \arg \operatorname*{opt}_{a^S \in A^S} \left\{ C^S(a^S) + \bar{C}^{TB}(a^S, a^{B^*}) \right\}.$$

If one is ultimately interested in the (strategic) investment decision a^S, Eqs. (12.3) and (12.4) might give a hint as to the significance of reaching a perfect compromise in the negotiation. Of course, if $C^S(a^S)$ dominates $\bar{C}^{TB}$ considerably, negotiations are only of a limited impact.

12.5 The Entire Negotiation Process

Summarizing the previous considerations, the top-level has a rich number of options available to control the negotiation process, in particular, it can choose the pair of scenarios, it can select the representative scenarios, and it can decide upon the strategic provision. To be more specific, the entire (strategic) planning and negotiation process may be organized as depicted in the chart diagram of Fig. 12.4.

A typical cycle of the process starts with the proposition of a vector $\boldsymbol{IN}_k^*$ of aspiration levels provoking, at the base-level, reactions $\boldsymbol{RE}_k^*$ (see Eqs. (12.2)). This concession step which is performed for a particular set of selected representative scenarios, might result in a compromise $\boldsymbol{IN}_k^* = \boldsymbol{RE}_k^*$. In this case, the strategic decisions a^{S^*} and a^{S^o} (see Eqs. (12.4)) are equal, and the process could stop. Only for a situation that the top-level believes the set of representative scenarios not to be sufficient, a total compromise is not yet reached and new scenarios must be selected. Of course, the more scenarios the base-level is confronted with, the tighter is the net of contingencies for which one has settled a commitment. On the other hand, negotiations are costly and should be restricted to a minimum.

Consider now the case a compromise has not been reached, i.e., $\boldsymbol{IN}_k^* \neq \boldsymbol{RE}_k^*$ and $a_k^{S^*} \neq a_k^{S^o}$. In this case, several options are available. First, one could try harder to find a compromise for the given set of scenarios which ultimately might end up with

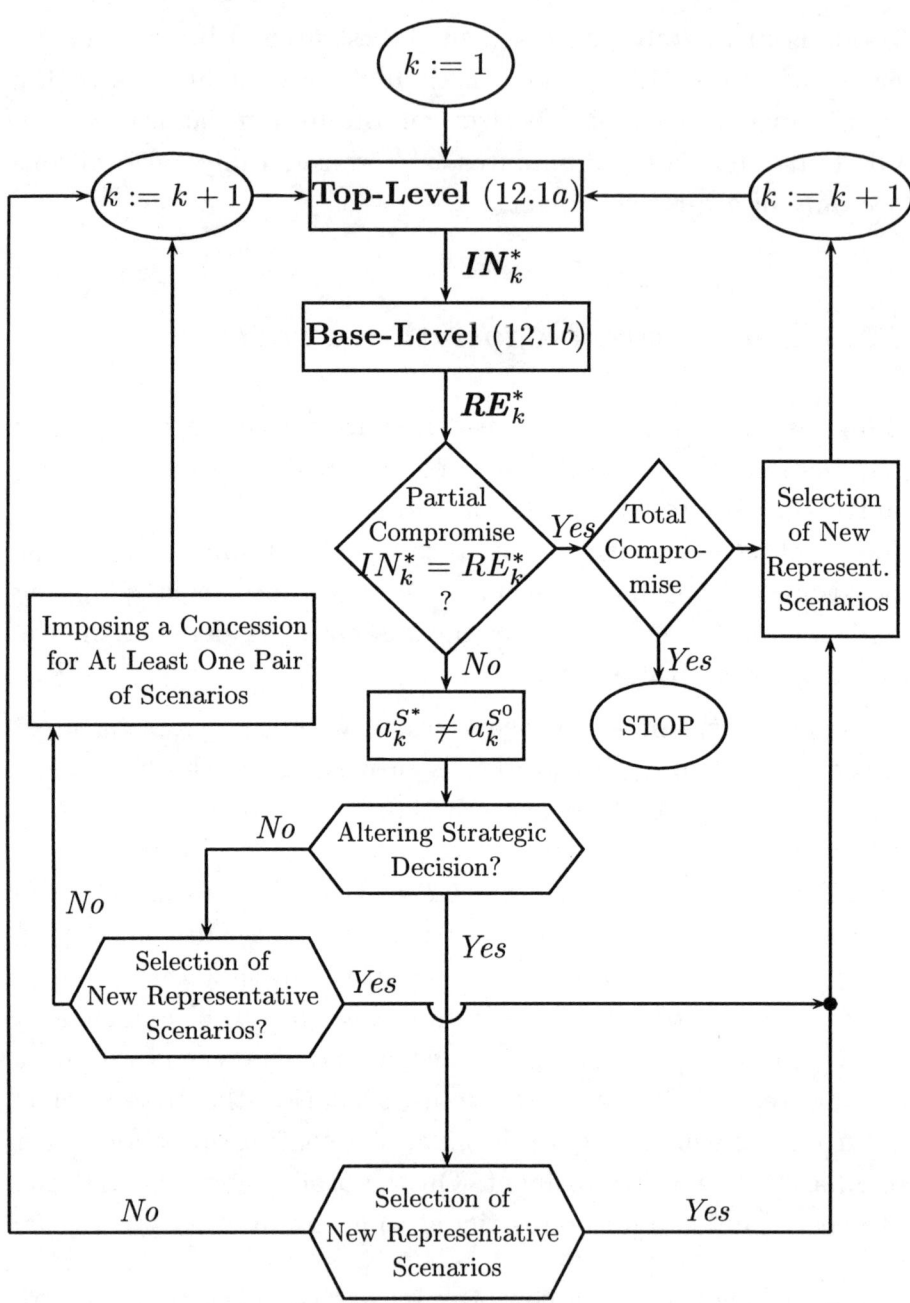

Fig. 12.4: The Total Planning and Negotiation Process

the top-level to impose a 'compromise' on the base-level. Second, new scenarios could be taken into consideration. Finally, as a third option, one could change the strategic decision normally resulting in a new negotiation making use, in general, of a new scenario. (Note that, in order not to overload the flow chart of Fig. 12.4, the case $IN_k^* \neq RE_k^*$ and $a_k^{S^*} = a_k^{S^0}$ is discarded from the discussion. This case is in principle possible but will not often be encountered.)

Of course, in view of the base-level, closing the negotiation gap between $\boldsymbol{IN}_k^*$ and $\boldsymbol{RE}_k^*$ or between $a_k^{S^*}$ and $a_k^{S^0}$ is not ultimately necessary. It should be clear, however, that for a participative leadership style both parties should try hard not only to reach a (transactional) compromise but a (transformational) conflict resolution (see Fig. 2.5d).

Incorporating negotiations into the planning process plainly shows these important features. First, it reduces, as just mentioned, the complexity of the optimization problem. Second, it reduces the uncertainty as to the future behavior of the contracting parties. In Section 8.1 we called this uncertainty *implementation disturbance*. Finally, negotiations were used not only to reduce formal and empirical complexity but they were simultaneously employed in conditioning the party's attitudes in favor of an overall acceptable decision and its reliable implementation.

Having arrived at a compromise, the strategic decision can now be made. This decision is no longer of a multi-criterion nature but, because C^{BB} is fixed to its aspiration level $AL^{B^*} = AL^{BT^*} = AL^{BB^*}$, a simple single objective optimization.

In Section 10.2.3 (and Fig. 10.8), we discussed the role of emotional (leadership) instruments in bringing about a transformational change in attitude. In view of the many well-defined quantities we used, this role might not be readily understood.

It should be clear, however, that the many concession steps and solutions of multi-criterion decision problems leave ample space for accommodating non-cognitive elements in using cognitive variables.

As a final remark, one may consider again the many hierarchical features of the total planning and negotiation process. Besides the choice of the scenarios and the strategic decision, the top-level was (ultimately) allowed to impose a compromise. Furthermore, it could make a first proposal for the aspiration level and was given the right to terminate the whole process, and finally it could, at least to a certain degree, manipulate the base-level in exerting control on the many decisions needed in driving the negotiation process.

Chapter 13

A Unifying Perspective of the Management Process

Distributed decision making follows the basic idea that complex decisions should be decomposed into more tractable components. For two and more decision makers, a decomposition seems almost natural. But even for only one decision maker, to reduce complexity, a separation often proves to be imperative. This is particularly the case for dynamic decisions that have to be decomposed over time.

For all the different separation devices, the partial models to be generated should be connected through well-defined distinct 'communication channels', such as the exchange of offers and counter-offers in negotiations or the 'virtual' instruction and anticipation exchange within hierarchical planning. This canalization of exchange is responsible for the desired reduction in complexity and guarantees the partial problems the required amount of autonomy.

Particularly, in case of distributed planning and also for leadership activities, distributed decision making exhibits a high variety of asymmetric and hierarchical features. But even in negotiations between *equally ranked* competitors, establishing the rules on how to negotiate can be considered as a hierarchically superposed decision. These negotiations do not need to take place between real-life systems but, as has been shown in Chapters 3 and 11, may occur within the hierarchical algorithm of the anticipation procedure imitating a rule-based real-life negotiation.

The developed theory of hierarchies in distributed decision making provides a unified approach to a large number of different management fields. Its particular strength may not only be seen in its capability to describe a wide variety of real-life hierarchical situations, but rather in its ability to handle the interface between different levels of description, such as 'quantitative – non-quantitative', 'analytic - holistic', or 'normative - empirical'. Identifying different stages of description with the levels of a hierarchy, one may, as in Section 10.1, describe the entire planning process as a hierarchically evolving sequence of decision problems. Hence, if one considers the management process as a process of interrelated planning and leadership activities, it might be worth investigating how much *hierarchies in distributed decision making* could contribute to a general theoretical understanding of this fundamental concept of an action-oriented science.

Before reflecting upon this central question, let us first, in Sections 13.1 and 13.2 summarize some of the major results of the general theory that has been presented and let us emphasize the contributions it is providing for specific theories in business administration.

13.1 Summarizing Key Notions of the Developed Theory

The theory on hierarchies in distributed decision making was presented in three steps. The first step laid the foundations of the theory, mainly confining itself to hierarchical planning problems. The second part then applied the general concepts to important questions and areas in business administration demonstrating their considerable theoretical potential. Finally, the third part extended the theory to less distinct hierarchical settings and tried to capture some typical leadership relationships.

Thus, the theory relies on two main stages of foundation. Chapter 2 provides the basic concepts, mainly focusing on hierarchical planning, whereas Chapter 10 extends the basic theory to include leadership problems. In doing so, we followed the general idea of passing from the one-person setting to multiperson interactions, simultaneously showing that the extreme ends covered by the theory (Chapter 3 and Part III) have a less distinct hierarchical character than the real life planning settings illustrated in Chapter 4 and Part II.

For hierarchical plannning the base-level only plays a passive role. No reaction is allowed, so that the anticipation of the base-level becomes the key concept of the theory. Various ways were considered to take the base-level into account, particularly the reactive and non-reactive anticipation. These anticipations (and this is the second significant concept) were re-evaluated by the top-level, allowing a distinct separation between the estimate of the base-level's behavior and the degree one would like to accept it. Hence, the top-down criterion and its relation to the base-criterion play a crucial role. The third important concept makes up the instruction and the way in which it is interpreted and incorporated into the base-level's decision model.

The three concepts are combined and effectively tied together in the coupling equations which provide a condensed representation of most of the theory, and form the nucleus for all further development. The coupling equations and particularly their optimization operators describe, in very general terms, the interrelations within a hierarchy. Hence, on the one hand, they allow an almost verbal interpretation, whilst, on the other, for quantitative settings, they may directly be employed for an analytic treatment of a specific problem.

This comprehensive generality of the coupling equations is of essential importance for an area such as management that involves phenomena of different levels of abstraction and measurement. In particular, considering the management process with its evolving sequence (and network) of hierarchies, the universality of the coupling equations provides a uniform framework within which a transition from a more holistic representation to an analytic description may conveniently be performed.

To be more specific, the coupling equations (2.5) accommodate different anticipations, criteria, and instructions. Moreover, they describe a possible information asymmetry and, by their criteria, capture different cooperation and communication schemes. In principle, all elements of the top-level can be affected by the anticipation and, in turn, every component of the base-level can be influenced by the instruction, thus giving rise to a learning process at the top-level and for an alteration of the decision processes at the base-level. This mutual influence was not fully made explicit in the coupling equations, but was elucidated in the discussion of the individual decision process in Chapter 10. Of course, in solving the top- or the base-equation, the employed optimization procedures are, within a learning process, open to new insights into a situation, and to exogeneous instructions.

Applying hierarchical planning to the comparatively simple one-person situation proves already to be of high conceptual significance. It has been shown that the individual (one-person) decision process is hierarchically structured such that the evolution from very loosely defined situations to more analytic descriptions may be considered as a sequence of hierarchically coupled levels.

It should be emphasized that in considering only two levels, we are not restricting our investigation to merely one or two decision makers. Indeed, particularly in Section 3.1.2 and in Chapter 11, the base-level consisted of a multitude of decision makers that were to be coordinated. Furthermore, in Section 4.2.4, in investigating the strategic-tactical-operational hierarchy and in Chapter 8, analyzing the implementation process, we explicitly considered more than two levels. Finally, it is evident that it is in the main stream of argument of hierarchical planning that network relationships between decision makers should be composed of a superposition of pairs of levels. Hence, for network relations, the analysis of pairs proves to be a necessary prerequisite.

Particularly, from the investigation of the individual decision process and the discussion of the implementation problem in Chapter 8, it became clear that the levels themselves may represent hierarchies consisting, for instance, of information gathering, coordination, implementation, and controlling activities. Sometimes the term 'recursiveness' [Beer (1985)], [Espejo et al.] is used for such 'incapsuled' systems. It is exactly these systems that the superposition of individual decision processes is describing.

The problem of how the base-level should be estimated and forecast was mainly treated in the far more involved situation of antagonistic levels. In cases the base-level are observable, well-established statistical estimation (screening) methods could be used. In cases where an observation (and control) was not achievable in a simple way, self-selection methods and/or incentives were necessary. In very general terms, one may state that gathering information and optimization should not be separated.

Besides these fundamental and more conceptual principles, the hierarchical planning part of the theory was mainly illustrated by its ability to cope with constructional and organizational hierarchies. For the negotiation part, on the other hand, the coordination of different departments possessing private information served as an illustration. Generally, the participation of the lower level in the top-level's strategic decision process demonstrated the ability of the theory to deal with fundamental leadership problems.

For constructional hierarchies, relaxations played an important role, implying a rather abstract interpretation of the notion of distributed decision making. In fact, physically one has the same system, and the two levels are generated by separating the differing grades of description. This is an important observation not only for the individual process but also for the more involved management process.

For constructional and organizational hierarchies, the concept of the pure top-down hierarchy played a prominent role. Of even more significance, however, proved to be the tactical-operational hierarchy, since many theoretical concepts in production planning and cost accounting rely on this fundamental type of hierarchy.

13.2 The Impact of Hierarchies in Distributed Decision Making on Specific Theories in Business Administration

Part II considered four important topics. Two of them, 'implementation' and 'design' discussed rather abstract and general management tasks. The remaining two topics, 'hierarchical production planning' and 'cost accounting' dealt with questions being more related to specific functional fields of application.

Obviously, **design problems** are of a hierarchical nature and, in fact, taking a broad enough perspective, hierarchical planning on the whole could be interpreted as a problem of design. Generally, however, design has to do with tactical or strategic decisions, and Chapter 7 demonstrated the capability of hierarchical planning to cope with these more involved decisions. One class of design decisions consisted in the design or redesign of a hierarchy itself showing a meta property of hierarchical planning. The other class involved the comprehensive design of all properties of a system. Flexibility with its extensive properties that affect all components of a system served as an example. Of particular importance was not just the task of configurating the elementary characteristics of flexibility, but rather the design of meta properties such as the system's learning and planning ability. Moreover, we briefly discussed the case of assuming the designed system to behave antagonistically.

Implementation problems are of similar generality as design problems. There is rarely a decision without some kind of implementation. Since implementation is one of the most important leadership tasks, it represents the first step into a comprehensive leadership theory. Particular emphasis was laid on treating implementation as part of the individual decision process and hence on the integration problem of planning and implementation. In a way, Chapter 8 may be viewed as an introduction to the more general considerations of Chapter 10 which described the implementation as the response of the affected level with respect to the instruction of the other level. In particular, Chapter 8 emphasized that the instruction usually has to be interpreted and operationalized by the (implementing) base-level and that the lack of knowledge about the base-level's interpretation causes the top-level an additional uncertainty. These still very general insights were made more explicit in the negotiation process of Chapter 12.

A possible foundation of a specific field in management science may be seen in the treatment of **hierarchical production planning (HPP)**. Using the general coupling equations, traditional HPP was shown to be just a special case. It was characterized as a strict top-down (non-reactive) constructional hierarchy. In view of the general frame given by the coupling equations, it is obvious that there is ample space for numerous substantial extensions. For the top-down constructional hierarchy, an important computational extension can be achieved in introducing at least an *implicit* reactive anticipation. A really substantial extension, however, may be seen in allowing for an explicit reactive anticipation of an *organizational* hierarchy as has been proposed in Sections 6.2 and 6.3.

Cost accounting is the second field in business administration we selected as an example to indicate how hierarchical planning could serve as a conceptual framework. Indeed, cost accounting and, more generally, management accounting seems to be an area for which hierarchical planning could provide a theoretical foundation. This is particularly necessary because of the tremendous development one has witnessed in this field in recent years. Cost accounting left its 'one-person paradigm' and hence its traditional cost theoretic foundation. Hierarchical planning with its richer structure seems to be able to fill this place for several reasons:

1. Hierarchical planning describes the hierarchical features of production planning. Since for these hierarchies cost accounting has to provide cost (preference) information, it seems natural to design cost accounting systems in parallel to the planning hierarchies. Hence, accounting systems should have a hierarchical structure as well.
2. The extension of cost accounting to the tactical and strategic level, to information asymmetry, and to the revenue aspect of a decision, calls for a sufficiently comprehensive hierarchical planning framework.

3. The various evaluations of cost parameters and opportunity costs can only be fully understood within the structure of hierarchical planning which explicitly formulates the necessary evaluating criteria on a meta level and gives a full description not only of a problem's cost function but also of its decision field.

Generally, hierarchical planning may replace traditional production and cost theory as a foundation of cost accounting. Modern production theory should provide a theoretical framework for the field of production planning. It should be able to capture asymmetries and multi-person decision situations. In addition, it should be able to describe hierarchical relationships and the various aggregation-disaggregation steps. Corresponding to this structure, modern cost theory should provide evaluation procedures and in general, should contribute to a comprehensive theory of managerial cost accounting.

13.3 The Management Process

After the summarizing remarks of the previous sections, let us now reflect on more general insights one might gain from a consideration of hierarchical relationships. In fact, a treatise on hierarchies in distributed decision making should not be concluded without some remarks on the general decision theoretic structure of the management process in which all our efforts are tied together. In doing so, it seems to be appropriate to dwell somewhat more on the notion of a theory we have used so far.

Generally, a theory may be defined as a (purpose-oriented) system of statements. According to the kind of statements, one particularly distinguishes between analytical, empirical, and normative theories, respectively. A theory of the management process comprises all three types of statements, possessing as a further property a distinct situative characteristic. Let us call such a theory action-oriented.

An **action-oriented theory** consists of a set of conditional normative statements defining the set of rules, i.e., the 'tool box' of the theory. This set comprises the *general* empirical knowledge which determines the framework that allows the decision maker to deal with a specific problem. To apply the framework, the decision maker must incorporate *specific* empirical knowledge in a situative way. In doing so, he might rely on empirically well-ascertained theoretical results. In most cases, however, this will not be possible. Empirical knowledge will not enter the decision process as 'theoretical' knowledge but simply through ad hoc hypotheses being valid only for the situation the decision process is just facing. Hence, an action-oriented theory is not just an empirical theory which is 'technologized' (see [Albert]), i.e., it is not a theory for which nomological empirical hypotheses (e.g., [Popper]) are simply converted into hypotheses for which the premises are replaced with the actual decision to be carried out.

In relying on empirically ascertained hypotheses, one would submit an action-oriented theory to a criterion of nomological empirical truth having the serious consequence that only the simplest situations could be dealt with. In fact, an action-oriented theory is not working with a criterion of empirical truth but with a normative wellfare criterion for which the existence of nomologically ascertained empirical results is useful but not a necessary prerequisit. However, in constructing contingent hypotheses, empirical theories might be at least used as a 'heuristic potential'.

In summary, an action-oriented theory consists of a set of rules which, for deriving a problem solution, has to be enriched with problem specific situative empirical knowledge. The individual decision process and the hierarchical superposition of such processes discussed in Chapter 10 might be considered as a conceptual framework for more specific action-oriented theories.

Characterizing the management process as an interplay of planning and leadership activities being describable as a superposition of individual decision processes, the management process may be considered as the object of investigation for an action-oriented theory. Of course, the interplay will usually be far more involved as to be describable by the notions of instruction, reaction, and anticipation of a single pair of models. As mentioned already in Chapter 10, an action-oriented theory must allow the management process to possess several interconnected 'top-level and base-level decision processes', and leadership interactions should be permitted simultaneously on several stages of these processes. Clearly, to describe such a dynamic type of interaction in formal decision theoretic terms proves to be a major challenge.

Despite these difficulties, the presented action-oriented theory on hierarchies in distributed decision making was shown to contribute valuable insights into conceptual aspects of the general management process. One of the most important properties of the hierarchical approach proved to be its ability to reconcile different levels of description as, for example, 'qualitative – quantitative', 'hermeneutic – analytic', or 'aggregate – disaggregate'. While these levels are granted a certain autonomy, they are cautiously integrated to support each other. Moreover, if the information state is changing, the hierarchical representation allows for a smooth transition from one level of description to the other. Thus, the decomposition of a complex decision problem into different layers of description and its reintegration using the concepts of hierarchical interactions may be considered as the essential contribution of an action-oriented theory of hierarchies in distributed decision making. It is this integrative property that renders a hierarchical representation to be particularly appropriate for a theoretical investigation of the normative characteristics of the management process.

Bibliography

Albert, H. 1972. "Theorie und Prognose in den Sozialwissenschaften". In: Topitsch, E. (ed.). Logik der Sozialwissenschaften, 8. Aufl., Kiepenheuer & Witsch, Köln.

Anandaligam, G., Friesz, T.I. (eds.) 1992. "Hierarchical optimization". Annals of Operations Research, Vol. 34, Baltzer, Zürich.

Ari, E.A., Axsäter, S. 1988. "Disaggregation under uncertainty in hierarchical production planning". In: European Journal of Operational Research 35, pp 182-186.

Arrow, K.J., Raynaud, H. 1986. "Social Choice and Multi-Criterion Decision Making". MIT Press, Cambridge, London.

Axsäter, S. 1981. "Aggregation of product data for hierarchical production planning". In: Operations Research 29, pp 744-756.

Axsäter, S. 1986. "On the feasibility of aggregate production plans". In: Operations Research 34, pp 796-800.

Axsäter, S., Jönsson, H. 1984. "Aggregation and disaggregation in hierarchical production planning". In: European Journal of Operational Research 17, pp 338-350.

Axsäter, S., Schneeweiss, Ch., Silver, E. (eds.) 1986. "Multi-Stage Production Planning and Inventory Control". Lecture Notes in Economics and Mathematical Systems, No. 266. Springer, Berlin, Heidelberg, New York.

Bamberg, G., Spremann, K. (eds.) 1987. "Agency Theory, Information and Incentives". Springer, Berlin, Heidelberg, New York.

Barbarosoglu, G. 1995. "Hierarchical production planning". In: Burton, R.M., Obel, B. (eds.). Design Models for Hierarchical Organizations: Computation, Information and Decentralization, pp 181-206, Kluwer, Boston.

Beer, S. 1966. "Decision and Control". Wiley, Chichester.

Beer, S. 1985. "Diagnosing the System for Organisations". Wiley, Chichester.

Benders, J.F. 1962. "Partioning procedures for solving mixed variables programming problem". In: Numerische Mathematik 4, pp 238-252.

Benjaafar, S., Morin, T.L., Tavalage, J.J. 1995. "The strategic value of flexibility in sequential decision making". In: European Journal of Operational Research 82, pp 438-457.

Bertrand, J.W.M., Wortmann, J.C., and Wijngaard, J. 1990. "Production Control. A Structural and Design Oriented Approach". Elsevier, Amsterdam.

Bisdorff, R. 1999. "Cognitive Support Methods for Multi-Criteria Expert Decision Making". In: Valdares Tavares, L., Dean, B.V. (eds.). EURO XV - INFORMS XXXIV Conference (Barcelona, 1997), special issue of the European Journal of Operational Research.

Bitran, G., Haas, E., and Hax, A. 1981. "Hierarchical production planning: A single stage system". In: Operations Research 29, pp 717-743.

Bitran, G.R., Tirupati, D. 1993. "Hierarchical production planning". In: Graves, S.C., Rinnooy Kan, A.H.G., and Zipkin, P.H. (eds.). Logistics of Production and Inventory, Vol. 4 in the series "Handbooks in Operations Research and

Management Science", North-Holland, Amsterdam, pp 523-568.

Bogetoft, P., Ming, C., and Tind, J. 1994. "Price-directive decision making in hierarchical systems with conflicting preferences". In: Journal of Multi-Criteria Decision Analysis 3, pp 65-82.

Burton, R.M., Obel, B. 1984. "Designing Efficient Organizations: Modelling and Experimentation." North-Holland, Amsterdam.

Burton, R.M., Obel, B. (eds.) 1995. "Design Models for Hierarchical Organizations: Computation, Information and Decentralization". Kluwer, Boston.

Caravilla, M., Sousa, J.P. 1995. "Hierarchical production planning in a make-to-order company: A case study". In: European Journal of Operational Research 86, pp 43-56.

Chen Chuan, J., Lasserre, J.B., Roubellat, F. 1981. "Hierarchical planning. A case study". In: Operational Research, pp 439-452.

Cooper, R., Kaplan, R.S. 1991. "The Design of Cost Management Systems". Prentice-Hall, Englewood Cliff, NJ.

Corbett, D., Debets, F., and Van Wassenhove, L. 1995. "Decentralisation of responsibility for site decontamination projects: A budget allocation approach". In: European Journal of Operational Research 86, pp 103-119.

Crowder, H. 1976. "Computational improvements for subgradient optimization". In: Symposia Mathematica 19, pp 357-372.

Dantzig, G.B., Wolfe, Ph. 1961. "The Decomposition Algorithm for Linear Programs". In: Econometrica 29, pp 767-778.

Dempster, M.A.H., Fisher, M.L., Jansen, L., Lageweg, B.J., Lenstra, J.K., Rinnooy Kan, A.H.G. 1981. "Analytical evaluation of hierarchical planning systems". In: Operations Research 29, pp 707-716.

Demski, J.S. 1994. "Managerial Uses of Accounting Information". Kluwer, Boston.

Demski, J.S., Sappington, D.E.M (1987). "Delegated Expertise". In: Journal of Accounting Research 25, pp 68-89.

Dirickx, Y.M.I., Jennergren, P. 1979. "Systems Analysis by Multilevel Methods: With Applications to Economics and Management". Wiley, New York.

Eichin, R., Schneeweiss, Ch. 1998. "Determining depreciations as a hierarchical problem". Discussion Paper No. 59, Department of Operations Research, Universität Mannheim, Germany.

Erschler, J.G., Fontan, G., Mercé, C. 1986. "Consistency of the disaggregation process in hierarchical planning". In: Operations Research 34, pp 464-469.

Espejo R., Schuhmann, W., Schwaninger, M., and Billelo, U. 1996. "Organizational Transformation and Learning. A Cybernetic Approach to Management". Wiley, New York.

Flippo, O.E., Rinnooy Kan, A.H.G. 1993. Decomposition in general mathematical programming". In: Mathematical Programming 60, pp 361-382.

Fransoo, J.C., Sridharan, V., Bertrand, J.W.M. 1995. "A hierarchical approach for capacity coordination in multiple products single-machine production systems with stationary stochastic demands". In: European Journal of Operational Research 86, pp 57-72.

French, S 1988. "Decision Theory: An Introduction to the Mathematics of Rationality". Hellis Horwood, Chichester.

Fudenberg, D., Tirole, J. 1993. "Game Theory". MIT Press, Cambridge, MA.

Gabbay, H. 1979. "Optimal aggregation and disaggregation in hierarchical planning." In: P. Ritzmann et al. (eds.). Disaggregation: Problems in Manufacturing and Service Organizations, Nijhoff, Boston.

Gelders, L.F., Van Wassenhove, L. 1981. "Production planning: A review". In: European Journal of Operational Research 7, pp 101-110.

Gelders, L.F., Van Wassenhove, L. 1982. "Hierarchical integration in production planning: Theory and practice". In: Journal of Operations Management 3, pp 27-35.

Gershwin, S.B. 1994. "Manufacturing Systems Engineering". Prentice-Hall, Englewood Cliffs, NJ.

Gfrerer, H., Zäpfel G. 1995. "Hierarchical model for production planning in the case of uncertain demand". In: European Journal of Operational Research 86, pp 142-161.

Goedhart, M. Spronk, J. 1995. "An interactive heuristic for financial planning in decentralized organizations". In: European Journal of Operational Research 86, pp 162-175.

Graves, S.C. 1982. "Lagrangean techniques to solve hierarchical problems". In: Management Science 28, pp 260-275.

Grossman, S.J., Hart, O.D. 1983. "An Analysis of the Principal-Agent Problem". In: Econometrica 51, pp 7-46.

Groves, T., Loeb, M. 1979. "Incentives in a divisionalized firm". In: Management Science 25, pp 221-230.

Günther, H.O. 1986. "The design of an hierarchical model for production planning and scheduling". In: Axsäter, S., Schneeweiss, Ch., and Silver E. (eds.). Multi-Stage Production Planning and Inventory Control, Lecture Notes in Economics and Mathematical Systems, No. 266, Springer, Berlin, Heidelberg, New York.

Gupta, Y., Goyal, S. 1989. "Flexibility of manufacturing systems: Concepts and measurements". In: European Journal of Operational Research 43, pp 119-135.

Harris, M., Raviv, A. 1979. "Optimal incentive contracts with imperfect information". In: Journal of Economic Theory 20, pp 231-259.

Hart, O.D., Holmström, B. 1987. "The theory of contracts". In: Bewley, T.F. (ed.). Advances in Economic Theory. MIT Press, Cambridge, Mass., pp 71-155.

Hauth, M. 1998. "Hierarchisch integrierte Planungsansätze in der Prozeßfertigung". Gabler, Wiesbaden.

Hauth, M., Schneeweiß, Ch. 1997. "Kapazitätsanpassung bei simultaner Losgrößen- und Reihenfolgeplanung. Adapting capacity for lotsizing and scheduling problems." In: OR Spektrum 19, pp 251-260.

Hax, A.C., Candea, D. 1984. "Production and Inventory Management". Prentice-Hall, Englewood Cliffs, N.J.

Hax, A.C., Meal, D. 1975. "Hierarchical integration of production planning and scheduling". In: M.A. Geisler (ed.). Logistics, TIMS Studies in the Management Sciences. North Holland, Amsterdam.

Held, M., Wolfe, P., and Crowder, H.P. 1974. "Validation of subgradient optimization". In: Mathematical Programming 1, pp 6-25.

Heinrich, C., Schneeweiss, Ch. 1986. "Multi-stage lotsizing for general production systems". In: Axsäter, S., Schneeweiss, Ch., Silver. E. (eds.). Multi-stage production planning and inventory control, Lecture Notes in Economics and Mathematical Systems, No. 266, Springer, Berlin, Heidelberg, New York.

Holmberg, K. 1995. "Primal and dual decomposition as organizational design: Price and/or resource directive decomposition". In: Burton, R.M., Obel, B. (eds.). Design Models for

Hierarchical Organizations: Computation, Information and Decentralization, pp 61-92, Kluwer, Boston.

Holmström, B. 1979. "Moral hazard and observability". In: Bell Journal of Economics 13, pp 324-430.

Holmström, B., Tirole, J. 1991. "Transfer pricing and organizational form". In: Journal of Law, Economics and Organization, pp 201-228.

Homburg, C. 1995. "Hierarchical Negotiations". In: Burton, R.M., Obel, B. (eds.), Design Models for Hierarchical Organizations: Computation, Information and Decentralization, pp 161-180, Kluwer, Boston.

Homburg, C. 1996. "Hierarchische Aushandlungen in Organisationen". Physica, Heidelberg.

Homburg, C. 1998a. "Hierarchical multi-objective decision making." In: European Journal of Operational Research 105, pp 155-161.

Homburg, C. 1998b. "Production planning with multiple objectives in decentralized organizations". In: International Journal of Production Economics, 56-57, pp 243-252.

Homburg, C., Schneeweiss, Ch. 1997. "Hierarchisch-partizipative Koordinationsprozesse". In: Zeitschrift für Betriebswirtschaft 67, pp 759-780.

Horngren, C.T., Foster, G., and Datar, S.M. 1994. "Cost Accounting: A Managerial Emphasis". 8th ed., Prentice-Hall, Englewood Cliffs, NJ.

Hotelling, H. 1925. "A general mathematical theory of depreciation". In: The Journal of the American Statistical Association 20, pp 340-353.

Houtem van, G.H., Inderfurth, K., Zijm, W.H.M. 1996. "Material coordination in stochastic multi-echelon systems". In: European Journal of Operational Research 95, pp 1-23.

332   Bibliography

Jelassi, M.T., Kersten, G.E., and Zionts, S. 1990. "An introduction to group decision and negotiation support". In: Bana e Costa, C.A. (ed.). Readings in Multiple Criteria Decision Aid, Springer, Berlin, Heidelberg, New York.

Jörnsten, K., Leisten, R. 1995. "Aggregation approaches to decentralized planning structures". In: Burton, R.M., Obel, B. (eds.). Design Models for Hierarchical Organizations: Computation, Information and Decentralization, pp 93-119, Kluwer, Boston.

Jordan, W.C., Graves, S.C. 1995. "Principles of the benefits of manufacturing process flexibility". In: Management Science 41, pp 577-594.

Kaplan, R.S., Atkinson, A.A. 1989. "Advanced Management Accounting". 2nd ed., Prentice-Hall, Englewood Cliffs NJ.

Keeney, R.L., Raiffa, H. 1976. "Decisions with Multiple Objectives: Preferences and Value Tradeoffs". Wiley, New York.

Kistner, K.P., Steven, M. 1991. "Applications of operations research in hierarchical planning". In: Fandel, G., Zäpfel, G. (eds.). Modern Production Concepts, Theory and Applications, Springer, Berlin, Heidelberg, New York.

Küpper, H.-U.. 1985. "Investitionstheoretische Fundierung der Kostenrechnung". In: Zeitschrift für betriebswirtschaftliche Forschung 37, pp 26-46.

Lasserre, J.B., Martin, J.B., Roubellat, F. 1983. "Aggregate model and decomposition method for mid-term production planning". In: International Journal of Production Research 21, pp 835-843.

Lasserre, J.B., Roubellat, F. 1985. "Measuring decision flexibility in production planning". In: IEEE Transactions on Automatic Control AC-30, pp 447-452.

Lasserre, J.B., Mercé, C. 1990. "Robust hierarchical production planning under uncertainty". In: Annals of Operations Research 26, pp 73-87.

Leisten, R., Jörnsten, K. 1995. "Comparison of iterative aggregation in hierarchical and decentralised planning structures". In: European Journal of Operational Research 86, pp 120-141.

Malek, L.A., Wolf, C. 1991. "Evaluating flexibility of alternative FMS designs – A comparative measure". In: International Journal of Production Economics 23, pp 3-10.

Martial, F. von, 1992. "Coordinating plans of autonomous agents". In: Lecture Notes in Artificial Intelligence, No. 610, Springer, Berlin, Heidelberg, New York.

Mehra, A., Minis, I., Proth, J.-M. 1995. "Hierarchical Production Planning for General Job Shops: Part 1 and 2 Rapport de Recherche No. 2633/2634". Institut National de Recherche en Informatique et en Automatique (INRIA), Metz, France.

Meijboom, B.R. 1987. "Planning in Decentralized Firms". Springer, Berlin, Heidelberg, New York.

Mesarovic, M.D., Macko, D., and Takahara, Y. 1970. "Theory of Hierarchical, Multilevel, Systems". Academic Press, New York, San Francisco, London.

Milgrom, P., Roberts, J. 1992. "Economics, Organizations and Management". Prentice-Hall, Englewood Cliffs, NJ.

Miller, B.L., Buckman, A.G. 1987. "Cost allocation and opportunity costs". In: Management Science 33, pp 626-639.

Mirrless, J.A. 1976. "The optimal structure of incentives and authority within an organisation". In: Bell Journal of Economics 7, pp 105-131.

Panne, C. van der 1991. "Decentralization for multi-division enterprises". In: Operations Research 39, pp 786-797.

Paulli, J. 1995. "A hierarchical approach for the FMS scheduling problem". In: European Journal of Operational Research 86, pp 32-42.

Pesenti, R. 1995. "Hierarchical resource planning for shipping companies". In: European Journal of Operational Research 86, pp 91-102.

Popper, K.R. 1992. "The Logic of Scientific Discovery". Hutchinson, London.

Pratt, J.W., Zeckhauser, R.J. 1964. "Risk aversion in the small and in the large". In: Econometrica 32, pp 122-136.

Rajan, M.V. 1992. "Cost allocation in multiagent settings". In: The Accounting Review, pp 527-545.

Rogers, L.M., Evans, R.J., Plante, R.D., and Wong, R.T. 1991. "Aggregation and disaggregation techniques and methodology in optimization". In: Operations Research 39, pp 611-626.

Rosenhead, J., Elton, M., Gupta, S.K. 1972. "Robustness and optimality as criteria for strategic decisions". In: Operational Research Quarterly 23, pp 413-431.

Sakurai, M. 1989. "Target costing and how to use it". In: Journal of Cost Management, pp 39-50.

Sawik, T. (1998). "A lexicographic approach to bi-objective loading of a flexible assembly system". In: EJOR 107, pp 101-113.

Schenk-Mathes, H. 1995. "The design of procurement contracts as a problem of delegation". In: European Journal of Operational Research 86, pp 176-187.

Schneeweiss, Ch. 1987. "On a formalization of the process of quantitative model building". In: European Journal of Operational Research 29, pp 24-41.

Schneeweiss, Ch. 1992. "Planung 2: Konzepte der Prozeß- und Modellgestaltung". Springer, Berlin, Heidelberg, New York.

Schneeweiss, Ch. 1995. "Hierarchical structures in organizations: A conceptual framework". In: European Journal of Operational Research 86, pp 4-31.

Schneeweiss, Ch. 1998. "On the applicability of activity based costing as a planning instrument". In: International Journal of Production Economics 54, pp 277-284.

Schneeweiss, Ch., Schneider, H. 1999. "Measuring and designing flexibility as a generalized service degree". In: European Journal of Operational Research 112, pp 98-106.

Schneeweiss, Ch., Schröder, H. 1992. "Planning and scheduling the repair shops of the Deutsche Lufthansa AG: A hierarchical approach." In: Production and Operations Management 1, pp 22-33

Schneider, H. 1981. "The effects of service levels on order-point or order-levels in inventory control models". In: International Journal of Production Research 19, pp 615-631.

Sethi, A.K., Sethi, S.P. 1990. "Flexibility in manufacturing: A survey". In: International Journal of Flexible Manufacturing Systems, pp 289-328.

Sethi, P.S., Zhang, Q. 1994. "Hierarchical Decision Making in Manufacturing Systems". Birkhäuser, Boston, Basel, Berlin.

Sherali, H.D., Sarin, S.C., and Desai, R. 1990. "Model and algorithms for job selection, routing and scheduling in a flexible manufacturing system". In: Annals of Operations Research 26, pp 433-453.

Siegel, G., Ramanauskas-Marconi, H. 1989. "Behavioral Accounting". South Western, Cincinnati, Ohio.

Silver, E.A. Meal, A.C. 1973. "A heuristic for selecting lot-size quantities for the case of a deterministic time-varying demand rate and discrete opportunities for replenishment". In: Production and Inventory Management 14, pp 64-74.

Silver, E.A., Peterson, R. 1998. "Decision Systems for Inventory Management and Production Planning". 3rd ed., Wiley, New York.

Söhner, V. 1995. "Hierarchisch integrierte Produktionsplanung und -steuerung". Physica, Heidelberg.

Söhner, V., Schneeweiß, Ch. 1995. "Hierarchically integrated lot size optimization". In: European Journal of Operational Research 86, pp 73-90.

Spremann, K. 1987. "Agent and principal". In: Bamberg, G. and Spremann, K. (eds.). Agency Theory, Information, and Incentives, pp 3-37. Springer, Berlin, Heidelberg, New York.

Stadtler, H. 1986. "Hierarchical production planning: Tuning aggregate planning with divergent sequencing and scheduling". In: Axsäter, S., Schneeweiss, Ch., and Silver, E. (eds.). Multi-Stage Production Planning and Inventory Control, Lecture Notes in Economics and Mathematical Systems, No. 266, pp 197-226. Springer, Heidelberg, Berlin, New York.

Steven, M. 1994. "Hierarchische Produktionsplanung". 2. Aufl., Physica, Heidelberg.

Ten Kate, A. 1972. "Decomposition of linear programs by direct distribution." In: Econometrics 40, pp 883-898.

Tind, J. 1995. "General mathematical programming models in multi-level planning". In: Burton, R.M., Obel, B. (eds.), Design Models for Hierarchical Organizations: Computation, Information and Decentralization, pp 121-134. Kluwer, Boston.

Tirole, J. 1988. "The Theory of Industrial Organization". MIT Press, Cambridge, Mass.

Varian, H.R. 1992. "Microeconomic Analysis". 3rd edition. Norton & Company, New York, London.

Vetschera, R. 1990. "Group decision and negotiation support - An ethodological survey". In: OR-Spektrum 12, pp 67-77.

Vollman, T.E., Berry, W.L., Whybark, D.C. 1997. "Manufacturing Planning and Control Systems".   4th ed., McGraw-Hill, Maidenhead.

Wassenhove Van, L.N., Vanderhenst, P. 1983. "Planning production in a bottleneck department". In: European Journal of Operational Research 12, pp 127-137.

Wagner, H.M. 1975. "Principles of Operations Research". Prentice Hall, Englewood Cliffs, NJ.

Wagner, H.M., Whitin, T.H. 1958. "Dynamic version of the economic lot size model". In: Management Science 5, pp. 89-96.

Weitzman, M.L. 1976. "The new soviet incentive model". In: Bell Journal of Economics, pp 251-257.

Whitt, W. 1983. "The queueing network analyzer". In: Bell System Technical Journal 62, pp 2779-2815.

Wild, B. 1995. "Die Flexibilität von Betriebsvereinbarungen". Physica, Heidelberg.

Wild, B., Schneeweiß, Ch. 1993. "Manpower capacity planning - A hierarchical approach". In: International Journal of Production Economics 30-31, pp 95-106.

Zeleny, M 1982.   "Multiple Criteria Decision Making". McGraw-Hill, Maidenhead.

Zimmerman, J.L. 1995. "Accounting for decision making and control". Irwin, Homewood, Ill.

Zionts, S., Wallenius, J. 1976. "An interactive programming method for solving the multiple criteria problem." In: Management Science 22, pp 652-663.

Zionts, S., Wallenius, J. 1983. "An interactive multiple objective linear programming method for a class of underlying nonlinear utility functions". In: Management Science 29, pp 519-520.

Index

Druck: Strauss Offsetdruck, Mörlenbach
Verarbeitung: Schäffer, Grünstadt